# Creating a Person-Centered Library

# Creating a Person-Centered Library

## Best Practices for Supporting High-Needs Patrons

Elizabeth A. Wahler and Sarah C. Johnson

BLOOMSBURY LIBRARIES UNLIMITED
NEW YORK • LONDON • OXFORD • NEW DELHI • SYDNEY

BLOOMSBURY LIBRARIES UNLIMITED
Bloomsbury Publishing Inc
1385 Broadway, New York, NY 10018, USA
50 Bedford Square, London, WC1B 3DP, UK
29 Earlsfort Terrace, Dublin 2, Ireland

BLOOMSBURY, BLOOMSBURY LIBRARIES UNLIMITED and the Diana logo are trademarks of
Bloomsbury Publishing Plc

First published in the United States of America 2024

Library of Congress Cataloging in Publication Control Number: 2023026526

ISBN: PB: 978-1-4408-8083-4
ePDF: 978-1-4408-8084-1
eBook: 979-8-2161-7114-0

Typeset by Deanta Global Publishing Services, Chennai, India

To find out more about our authors and books visit www.bloomsbury.com and
sign up for our newsletters.

*This book is dedicated to all of the courageous, kind, caring library staff who show up every day to make a difference in the lives of the people who walk through their doors. Keep showing up. The world is a brighter place because of you.*

*To Chase from Mom B: When you walk into a library, you light up. I hope you never lose that sense of wonder at the magic inside their doors. I love you!*

*To Aunt Marty from Sarah: Thank you for guiding me during the early steps on my professional path and continuing to share your love of libraries with me.*

# Contents

# Acknowledgments

This book would not be possible without the many individuals who have helped us both directly and indirectly. First, we would like to offer our sincere thanks to everyone who participated in our interviews and helped inform the content of this book. The information we present stemmed from our many conversations over the years with innovative, caring, and creative library staff, administrators, and library-based social workers, social work students, and peer navigators who are eagerly trying to meet the needs of their communities. We are continually impressed with their dedication to this work and the patrons they serve, despite the many challenges they face.

We are also grateful to Rob A., Taylor Atkinson, Kylie Carlson, Emily Dalton, Ahmed Farah, Anita Favretto, Tonya Garcia, Karina Hagelin, Sean Harris, Jana Hill, Kevin King, Noah Lenstra, Patrick Lloyd, Anna Lockwood, Peggy Morton, Mary Nienow, Lydia Ogden, Tracey Orick, David Perez, Anne-Maree Pfabe, Shay Pounds, Tiffany Russell, Caroline Sharkey, Darren Smart, Ashley Stewart, Diana Brawley Sussman, Charles Sutton, Mary Jo Vortkamp, Rachel Williams, Julie Ann Winkelstein, Sara Zettervall, members of Whole Person Librarianship group, and the former PLA Social Worker Task Force. Your expertise on library challenges, opportunities, and next steps for improving services to high-needs patrons while also supporting library staff was instrumental in shaping what we included in the book.

We express our gratitude for and appreciation to the front-line library workers across the world who continue to show up, ready to serve despite growing patron needs, reduced library funding, and significant demands and challenges from their communities. We firmly believe that libraries are essential to a healthy, well-functioning, and well-informed society, and we have great respect and gratitude to everyone who has chosen this line of work. Your service to your community is invaluable and deeply appreciated.

Sarah would like to thank her students at the University of Illinois Urbana-Champaign School of Information Sciences. Additional gratitude goes to Mark Giesler, Margaret Ann Paauw, and Maria Bonn. Thank you to Leslie Kahn for being one of the first public librarians to encourage my interest in social work/library collaborations. There is special love in Sarah's heart for her childhood library: the

College Hill branch of the Cincinnati & Hamilton County Public Library. Thank you, Keith, for being the ever-steady presence throughout this process and continually supporting my work.

Beth: I would like to thank John Helling and Mike Williams, the two librarians who first introduced me to the idea of library social work, and Kim Bolan, Nate Burnard, Colleen Rortvedt, and Tasha Saecker. It is through conversations with all of them that I began to better understand the reality of contemporary library work and conceptualize the mutually beneficial relationship between social work and libraries. I would not be in this line of work without their initiative, openness to discussing difficult topics, willingness to problem-solve and take risks, and collaborative spirit. Most of all, I thank Kristy—for taking care of things at home, giving me space and time to endlessly write and edit, and doing your #wifebrag thing; this book got written largely because of you and your support. Thank you from the bottom of my heart.

# Preface

The timing of this book is not a coincidence. With the ongoing Covid-19 pandemic eliciting more mental health issues, poverty-related needs, housing instability, and health concerns across the world, public libraries are adapting to these growing needs with their communities, patron populations, and their own staff.[1] In our conversations with libraries around the world, many staff with decades of library experience are describing the behavioral concerns and mental health challenges they witness in their patrons on a daily basis as more extreme than previously experienced. In many cases, budgets for public services are being cut, requiring that libraries "do more with less" to ensure efficiency of services while adequately targeting and addressing their patrons' highest needs. Libraries are often pressured to be all things to all people, and the pandemic has only heightened this expectation.

In addition to the Covid-19 pandemic, the United States is undergoing a reckoning of long-term racial injustices permeating all institutions, including libraries. Libraries are attempting to diversify their staff and collections, as well as ensure programming meets the needs of the increasingly diverse communities around them. Some libraries have long maintained an active security presence in their library and are now questioning this choice due to the growing awareness of the ways law enforcement, security, and the criminal justice system can further perpetuate racial injustice. Some libraries are replacing security personnel with social workers or the like, attempting to respond to patron crises with compassion and support rather than merely enforcing rules or using a carceral approach. Other branches are trying to ensure security officers are trained in person-centered, recovery-oriented approaches. The bottom line is that many libraries are currently at a crossroads.

Over the course of our work with public libraries across the United States, we have had the pleasure of learning about a multitude of innovative ways libraries are improving the health and well-being of their communities and the lives of the individuals visiting their spaces. We have observed libraries, both big and small, initiating new programs, offering innovative services, and building community collaborations to create warm, comfortable, and inviting spaces that positively serve the various patron populations coming through their doors. We have met spectacular people who have great compassion and a huge willingness to help. However, because of this strong inclination to serve, we have also met with libraries that have jumped into new programming or services too quickly without considering the potential ramifications or the cultural change required for long-term sustainability. This book is our attempt to provide suggestions and solutions to guide you and your library through these crossroads in order to create sustainable change, while also understanding the ramifications and avoiding potential landmines commonly encountered by other libraries.

As social workers, it is important for us to clarify that this is *not* a social work book. Instead, our aim is to speak to current and upcoming library and information science (LIS) students, early career library staff, and administrators trying to grasp the lay of the land with your patrons and communities, as well as seasoned library professionals navigating the rapidly changing needs of your patrons. Although social work collaborations are one of the options addressed in this book, we aim to provide an extensive overview of the various services, programs, and collaborations that can help public libraries address their patrons' psychosocial needs and support their staff with these types of patron needs. We aim to include options for libraries of all sizes while being mindful of budget restrictions experienced by many—especially small or rural—libraries. We share best practices for libraries in providing person-centered services while offering lessons learned along the way.

We hope our presentation of the concept of "person-centered libraries" builds upon and adds to the seminal work of Sara Zettervall and Mary Nienow, *Whole Person Librarianship*.[2] Their book, published in 2019, was originally written to educate librarians and library staff on social work concepts and tools that could help them in their work. We asked Sara[3] about her observations on the changes she sees in libraries and with social work/library collaborations since her book's publication. Though the distance between now and 2019 is objectively brief, much has happened in the United States since that time, as mentioned earlier. Zettervall views the birth of the initial social work/library partnerships as having occurred during a time of abundance. While we are still in a space of determining the full impact of the pandemic on libraries, throughout the country many branches recently experienced hiring freezes, furloughs, and staff layoffs. Fewer employees invariably put more pressure on existing staff to cover their service desks instead of taking regular breaks and the necessary self-care steps we advise in this book. As a result, Zettervall observes, library staff are asking more questions about self-care and fewer about how to better understand their patrons, not because they care any less than they once did, but rather because they are more focused on establishing boundaries for themselves. This increased awareness and insistence on self-care help staff to realize that it's okay that they aren't able to do and fix everything; the library does not have to pick up the remaining slack. We hope our book helps address this concern and strikes a balance between providing strategies about what libraries can do to help their patrons while also emphasizing the need for staff and their leaders to set boundaries, practice reflection and self-care, and create healthy workplaces for library employees.

In this book, we begin by providing an overview of patrons' increasing psychosocial needs, structural and societal reasons for this shift observed in library patrons' needs, and how these changes impact libraries and library staff. The introduction focuses on the "why" behind this work. Then, the bulk of the book focuses on best practices for libraries in providing person-centered services and shares lessons learned, including special considerations for certain patron populations that might be served by your library. We conclude with information about organizational approaches to supporting public library staff and ways you can anticipate and approach common challenges to the change process.

If you're reading this book, we know you are someone who is concerned about your patrons and staff and you want to build, lead, or contribute to the best library services on offer. We sincerely hope that this information is helpful in your journey.

## Notes

**1**  InfoPeople, *We Are Not Okay: Library Worker Trauma Before and During COVID-19 and What Happens After* (InfoPeople Webinar, 2022), https://infopeople.org/civicrm/event/info?id=1019&reset=1.

**2**  S. K. Zettervall and M. C. Nienow, *Whole Person Librarianship: A Social Work Approach to Patron Services* (Santa Barbara, CA: Libraries Unlimited, 2019).

**3**  S. Zettervall, personal communication, September 26, 2022.

# Introduction

## What Do We Mean By "High-Needs Patrons"?

Throughout this book, we use the term "high-needs patrons" interchangeably with patrons who have "psychosocial needs." Although definitions vary, psychosocial needs refer to psychological, social, or environmental needs which can lead to chronic stress and strain and ultimately result in poor health outcomes or decreased life satisfaction and well-being. Psychosocial needs can include mental health challenges, substance use–related problems, housing instability, food insecurity, or other poverty-related needs such as difficulty with transportation, obtaining clothing, or the like. Needs may also include social isolation, relationship problems, struggles with parenting and childcare, or difficulties with employment.

You may be reading this book and wondering why libraries are concerned with these types of needs when they are often addressed by freestanding social service organizations in your community. Due to factors we'll discuss, the reality is public libraries have many patrons who have existing psychosocial needs and are faced with the necessity of addressing them. Some patrons are in the library space exhibiting symptoms of their need (such as mental health or substance use–related challenges) while others are directly asking library staff for help finding resources for housing, mental health, or poverty-related issues. Whether libraries want to address these types of needs or not, it has become a necessity in many cases.

## Overview of Data about Psychosocial Needs

Library patrons' psychosocial needs are a growing concern across the United States. It is unsurprising that with the large number of people experiencing homelessness who regularly visit libraries, the most frequently mentioned psychosocial need of library patrons in the existing literature is housing.[1] The pronounced presence of patrons experiencing homelessness connects to the fact that libraries are one of the last free public spaces in most communities, requiring zero resources to access them. People without housing may not have anywhere to go during the day and therefore use the library as a climate-controlled space with comfortable seating, public restrooms, water fountains, computer and internet access, and some familiar faces. Also, people staying in temporary shelters are often required to leave during the day and might use the library for a place to be until returning to their shelter for the evening.

Sometimes observed in, but not limited to, patrons experiencing homelessness are mental health challenges. Libraries report having patrons who exhibit symptoms of mental illness that include delusions, hallucinations, depressive symptoms, and anxiety. Library workers frequently report stress associated with working alongside these patrons. Staff express that they don't have the necessary training to assist such individuals, are concerned these patrons might be a danger to themselves or others in the library, and are frustrated that helping high-need patrons absorbs considerable time and detracts from helping all patrons in the library. Although people with mental illness are more likely to be victimized by others than to hurt someone else,[2] several libraries have recently made national news due to patrons exhibiting symptoms of mental illness, dying by suicide in the library space, or assaulting someone. Because of these incidents, library staff are sometimes fearful of patrons experiencing mental illness. Due to the symptoms of some mental illnesses, library staff also hear complaints from other patrons who are bothered or upset by patrons experiencing mental illness in the library space. This can generate tremendous strain for library staff trying to satisfactorily serve all of their patrons.

Another considerable psychosocial need of library patrons is substance use. As the opioid crisis rages in the United States[3] and overall substance use and related health problems continue to ravage countries throughout the world,[4] library staff report finding used needles or other dangerous drug paraphernalia in bathrooms, while others witness patrons overdose and experience life-threatening drug-related emergencies. These occurrences are becoming so frequent that some public libraries are training employees on administering Naloxone and stocking it on library property to quickly reverse the effects of an overdose when needed.

Poverty-related needs are also a significant psychosocial factor of patrons in libraries across the United States. Branches frequently report patrons experiencing food insecurity. To counter this, some libraries provide snacks to patrons, host on-site food pantries, or maintain partnerships with local food organizations offering meals or groceries on library property. Transportation is another common poverty-related need, so many libraries provide bus passes, tokens, or vouchers to help patrons access medical care, interview for jobs, and so forth.

Although the areas of need listed before are the most commonly experienced in libraries, there are other psychosocial needs also experienced by patrons, although their frequency and prevalence vary by population and community context. For example, some libraries serve a significant number of immigrants who may have needs related to immigration or English proficiency. Other libraries serve senior adults who may have aging-related accessibility challenges, need dementia support, or have caregivers that desire resources. It can be helpful to conduct a needs assessment of your specific library branch to determine its highest priority needs and to guide the planning and implementation of appropriate services and programming. The process of conducting a needs assessment will be addressed in the next chapter.

## How Patrons' Psychosocial Needs Impact Staff

While a growing body of literature rightly speaks to the various needs of library patrons, the impact on library staff is often overlooked. It's critical to consider how the growing psychosocial needs of patrons contribute to the strain on library staff as they work to meet the needs of all patrons. Library staff report significant stress from attempting to address patrons' psychosocial needs, especially because many feel unprepared to do so. Most library staff have undergone little training addressing these types of needs and the instruction they've received doesn't always teach practical or useful skills. For example, staff frequently need to de-escalate agitated patrons yet are rarely taught or have opportunities to practice effective de-escalation skills. Many staff want to increase their knowledge base through training about serious mental illness, conflict resolution, de-escalation techniques, or Mental Health First Aid.[5]

Although many libraries and staff want more training, staff also feel strain from the time and energy it takes to assist some patrons with psychosocial needs. Due to budget constraints, many libraries are already understaffed, and few have the time to assist patrons with completing job applications, searching for housing resources, or even listening to those who simply want someone to talk to. Apart from the time and energy it takes to address patrons' needs, we would be remiss if we did not address the psychological impact this work has on staff. Patrons' challenges can contribute to library staff experiencing burnout and vicarious trauma, and they are the most commonly identified source of stress among library staff.[6] Research suggests that many library workers experience trauma in the course of their job, which may exacerbate underlying mental health conditions or elicit trauma-related symptoms. Many staff report burnout and dissatisfaction with their job, while others are leaving the field altogether due to these workplace stressors. In our experience, it is not uncommon for library staff to be at odds about the library's role regarding these types of patron needs, and some understandably argue that they are not social workers and should not be carrying out similar job responsibilities as those of social workers. There is a lack of consensus about if and when it is staff's professional responsibility to address patrons' psychosocial needs at all.[7]

## History of Libraries Addressing Psychosocial Needs

Attempts to address patrons' psychosocial needs are nothing new, although the frequency and severity of those needs, alongside the innovative approaches to address these needs, are somewhat different today compared to the past. Public libraries have been addressing the broad range of their patrons' needs since their inception. Beginning in the Progressive Era, libraries offered "services and programs outside of traditional library service such as access to bathrooms and kitchens, lecture and concert series, and children and family centered services."[8] During this time, the benefactor of nearly 1,700 US public libraries, Andrew Carnegie, sought to endow "nobility on people who can't otherwise afford a shred of it."[9] Carnegie proclaimed the library is for everyone as "it is emphatically the people's library . . . where neither rank, nor office, nor wealth receives the slightest consideration."[10]

Librarians of the Progressive Era like Edith Guerrier responded to the "intense socioeconomic churn"[11] of its time by developing programming that met specific community needs. She aimed to value the lived experiences of young, immigrant girls in Boston through an egalitarian means of encouraging them to select the types of books they chose to read. This position stood in contrast to the underlying tone of the era, in which adults in a position of authority sought to instruct immigrant children on the "proper" and "correct" way to live.

As an essential place of social infrastructure and cohesion, libraries have a history of offering spaces "committed to openness and inclusivity."[12] For example, when Washington DC's oldest library opened its doors in 1903, it was the only place African Americans could use a public bathroom. During the Depression of the 1930s, the library was considered the "intellectual breadline" where people fed their minds, even when work was scarce.[13] In the 1970s, Information & Referral (I&R) services coincided with reference work so librarians could link patrons with resources outside the library's walls. In the 1980s, social work and library students worked together to assist Nassau County Public Library's elderly patrons' complete Medicare and Medicaid applications.[14]

More recently, a growing number of libraries employ or explicitly dedicate a sector of their services to community outreach, even if they do not engage in formal partnerships with social workers or the like. Many libraries advertise a list of community resources on their websites that are not directly related to library services. Even with official policies, statements, and task forces set forth by the American Library Association,[15] there is no consensus among library staff about providing services viewed as outside their scope of practice[16] and it's not without controversy that some libraries remained open during times of civil unrest[17] and during the early stages of the Covid-19 pandemic. Considering the needs of a community alongside the health and safety of library staff can be a challenge to negotiate.

## Aim of This Book

Given this context about the growing psychosocial needs of patrons and its impact on library staff, the aim of this book is to review and discuss best practices for how libraries can meet the diverse needs of their patrons while also supporting staff. In the following chapters, we will discuss steps your library can take to assess the unique needs of your staff, patrons, and community, the services and collaborations you can offer to address these needs, and how you can transform your overall organizational culture to be as supportive and welcoming as possible for all. We will also examine ways to help staff take care of themselves to avoid burnout and maintain a healthy sense of enjoyment in their work, even while engaging with patrons experiencing life challenges. We include examples to illustrate the points we make and to feature the innovative work libraries are already doing. As authors based in the United States, much of this book focuses on American libraries, yet we have included international examples as well. Therefore, we hope this book finds application and relevance to other libraries throughout the world.

## Terminology Used

Throughout this book we try to be inclusive in the terms used. Recognizing that all library staff are not librarians, we broadly use "library staff" to mean any persons working in a library including, but not limited to, librarians. The majority of this book applies to people in all types of library positions. When we use the term "librarian," it is because we are referring specifically to people who have a degree in library and information science.

Similarly, we recognize that there are many different types of libraries, and content in this book may apply to them as well. We have heard from many academic libraries, for example, that are seeing similar patron challenges as are public libraries. However, a substantive part of this book is informed by our work with public libraries, and when we use the term "library," we are primarily considering public libraries.

Lastly, we recognize that libraries use different terms for the people who use their services, including "patrons," "visitors," "consumers," "customers," and "users," and that there are preferences and reasons library staff or administrators prefer one term over another. For consistency's sake, we chose one word to use for this group of people and selected the term "patrons" for its broad application to people using the library in a variety of ways.

## Notes

**1**  M. A. Provence, E. A. Wahler, J. Helling, and M. A. Williams, "Self-Reported Psychosocial Needs of Public Library Patrons: Comparisons Based on Housing Status," *Public Library Quarterly* (2020): 1–14, https://doi.org/10.1080/01616846.2020.1730738.

**2**  S. L. Desmarais, R. A. VanDorn, K. L. Johnson, K. J. Grimm, K. S. Douglas, and M. S. Swartz, "Community Violence Perpetration and Victimization among Adults with Mental Illnesses," *American Journal of Public Health* 104, no. 12 (2014): 2342–9, https://doi.org/10.2105%2FAJPH.2013.301680.

**3**  F. B. Ahmad, J. A. Cisewski, L. M. Rossen, and P. Sutton, "Provisional Drug Overdose Death Counts," *National Center for Health Statistics, Center for Disease Control,* 2022, https://www.cdc.gov/nchs/nvss/vsrr/drug-overdose-data.htm.

**4**  United Nations Office on Drugs and Crime, *World Drug Report 2022,* 2022, https://www.unodc.org/res/wdr2022/MS/WDR22_Booklet_1.pdf.

5   "63% of patrons and 86% of library managers said more training for librarians on detecting the signs of mental health issues would help" (p.11). L. A. Urada, M. J. Nicholls, and S. R. Faille, "Homelessness at the San Diego Central Library: Assessing the Potential Role of Social Workers," *International Journal of Environmental Research and Public Health* 19, no. 14 (2022): 8449. MDPI AG. Retrieved from http://dx.doi.org/10.3390/ijerph19148449.

6   D. L. Smith, B. Bazalar, and M. Wheeler, "Public Librarian Job Stressors and Burnout Predictors," *Journal of Library Administration* 60, no. 4 (2020): 412–29, 422–3; 426, https://doi.org/10.1080/01930826.2020.1733347.

7   R. Cathcart, "Librarian or Social Worker: Time to Look at the Blurring Line?" *The Reference Librarian* 49, no. 1 (2008): 87–91, https://doi.org/10.1080/02763870802103845.

8   M. Bausman, "Two Noble Professions," *Reflections: Narratives of Professional Helping* 23, no. 3 (2017): 1–8 (p. 5).

9   E. Klinenberg, *Palaces for the People: How Social Infrastructure Can Help Fight Inequality, Polarization, and the Decline of Civic Life* (New York: Crown, 2018), 53.

10   The Library Association, *The Library Association Record* 7, no. 6 (1905, June 15): 295.

11   Bausman, "Two Noble Professions," 1–8.

12   Klinenberg, *Palaces for the People*, 36. Klinenberg further reflects that "public institutions with open-door policies compel us to pay close attention to people nearby. After all, places like libraries are saturated with strangers, people whose bodies are different, whose styles are different, who make different sounds, speak different languages, give off different, sometimes noxious, smells. Spending time in public social infrastructures requires learning to deal with these differences in a civil manner" (p. 45).

13   S. Stamberg, "How Andrew Carnegie Turned his Fortune into a Library Legacy," *NPR*, August 1, 2013, https://www.npr.org/2013/08/01/207272849/how-andrew-carnegie-turned-his-fortune-into-a-library-legacy.

14   R. Tifft, "The Growth and Development of Information and Referral in Library Services: A Selective History and Review of Some Recent Developments," in *Information and Referral in Reference Services*, ed. M. S. Middleton and B. Katz (Haworth, 1988), Vol. 21, 229–59.

15   American Library Association, *Library Services for the Poor*, 2007, https://www.ala.org/ala/ourassociation/governingdocs/policymanual/servicespoor.htm.

16   "historically, librarians have had mixed attitudes about serving patrons in crisis that have changed over time" (p. 63). R. D. Williams and L. Ogden, "What

Knowledge and Attitudes Inform Public Librarian Interactions with Library Patrons in Crisis?" *Journal of Librarianship and Information Science* 53, no. 1 (2021): 62–74, https://doi.org/10.1177/0961000620917720.

**17** J. N. Berry, III, "2015 Gale/LJ Library of the Year: Ferguson Municipal Public Library, MO, Courage in Crisis," *Library Journal* 140, no. 11 (2015): 28–32.

# 1 Understanding Your Library's Unique Needs

Every library is different, based on its community context, organizational structure, funding model, patron population, and available resources. We hope readers recognize that a "one size fits all" approach to all of the collaborations, programming, and services mentioned throughout this book will not work due to these differences. What is useful for one community might not apply to others, and often libraries need to take a design-thinking approach to services. Design thinking is a process whereby someone analyzes a problem or challenge, creates and tries various initiatives or solutions to address the problem, gathers feedback about how the initiative has been working (or not), then uses that feedback to redesign and modify the initiative as needed.[1] The process is ongoing and iterative, making changes as needed to create a solution that will work for the unique challenge and context. To guide the design-thinking approach, we recommend beginning with a needs assessment. Needs assessments are a great way to gather data that will help you understand your library's unique needs and challenges and inform your first iteration of a service or initiative to address the challenges.

## What Is a Needs Assessment?

Conducting a "needs assessment" can sound intimidating, but it doesn't have to be. Anyone can carry out a basic needs assessment without having any specialized research training. We define the term as using a systematic method to uncover the biggest areas of opportunity for your library, and a means of measuring potential barriers and challenges that should be addressed so you can pursue opportunities at hand. Needs assessments are created to be as objective as possible, and the results can be used to determine future service and programming needs. They can also help establish a specific area of need to gain buy-in from your board, city administrators, or funders. In this chapter, we'll review some relatively simple ways you can do a basic needs assessment to help inform your library's programming and services.

# Why Are Needs Assessments Important?

You might be asking yourself why a needs assessment is even necessary. After all, many organizations start programs or new services without first doing a needs assessment, and you may feel confident you have a solid grasp of your library's needs. While that may be true, without a needs assessment it's impossible to know whether the programming or services you are offering directly address a patron's need, how well the services or program will be received and attended, or if you're using your time wisely to address the most urgent or pressing needs. It's essential that libraries understand who is using their library as well as who is not, thereby intentionally designing programs and services to reach constituents and address their related needs. Needs assessments can also help us uncover reasons why people are *not* using our services so we can make changes if needed. When we take the time to do a needs assessment first, we can make data-driven decisions about how we will use our limited staff, time, or financial resources. Why waste time, energy, and money on something that your users don't want or perceive that they need? Having information about the most important needs of your service users, gaps that exist in your communities, and barriers or threats to your programming or services helps to plan initiatives that are likely to be well-attended and well-received. These factors help ensure that you're using your limited resources as efficiently as possible on things that will directly benefit your constituents.

In addition to aiming for efficiency, needs assessments are useful to help justify your services or programming to decision-makers such as city/county administrators, boards of directors, or funders/grant-making organizations. Libraries frequently find themselves requesting additional funding or rationalizing choices to use resources for specific kinds of programming or services. A purposeful needs assessment makes the process of requesting and gaining funding, or justifying the use of funds in a specific way, much easier. It's hard to argue with data!

# The Basic Components of a Needs Assessment

Although libraries with larger budgets might pay a consultant or researcher to conduct a needs assessment, many libraries find themselves without the financial resources to do so. This chapter is for you! We'll lay out the steps necessary to design and conduct a basic needs assessment of your library or community.

When planning a needs assessment, the first things to consider are the *who, what, when, where, why,* and *how* of the process:

*Who* needs to be interviewed or surveyed? *Who* will have knowledge about the need you're trying to understand or define? *Who* will know if data already exists that can inform the assessment?

*What* exactly do you need to know? *What* is it you hope to accomplish with the assessment once finished? *What* resources do you have to put into the needs assessment?

*When* is the best time to collect the information? *When* do you need this information?

*Where* can you find the people you need to ask? *Where* can you find the information you need to know?

*Why* are you doing this needs assessment? *Why* is it important?

*How* will you obtain the information?

Here we walk you through thinking about these details, but we have slightly changed the order of questions to match how we typically walk through the steps involved in the needs assessment process.

## Why

To best plan a needs assessment, it helps to answer the "why" first and think through your objectives. Thinking through why the information is needed will help you plan the rest of the details in a way that will make sense and help explain both the methods you used and the results to whomever will review the report or the findings. For example, will you conduct a needs assessment because you want to design a new program that will cost money and you need to request resources to carry out the program? Do you require a needs assessment to demonstrate your library has a need for additional staff and to justify to your city/county officials that your budget needs increased? Or is a needs assessment necessary to show your board why a policy needs revising? The "why" of your needs assessment will guide in determining which pieces of information you need to include in the process.

## What

Once you're clear about the reasons you're doing the needs assessment, think through exactly what kind of information you need to collect and what resources you have in terms of personnel, time, and money to put into the assessment. What is the purpose of this needs assessment and what do you hope to learn by the end? Does that information already exist in secondary sources, or do you need to collect primary data? In research terminology, *secondary data* means that the information has already been collected in the past and exists in a format we can access and use to answer a new question. *Primary data* means that the data have not previously been gathered and we must collect it ourselves directly from the source. Needs assessments using secondary data can sometimes be completed faster, but one of the pitfalls is that the data were collected by someone else and may not have been gathered in the way we would choose, or it doesn't measure exactly what we prefer. Collecting primary data gives us control over the methods of what information we gather and under what circumstances.

If you determine you will collect primary data, the next "what" question to answer is about what you need to ask. Be specific and clear. Determine whether you need to ask an open-ended question or a closed-ended one. *Open-ended* questions allow participants to elaborate or explain a situation, while *closed-ended* questions require participants to respond yes/no or with multiple-choice predetermined responses. There are important guidelines for question development to ensure the responses obtained give you the information you need and not inadvertently provide something different. Careless or quickly written questions can result in poor, unusable responses. For example, good survey or interview questions should:

- Be direct, using clear, simple, and understandable language. Avoid ambiguous language and define any terms that might mean something different to participants. Create questions that use basic terms people can answer, even if they did not complete primary education.

- Consider the cultural backgrounds of people who will be taking the survey or participating in an interview to ensure that the terms and questions used are clearly defined to obtain accurate responses from participants, no matter their background. Also consider when your survey should be translated into another language, especially when the needs of a particular cultural group are being assessed.

- Ask about only one thing at a time. Often novice question-writers accidentally craft questions asking about more than one concept (a "double-barreled question") which creates the possibility that participants will only answer one part of the question. Alternatively, they may not be able to accurately answer the question because their responses are potentially different for the two concepts comprising the single double-barreled question. For example, "Do you prefer to visit the library for reading material and internet usage?" is a double-barreled question. It's preferable to separate such questions in two, one asking about visiting the library for reading material and a separate question asking about internet usage.

- Ensure there is no bias in the questions or wording that could potentially offend participants. An example of a biased question is, "Do out-of-control teens bother you when using the library space?" Rather, reframe your question by asking, "Have you had experiences in our library that you find troubling? If so, please describe your experiences."

- Avoid leading questions, which are worded in such a way that they influence the response. For example, the question "don't you agree that the library is a safe haven for people in need of community services?" can influence participants to answer in a way they think is expected. It is more neutral to ask, "do you view the library as a safe haven for people in need of community services?"

Best practice for survey development is to craft the survey in collaboration with at least one or two people from the group you are planning to survey. Discussing and determining questions with someone from the targeted group can help ensure your questions will be clear and understandable to potential participants. Additionally, plan to pilot the survey with a small group of people before rolling it out to a larger group. Sometimes questions we deem clear are actually confusing to others. This is a hard lesson to learn when we've already distributed the survey to hundreds of people and then learn that the information we gathered isn't meaningful because the questions were confusing.

## Who

Consider the best source(s) of information for your needs assessment. It's not uncommon that we need to survey or interview multiple groups of people to gain a holistic picture of the needs we're trying to assess. As mentioned earlier, there are also times when someone may have secondary data that's appropriate for our needs assessment or can supplement data we may gather.

## When

When is the best time to collect information? Do patrons in specific groups primarily visit the library at certain times of the day or on particular days of the week? Are you planning to survey people when it's close to a holiday or a time of year the library may be used differently than its typical schedule or pattern? If you need to survey or interview city officials, is there a municipal initiative happening simultaneously that might make it difficult to find people who will engage with you for the needs assessment? Have there been other surveys sent recently that might cause "survey fatigue" and prevent people from responding to yours?

## Where

Lastly, to find participants who have the information you need, where is the best location to interview or survey them, or where can you find secondary sources of data to supplement or inform your needs assessment? If the survey or interview enquires about sensitive information, having a private location is critical. Equally important is inviting people to participate in the survey or interviewing them when they have adequate time and aren't rushed. Thinking through where to reach your ideal participants is an essential part of the needs assessment planning process.

## How

There are a number of different methods you could choose for a needs assessment, including electronic or paper surveys, focus groups, or in-person or phone interviews with patrons. The type of questions you can ask will depend on how you hope to obtain the information. Electronic surveys are quick, anonymous, inexpensive, and easy to analyze, but questions have to be very clear and the overall survey needs to be short. This type of survey also tends to inadvertently exclude people who have low computer literacy or difficulty accessing a computer, which may generate results biased against senior or low-income patrons. Because of the large number of patrons who may use electronic library resources but do not physically use the library space, and depending on what information you're trying to obtain, this may or may not be the group of patrons you hope to reach.

**Table 1.1** *Example of the Needs Assessment Planning Process*

| | |
|---|---|
| **Why** | To assess the need for social work services in the library and, if needed, to justify to the board of directors and city officials that the library needs to pursue funding for this new position. |
| **What** | The library needs to collect information about patrons' unmet poverty-related, mental health, substance abuse, or other needs that would benefit from a trained social worker (questions to be asked for this needs assessment are included in Appendix A). The library needs to know how often these needs arise and how they impact staff. They also need to assess whether staff think the library should address these needs or not. |
| **Who** | Both front-line staff and patrons should be surveyed or interviewed. Security personnel would also be helpful to survey because they interact with patrons on a regular basis, including those who are in crises. |
| **When** | High-need patrons—who would most likely benefit from a social worker—visit the library daily and often stay in the library space from opening until closing. Because a local food organization serves lunch on Mondays and Wednesdays in the park outside of the library, the library sees an increase in patrons with poverty-related challenges on those two days. A survey of patrons could be done any day of the week, but should certainly include Mondays and Wednesdays at lunchtime. |
| | Front-line staff are present every day that the library is open, although they are often busy and might not have adequate time to participate in an interview or survey. Therefore, the survey should be easily accessible, completed according to their own schedule, and available for a couple of weeks to ensure they have an adequate amount of time to respond. |
| | Security staff are in the library only during the hours of 10–6 Monday–Friday so the survey needs could be accessible to them during those times. |
| **Where** | Surveys will be distributed to patrons in the library space to reach people who use the physical library facilities. |
| | Staff from all branches will be included in the survey procedures. |
| **How** | To best reach patrons in this library, a paper survey will be used and distributed to patrons as they enter the library. Volunteers will invite patrons to respond to the survey and will assist them if needed. |
| | For staff, including security, the survey will be available online so it can be completed at their convenience. It will be available for a minimum of two weeks to allow them time to complete it. |

Paper surveys are often a good way to obtain opinions of people who physically enter the library space. However, these types of surveys can take a lot of staff time to enter participants' responses into a spreadsheet for analysis. Additionally, if using paper surveys, it is important that patrons have a way to submit these anonymously so they will be more inclined to answer honestly.

Focus groups are an option for obtaining patron information from targeted groups of patrons. Such groups allow you to ask open-ended questions and seek clarification for any answers that are not clear. They allow the library to identify the themes of responses. However, focus groups make it difficult to attain dissenting opinions from patrons who may have an opinion different from the majority.

## Basic Needs Assessment Ideas

There are many ways to carry out a needs assessment, depending on its specific objectives, resources, and available data sources. In this section, we'll offer some suggestions about simple ways you can begin to assess your patrons', staff's, or community's needs. We have intentionally selected methods that will not require much staff time, financial resources (if any), or advanced research skills. Basic needs assessments can be accessible and approachable for all public libraries and library staff.

### *Patron Needs*

Patron needs assessments can be one of the most informative types of assessments you can do, since they can reveal the views of people who are actually using your library space. Be sure to limit questions to those the library can actually address, either through education, programming, collections, resource lists, or partnerships. When conducting patron needs assessments, consider whether you need to know the opinions of broad patron groups or just subgroups, and plan your methods accordingly. For example, if you're interested in the opinions of your whole patron population, you might consider surveying patrons through the email list as well as through paper surveys made available in library locations. If you're only interested in the opinions of teen or senior patrons, you might pass out paper surveys in programs or locations of your library that primarily serve those subgroups. One library needs assessment that Beth conducted with a practicum social work student specifically targeted patrons experiencing homelessness, so the survey was administered during free meal programs offered at that particular library. As we discussed earlier, plan your needs assessment methods in the best way possible to reach your targeted patron groups.

Common questions for patron needs assessments focused on psychosocial needs include the following:

- What unmet or under-met needs do you have? (Responses commonly include a list of needs and ask participants to check all that apply.)
- How can the library assist you with these needs?
- If the library were to offer programming in the following areas, which might you be interested to attend?
- What resources would you like to see added to the library?
- If the library were to offer the following services, in which might you participate?
- Do you prefer virtual or in-person programs and services?
- Is there anything else you would like us to know about your needs and how the library might help?

See Appendix A for a sample patron needs assessment, which can be modified to fit your library's specific needs.

## Staff Needs

Staff needs assessments can be an important way to determine training needs or to uncover the attitudes or beliefs of staff about their jobs and the patrons they serve. Although many library cultures might encourage free expression of ideas, some staff do not feel comfortable speaking freely in front of their colleagues. This can be particularly true when discussing something that is considered taboo, sensitive, or where their opinion might differ from the majority. This can also be true in diverse staff groups, in which people from marginalized demographic groups or who are in lower-status positions may not feel safe or comfortable revealing their true opinions. Because of these factors, anonymous staff surveys can be particularly helpful to use. These are easy to administer and keep anonymous by using electronic surveys software like SurveyMonkey or Qualtrics.

Staff needs assessments can be used to understand training needs such as de-escalation tactics, a greater understanding of mental health in general, the concepts of trauma-informed care, or what types of self-care or supportive strategies are needed. They can also be used to determine staff readiness for adding a new service or collaboration. Keep in mind that the bigger the staff group who completes the survey, the more you can assume the results are representative of the larger staff group. To increase the likelihood that staff will participate, discuss the importance of the survey with staff and let them know how the information will be used. People are more likely to spend time completing a survey if they know the information will be considered and used to inform services or policies. Assure them that their information will be anonymous and that the library will not be able to identify them unless participants opt to self-identify. Again, people are more likely to disclose sensitive information or to state disagreements if they know they can do so without being identified and without repercussions.

When considering the addition of new services or collaborations to address patrons' psychosocial needs, we encourage libraries to ask questions gauging their staff's attitudes about the roles and responsibilities of the library with these types of needs. If it's determined that a sizable portion of your staff think these services are outside of the scope of the library, this finding is important. It suggests that administration needs to ensure a broad understanding of how these activities fit within libraries and to achieve staff buy-in before moving forward.

Sample staff needs assessment questions include the following:

- What assistance or support could administration provide to help you better serve patrons with psychosocial needs (list examples)?
- Are there library policies that interfere with you serving patrons with these needs?
- What training topics would be helpful to you?
- What community collaborations could help us serve patrons with these needs?
- In your opinion, is it within the scope of the library to add resources (list examples) for patrons with psychosocial needs?
- In your opinion, is it within the scope of the library to provide information (list examples) for patrons with psychosocial needs?

- In your opinion, is it within the scope of the library to offer services (list examples) for patrons with psychosocial needs?
- Is there anything else you would like us to know about what you need to most effectively serve patrons with these needs?

See Appendix B for a sample staff needs assessment, which can be tailored to fit your library's unique needs.

## Community Needs

Community needs assessments are broader than those conducted to evaluate either patron or staff needs. They are designed to identify issues in the wider community that can inform what the library might offer. These types of needs assessments usually focus on identifying widespread community concerns or existing resources and can help identify topics of programming that the library might consider offering. Community needs assessments can ensure that services offered through the library will not duplicate existing community services and may be able to identify gaps existing in the community. Although the library cannot be all things to all people or meet all community needs, it is particularly useful for connecting resources, compiling accurate and unbiased sources of information, and serving as a location to bring together diverse groups of people. These functions position the library to directly address community needs in various ways that will be detailed throughout this book.

Community needs assessments may be completed through direct methods—through surveys or direct contact with people in the community— or indirect methods via existing sources of data. The library may be particularly suited for conducting a needs assessment through indirect methods since library workers are experts in searching available resources and finding and compiling sources of accurate information. For direct methods, libraries may choose to assemble a team of people from across the community who have expertise in a variety of areas, depending on what specific sector of the community is being assessed. For example, if the library wants to identify gaps in services for people experiencing homelessness, they may ask representatives from various homelessness-oriented agencies to assist with the needs assessment process.

To conduct a community needs assessment, you should first determine what question you are trying to answer, or what are the specific areas of need being assessed. For example, a needs assessment focused on identifying broad, general gaps in services for low-income individuals is very different from that specifically focused on understanding the mental health needs in the community and how the library might help. The subsequent methods should derive directly from and relate to this primary goal or question.

See Appendix C for sample community needs assessments.

## A Final Note about Needs Assessments

Needs assessments are a useful tool for determining where to begin when planning a new initiative. However, keep in mind that the results of a needs assessment *inform* your programming and services, but cannot give you all the answers about exactly what type of approach will best address the identified needs. Use the results of your needs assessment as a starting point, look at relevant literature, communicate with library networks or associations, or use strategies mentioned in this book to design your first attempt at a program or service to address your library's needs. As we mentioned at the beginning of this chapter, every library is unique, and what works in one library or community may not work in another. Don't be disheartened if your first attempt fails or has significant challenges. It is through these challenges that we all learn what is needed to grow, improve, and ultimately develop initiatives tailored to our specific patron population, staff, or community's unique needs.

## Summary and Key Takeaway Points

- Needs assessments are useful tools for helping libraries to identify patron, staff, or community needs that can inform programming or services.
- Taking the time to complete a needs assessment prior to beginning a new initiative can ensure that the initiative will best address the specific needs of the individuals your library is attempting to help.
- Needs assessments can also assist the library by gathering data that can be used to write a grant or other funding proposal to obtain financial support for the library's new program.
- Needs assessments inform and relate to a design-thinking approach, knowing in advance that you will have to take a risk by crafting a new

initiative, implementing it, gathering ongoing feedback, and making edits or revisions to the initiative as needed based on the feedback accumulated.

- To plan a needs assessment, consider the "who, what, when, where, why, and how" of the process before getting started.

- There are sample needs assessments available that can serve as templates for patron, staff, or community needs assessment.

# Note

1   R. Razzouk and V. Shute, "What is Design Thinking and Why is it Important?" *Review of Educational Research* 82, no. 3 (2012): 330–48, https://doi.org/10.3102/0034654312457429.

# 2 Transforming Library Culture

*The intention of every deliberately developmental organization's leader in the pages ahead is crystal clear: he or she is working hard on the culture every day as much to enhance the business as its employees. These leaders do not see two goals or two missions, but one. The relationship between realizing human potential and organizational potential in these companies is a dialectic, not a trade-off.*[1]

In this chapter, we'll focus on the cultural shifts that must be planned for and fostered by library leaders to transform the library into a person-centered organization. This includes examining the ways libraries can create a welcoming, supportive organizational culture for staff as well as patrons. As the quote at the beginning indicates, leaders need to focus on people as much as the day-to-day responsibilities of the organization to move forward and grow. Transforming the culture of the library to be person-centered cannot be done without genuinely supporting, encouraging, and challenging staff to reach their full potential as individuals and focusing on their well-being as well as their professional and personal development. Shifts in library services or programs without prior and current emphasis on staff, efforts at clear communication, and attempts to gain consensus around the desired cultural transformation can result in unsustainable programs, disgruntled patrons, and frustrated staff. Meaningful empowerment among librarians stems from a genuine change in the branch's culture, which benefits staff and patrons alike.[2]

## Toxic Workplaces

All organizations have the possibility of becoming "toxic workplaces" to the employees, and libraries are no exception. A toxic workplace is one in which employees feel uncomfortable, unsupported, devalued, stuck, and micromanaged, and sometimes results in employees becoming physically or psychologically unwell. Bullying, manipulation, defensiveness, and abuse may be present, and employees may feel unsafe speaking up or asserting themselves. Negative behaviors become woven into the fabric of workplace culture and may even be rewarded in a particular job, while attempts to improve the environment are unsuccessful or punished.

A quick web search of toxic libraries brings up numerous news articles about library boards and city officials called upon to investigate specific branches due to employee allegations of destructive or unsafe work environments. Staff complaints leading to these investigations include allegations of verbal abuse, racism, heterosexism, favoritism, absent leadership, bullying, staff manipulation and dishonesty, and condescending attitudes and behaviors toward staff by administrators or coworkers. Some libraries have lost funding because of substantiated claims about workplace abuse and toxicity. There's even a Facebook support group for library staff called "Renewers: Recovering from Low Morale in Libraries" where group members process and discuss harmful environments in the field and their resultant experiences of burnout.

Libraries that have become vicious workplaces usually get this way from unprepared administrators who may not know how to effectively manage others. These administrators then use hostile, abusive, or controlling management techniques to try to motivate employees lower in the organizational structure, apply consequences or policies unfairly to different groups of employees, or refuse to address or correct negative behaviors of other staff they supervise. In addition, unresolved trauma can also contribute to unhealthy workplaces and lead to administrators who may have their own difficulty coping with stress, setting boundaries, or otherwise managing the library. As a microcosm of a community, libraries are also environments that are as equally impacted by all of the societal "isms" present in other environments, such as racism, sexism, and heterosexism. No matter the cause, these workplaces have negative cultures felt by everyone who works in them as well as the patrons who visit. Libraries committed to creating a person-centered organization must be as committed to creating and sustaining a positive, healthy work culture for employees as they are to creating a positive culture for their patrons. One way this can be accomplished is by pledging to holistically implement a trauma-informed organizational approach.

## Cultural Shift: Becoming a Trauma-Informed Library

"A trauma-informed approach to our work realizes every choice we make, every interaction we have, every policy we create . . . they all have the potential to be retraumatizing or healing for our patrons and each other," says librarian, consultant, and trainer Karina Hagelin.[3] Anna Scheyett, faculty member at the University of Georgia School of Social Work and collaborator with the Athens-Clarke County Library's Trauma-Informed Library Transformation project, states, "A trauma-informed library is a place where people who have been affected by trauma are welcomed, respected, and helped to find the resources they need, where library staff are supported to understand the challenges of patrons who have experienced trauma and to respond in a positive and non-judgmental way, and where the space of the library itself conveys a message of safety and caring . . . it transforms the library . . . into a place of guaranteed respect, help, and healing."[4] A trauma-informed library is one in which all staff are trained to understand the prevalence of trauma, its potential impacts, and ways to interact with people (including both patrons and fellow employees) that promote healing and health instead of retraumatization.

## What Is Trauma?

Nearly every adult has been touched by trauma of some kind in their life, either by experiencing one or more traumatic events firsthand or by having a close relationship with someone who has experienced trauma themselves. Traumatic events include experiencing violence of any kind, living through an event in which one thought they might be assaulted or killed or saw someone else be attacked or killed, undergoing a serious medical event, or other experiences in which their security or safety was threatened. Globally, about 70 percent of adults report experiencing at least one traumatic event in their lifetime.[5] Adverse childhood experiences (ACEs) are traumatic experiences that occur before the age of eighteen. These occurrences undermine a child's sense of safety, stability, and bonding and may include the traumatic events listed before as well as family poverty, housing instability, food insecurity, parental separation, or parental incarceration. Nearly two-thirds of US adults report experiencing at least one ACE and one out of six adults report experiencing four or more ACEs in their lifetime.[6]

Events may be traumatic for one person but not for another; for something to be considered traumatic, the US Substance Abuse and Mental Health Services Administration (SAMHSA) uses a "3 E Framework." It stipulates that an *event* must have occurred, followed by the *experience* of the event as scary, life threatening, or life changing, and is then followed by *effects* as a result of the event.[7] Moreover, those who are deemed as having post-traumatic stress disorder experience the effects of the trauma longer than six months after the initial event occurred.[8] Therefore, multiple people can experience the same event but have a different interpretation of it and varying effects from it. This is important for libraries to keep in mind, because even experiences in the library can be perceived as highly traumatic for some staff and not bothersome for others.

All demographic groups experience traumatic events and, in general, most individuals recover from them without experiencing any long-term, harmful effects. Yet some groups are at higher risk for experiencing trauma events than others due to ongoing oppression and discrimination. In the United States, people of color, women, people who are gender diverse such as trans or nonbinary individuals, people living in poverty, and those experiencing homelessness are at higher risk of facing traumatic events than people who are not in any of these groups. Since libraries serve the entire public and are often visited by groups of people who are otherwise vulnerable or oppressed, it can be assumed that many people visiting the library have experienced trauma in their lives. Additionally, many people working in libraries have experienced their own personal traumas, sometimes due to workplace incidents but also due to external events that have occurred in their lives.

## The Impact of Trauma

Trauma impacts everyone differently, so library staff will observe people behaving in various ways that could be related to experiences of trauma. However, having some type of trauma response is very common and is the body and brain's way of adapting to harmful circumstances. These adaptations may remain long after the trauma has ended, and the severity of the trauma response may differ based on factors such as the age of the individual when they experienced trauma, the chronicity of the traumatic experiences, and the number of different traumatic events experienced.

Trauma responses may include some, many, or all of the following:[9]

- Difficulty with emotional regulation, such as impulse control or interpreting emotional cues
- Relationship trouble, including the ability to identify and form healthy relationships, trust people, express needs and wants to loved ones, and set boundaries with others
- Cognitive changes, including the ability to form memories, learn new information, concentrate, make decisions, and process language

- Mental health problems, including depression and suicidality, anxiety, or engaging in substance use or other risky behaviors
- The ability to have hope or optimism about the future, or overall feelings about the world being a dangerous and negative place.

Some people who experience trauma develop post-traumatic stress disorder (PTSD). PTSD includes symptoms such as the following:[10]

- Intrusive nightmares, flashbacks, or memories of the trauma
- Intentional avoidance of triggers associated with the traumatic events
- Mood changes such as depression, decreased interest in typically enjoyable activities, and changes in how the individual views the world (i.e. seeing it as dangerous, harmful, scary, or a place where everyone is "out to get you")
- Irritability, over-reactivity, a heightened startle response, hyperarousal (feeling "on edge"), hypervigilance (always being alert to potential danger), difficulty concentrating, or sleep disturbances.

Risk factors for developing PTSD include having a history of previous traumatic events, a personal or family psychiatric history, poor social support, and experiencing physical injury as part of the traumatic event. Although PTSD has a distinct set of symptoms, remember that trauma can and often does impact our behavior even if it does not result in PTSD.

## Trauma and Public Libraries

Jean Badalamenti and Elissa Hardy draw on their experiences as library-based social workers to explain what a trauma-informed approach is and how this relates to libraries:[11]

A trauma informed approach is a clinical social work approach that provides a framework for addressing behaviors. In social work, we . . . understand that a person has experienced adverse life challenges, and as a result views their world through the lens of their trauma experience. This may manifest in what can be viewed as a "behavior issue" or "defiance," or "disruptive behavior." By accepting a trauma-informed approach in libraries, we come to the understanding that what may be viewed as "defiance" etc., is a trauma response for this person, and how this person has learned to cope in their environment . . . View everything you do through a trauma-informed lens, remember that behavior is a person's response to their experiences and environment.

In the library setting, staff often interact with patrons who have experienced trauma, and their traumatic experiences in turn shape patrons' behavior. A trauma-informed framework can provide library staff with context to understand certain patron behaviors such as the following:

- Difficulty with social interactions or reading social cues
- Irritability, rudeness, or being easily escalated and angered
- Staying isolated and keeping to themselves *or* being overly social and talkative
- Using drugs and alcohol
- Wanting the library to be quiet *or* seeking stimulation/chaos
- Anger when things happen that are unplanned
- Inappropriate sexual advances or touching themselves or others.

Having a broader understanding of the reasons why someone may be behaving a certain way helps us have empathy and can depersonalize inappropriate or aggressive behavior we may witness in the library. That being said, understanding the reasons why someone is behaving in a certain way does not mean that we excuse the behavior or allow something to continue that is harmful or abusive to others. Staff should still enforce library behavioral policies and maintain boundaries with patrons about their behavior. Often, it is the library staff who are highly conscientious about patron experiences with trauma that may have difficulty setting boundaries out of compassion for the patron. Understanding trauma does not mean we eliminate or blur boundaries with patrons; rather, it can shape *how* we set those boundaries. We'll discuss this more in this chapter and later in this book.

Additionally, understanding the prevalence of trauma, we must be mindful that many library staff and administrators have also experienced trauma themselves. Any conversation about trauma-informed librarianship is lacking if it doesn't consider staff as well as patrons when discussing how trauma impacts libraries. Many staff have experienced their own ACEs, personal traumatic experiences, and/or workplace trauma. Although library staff may have their own experiences with trauma that occur outside the library context, there is a growing awareness that library work often places staff at a risk of experiencing trauma during the course of their jobs. Karen Fisher, faculty member at the University of Washington School of Information, found high rates of workplace trauma in her research on both urban and rural library staff.[12] Similarly, the Urban Library Trauma Study surveyed 435 urban library staff who reported experiencing job-related trauma and found that 416 of them reported experiencing violence or aggression by patrons.[13] Beth's own research with public library staff has found nearly half of all participants reported experiencing workplace violence or threats of violence and that rates are similar between urban, suburban, and rural staff.

Library-based trauma does not only stem from patron behavior but also from other staff in the library and sometimes directly or indirectly by library administration and management. Notably, the Urban Library Trauma Study found that nearly one-third of participants reported experiencing aggression or violence by their coworkers and twenty by their own managers. Of participants who reported patron-related violence or aggression, many indicated the actual trauma that resulted was more from the mishandling of a situation by the library than from the actual patron incident. The report's authors explain:

> Respondents frequently described situations where staff were not supported during or after an incident, where they were made to feel forgotten, neglected, were not believed by managers or administrators, where they were frustrated by the lack of communication and understanding, or the inconsistent or unequal application of policies and procedures. The predominant themes of survey respondents revolved around library power dynamics (e.g., communication between organizational levels, decision-making power, administration being out of touch with everyday library work, etc.), having (or not having) a supportive work environment (e.g., support form management, administrators, and coworkers, space to speak openly and honestly, incident debriefing, proper training and education, etc.), addressing staffing issues (particularly by increasing the number of staff and security personnel), and creating worker-centered library policies and procedures (e.g., streamlined and equally applied incident reporting, timely follow-up to incident reporting, quicker resolutions to worker complaints or concerns, etc.).[14]

These findings have important implications for library administrators who are attempting to bring about cultural change and create a more trauma-informed organization. *Institutional betrayal*, a term coined by psychologist Jennifer Freyd, refers to "wrongdoings perpetrated by an institution upon individuals dependent on that institution, including failure to prevent or respond supportively to wrongdoings by individuals committed within the context of the institution."[15] Freyd's work has found that experiencing institutional betrayal, such as that experienced by the Urban Library Trauma Study participants, can magnify or worsen the trauma for the person who experienced it. It is essential that library administrators respond swiftly and supportively to employees who have experienced workplace trauma.

In addition to their own personal experiences with trauma, many library staff experience *secondary* or *vicarious trauma* in the course of their jobs. Secondary/vicarious traumatization is when someone experiences a trauma response or symptoms of PTSD stemming from exposure to other people's traumatic experiences. This is considered a common occupational hazard for people in helping professions which, in our opinion, includes library workers. The risk of secondary or vicarious traumatization is greater for women, people who are highly empathetic by nature, or those who are trauma survivors and may have unresolved personal trauma.[16] Notably, the risk of secondary traumatization is higher for people who do not have adequate training, coping mechanisms, or support to deal with others' trauma, which includes library workers as this is not a common component of their academic or professional training. When a worker experiences secondary trauma, it can compromise their own health and well-being, and it can negatively impact their ability to do their jobs. It can also result in people leaving their jobs or the profession altogether.

Staff who experience trauma responses might feel depressed, irritable, or on edge. They might describe feeling burned out, lacking creativity, struggling to concentrate, dreading coming into work, having difficulty sleeping, or using unhealthy coping mechanisms such as drugs, alcohol, or overeating to deal with their trauma-related stress. They might say they're tired of dealing with people or frequently call in sick. Coworkers might observe them isolating, notice that they have poor boundaries with patrons or other staff, or become concerned they no longer approach work or life with the same enthusiasm or excitement they once had. These are all normal behaviors for someone who has experienced trauma, but they have an impact on the library for the staff who have experienced trauma, their coworkers, and the patrons they serve.

**A Note about Burnout.** Burnout is a concern of library workers and administrators everywhere, especially in public libraries that frequently deal with high-needs patrons. Although related to workplace stress and sharing some of the same symptoms discussed earlier, burnout differs from a trauma response and can occur in those who have no previous trauma history and are not experiencing secondary traumatic stress. Burnout is the result of unmanaged workplace stress and includes feelings of exhaustion, increased negativity and cynicism about one's job, and reduced effectiveness at work.[17] The risk of burnout increases for people who have little control in their work, lack the resources necessary to effectively do their job, have unclear job expectations, have dysfunctional work dynamics, have work-life imbalance, or have an absence of social support at work or at home.[18] Burnout has been occurring in many libraries and impacts not only the staff member experiencing it but also coworkers and the patrons served. Although the focus of this chapter is on creating mechanisms for the library to protect workers from trauma-related stress, the benefits of creating a trauma-informed library also extend to staff experiencing burnout. All of these complex workplace problems of firsthand traumatic experiences, secondary traumatic stress, and burnout need comprehensive, holistic approaches to workplace health to be effectively managed and prevented.

## Trauma-Informed Librarianship

One approach to preventing and managing workplace-related trauma and stress for both employees and patrons is to implement a trauma-informed librarianship approach. Although some have heard of trauma-informed care as it relates to healthcare or mental health care, it is less common to see workshops or articles focused specifically on trauma-informed libraries. Yet libraries are the perfect place to implement trauma-informed approaches due to their accessibility by the public, the large number of people who visit libraries every year who have experienced trauma, and the service-oriented nature of library staff. In this section we describe and demonstrate how the trauma-informed principles apply directly to a library context and how libraries can implement these principles as a guide for their policies, practices, and services.

What does it mean to be a trauma-informed library staff member or library? There are six guiding principles of trauma-informed care[19] that should be present and observable in any library claiming to be trauma-informed. See Figure 2.1 for these principles.[20]

Here, we provide a detailed description of each of the trauma-informed principles and describe how libraries can apply them. We also include a scenario to help demonstrate what each one of the principles looks like in a library setting.

## 6 GUIDING PRINCIPLES **TO A TRAUMA-INFORMED APPROACH**

The CDC's Center for Preparedness and Response (CPR), in collaboration with SAMHSA's National Center for Trauma-Informed Care (NCTIC), developed and led a new training for CPR employees about the role of trauma-informed care during public health emergencies. The training aimed to increase responder awareness of the impact that trauma can have in the communities where they work.

Participants learned SAMHSA'S six principles that guide a trauma-informed approach, including:

| 1. SAFETY | 2. TRUSTWORTHINESS & TRANSPARENCY | 3. PEER SUPPORT | 4. COLLABORATION & MUTUALITY | 5. EMPOWERMENT VOICE & CHOICE | 6. CULTURAL, HISTORICAL, & GENDER ISSUES |

Adopting a trauma-informed approach is not accomplished through any single particular technique or checklist. It requires constant attention, caring awareness, sensitivity, and possibly a cultural change at an organizational level. On-going internal organizational assessment and quality improvement, as well as engagement with community stakeholders, will help to imbed this approach which can be augmented with organizational development and practice improvement. The training provided by CPR and NCTIC was the first step for CDC to view emergency preparedness and response through a trauma-informed lens.

**Figure 2.1** *6 guiding principles to a trauma-informed approach.* Source: *Center for Preparedness and Response. "Infographic: 6 guiding principles to a trauma-informed approach." U.S. Department of Health & Human Services. September 17, 2020. https://www.cdc.gov/cpr/infographics/6_principles_trauma_info.htm*

**1.** Safety: The first trauma-informed principle is safety, meaning that the library ensures the atmosphere is safe for everyone, both physically and psychologically. For physical safety, the library attempts to maintain a comfortable, well-lit, and clean physical environment. There are policies in place that attempt to ensure library patrons are safe from physical harm, destructive behavior, weapons, sexual violence, and so forth. Even if the library cannot guarantee physical safety due to unpredictable patron behavior, actions that threaten others' physical safety will be swiftly and consistently addressed. It should be clear that everyone's (both patrons' and staff) safety is of the utmost importance. In addition to having safety-related policies in place, the library ensures that staff are trained and prepared to respond to all types of emergency situations. To ensure psychological safety, the library intentionally creates an atmosphere that welcomes everyone. Staff model supportive and caring relationships with everyone who walks through their doors, literally and metaphorically. All persons who walk through the library's doors are treated with respect, even when there are disagreements or conflict between staff or among patrons. All library policies are clearly communicated and consistently enforced, so everyone knows what to expect of the library. Consequences and behavior of staff should be predictable. They should set clear boundaries and expectations with patrons and with one another. Library administration and staff seek opportunities to ask what people need to feel safe and implement their suggestions when possible.

> Both physical and psychological safety are essential to be a trauma-informed library, because without safety it is impossible to demonstrate the other five principles discussed here. Library director Ashley Stewart gives examples of how she addresses this principle at Caseyville Public Library (CPL), a small rural library in southern Illinois. In addition to being registered as an official Safe Space,[21] CPL does everything possible to ensure the physical building itself feels warm and inviting to all. Stewart notes that "our library is small but it doesn't take much to ensure we provide an inviting space that helps make patrons feel safe. If a library our size can do it, any library can do it. For instance, we offer sanitary and hygiene kits, water and snacks, diapers and charging stations. We have comfortable chairs and free school supplies at our homework station."[22] Even small, inexpensive strategies can help communicate a feeling of warmth and safety to patrons visiting your library.

## Scenario

Wayne was a public librarian at a large urban branch in the Midwest for nearly twenty-five years. He observed[23] that patrons who appeared to be homeless and might benefit from the library's robust list of community partnerships and resources often weren't interested in getting connected and preferred to be left alone. He reasons that this is understandable as most people experiencing homelessness live their lives in public. Privacy and undisturbed quiet are rare when living on the street, in a car, or with others in someone's home or in a community shelter. At Wayne's library, he found the nature of its sizable space provided a refuge for patrons seeking such respite. He acknowledges the library's large campus permitted it to sidestep potentially challenging encounters with patrons pertaining to their hygiene or sizable possessions (i.e., carts).

In this scenario, Wayne's library illustrates the importance of creating a safe environment for everyone and acknowledges that many patrons may not feel safe in other locations like they do at the library. This situation helps to demonstrate that ensuring safety doesn't have to be a constant, active process generated by staff. The library may feel like a safe refuge simply due to its comfortable, welcoming environment and physical space. Following is a scenario that demonstrates the principle of safety from a more active standpoint.

## Scenario

Katrina manages the facilities at her library, which includes overseeing safety and security-related policies and procedures. When she started her position, she implemented a number of practices to help maintain safety: (1) she created a safety-related policy manual and trained all library staff to ensure they were familiar with the policies, emphasizing a trauma-informed, harm reduction approach that focuses on de-escalation when possible, (2) she posted clear signage throughout the library about behavioral and safety-related policies so all patrons would know the expectations, (3) she collaborated with library administration to create a comprehensive library behavior manual detailing behavioral expectations for using the library and describing the standard consequences for behavioral violations, (4) she designated several senior staff members as "persons in charge," worked with administration to ensure one of them was always on the schedule during open hours, and ensured these individuals had training in emergency procedures and de-escalation tactics above and beyond the training of other staff, and (5) she regularly conducted drills of various emergency procedures with staff, including procedures for both physical and mental health emergencies.

---

In this scenario, Katrina actively implemented various policies and practices to maintain library safety and planned for all types of potential emergencies. As you can notice in this scenario, Katrina focused on ensuring staff were trained to deal with library emergencies but also ensured that patrons were aware of safety-related and behavioral policies and understood the consequences for violating them. This type of environment helps to create a sense of both physical and psychological safety in the library.

2. Trustworthiness: The second trauma-informed principle is trustworthiness. In a library context, this means the library is transparent in its decision-making processes and actions, with administration intentionally communicating to staff and constituents why decisions have been made or what information was considered when making decisions or creating

new policies. To demonstrate trustworthiness, administration upholds commitments and ensures that the actions of the library match the stated values and priorities. Behavior of all library employees communicates trustworthiness, or lack thereof, so staff are oriented to the values of the library, expected to behave consistently and respectfully, with consequences enforced if staff are uncivil or inappropriate with patrons or one another. Even when a policy must be enforced, it is done in a compassionate, kind, and transparent way. In a trustworthy library, both staff and patrons know what to expect because behavioral expectations are communicated clearly and policies or the consequences for inappropriate behavior are applied fairly and consistently.

## Scenario

Maurice is the director of a small, rural library. Maurice covers most library duties himself, but he has four part-time staff that assist him. The library's behavioral policies are posted on the website as well as being available on a poster at the front door of the library. There are clear expectations for staff behavior as well, publicly posted and included in staff training and orientation materials. Maurice has received a number of complaints lately about the behavior of one of the new library assistants, namely that the person is sometimes perceived as rude or disrespectful to patrons and other staff and volunteers. This person has just moved to the area and Maurice and others are still getting to know her. Maurice requests a meeting with this assistant and discusses the complaints openly with her to obtain her perspective on what is happening. The library assistant seems shocked at the complaints and embarrassed that Maurice might think she is not doing a good job at work. They discuss that the assistant talks this way with others in her life and what has been deemed inappropriate at the library differs from how she normally talks in her family and social relationships. Maurice understands there could be some cultural differences impacting communication, specifically that the assistant is not from the local area and may not be familiar with customs and expectations. In this meeting, Maurice communicates this with the employee. He states that "we all make mistakes at times" and that he wants to support her professional development and growth. He shares that he believes in supporting employee growth rather than punishing people for mistakes made, especially in relatively minor instances such as this. They spend time talking about examples of what is considered rude and Maurice gives examples of how these conversations could have been handled in a way that would be more positively perceived. He and the employee collaborate to come up with a doable plan for improvement as well as clear communication about what the next steps will be if the problems continue.

---

In this scenario, Maurice acted in a transparent and trustworthy manner while also expecting the same from the employee. When he received complaints, he acted upon them to uphold the behavioral standards he had for the whole library. He held the staff member accountable for her behavior while being fair, kind, compassionate, and acknowledging factors that impacted her behavior. Genuinely caring about her well-being and growth, he clearly communicated support for her professional development and collaborated with her to mutually create a plan for her improvement. He also clearly communicated what would happen if the problems continued. All of these factors demonstrate Maurice acting in a trustworthy manner and also upholding the trustworthiness of the library as a whole.

3. Peer Support: The third trauma-informed principle is that of peer support. Generally, this means that an organization tries to minimize hierarchical structures and intentionally creates opportunities for peers to communicate with, learn from, and support one another. In a library context, this means the structure is created so people at all levels can learn from and receive encouragement, knowledge, and support from one another. This pertains to both patrons and staff. For patrons, this may mean the library offers nonclinical mutual aid or support groups for patrons in the library space. These can entail groups such as twelve-step meetings or other recovery-focused groups, cancer support groups, or abuse survivor groups. In many communities, these types of groups are seeking conveniently located facilities for them to meet free of charge, and libraries are perfect locations for these. Other types of patron-focused peer support might be offered by the library hosting book discussions on biographies or self-help books by authors with lived experiences of discrimination, mental health problems, or living with a disability. Libraries are often quite good at creating opportunities for people to commune over a common interest, typically art

or literature, and these groups or events are no different other than their focus on a particular psychosocial need.

Libraries may not be as experienced offering peer support for their staff, yet this option is equally important in a trauma-informed library. Applying trauma-informed principles to staff means looking for and supporting opportunities for them to develop relationships with one another and encouraging them to support one another in their work. Peer support has actually been demonstrated as an effective way to help people cope with stressful work circumstances and to learn from one another to improve how they handle stressful situations.[24] Libraries might consider offering peer support groups for staff to encourage relationships among them, create opportunities for staff to process difficult work situations, and allow them an intentional space to learn new skills together.

For peer support to be successful, administration needs to set aside time for staff to engage in this rather than expecting it to happen organically. Staff need dedicated time to form peer support groups and often require a structure created specifically for the group, at least until it is established enough to be self-facilitated. It can be helpful to have groups initially facilitated by someone trained in reflective practice or curating support groups, who can then train and model for staff how to self-facilitate the group moving forward. Another way a library can apply the principle of peer support is to intentionally pair new staff with a mentor. Creating clear expectations for mentoring relationships is important to ensure it is as supportive as possible for new staff.

## Scenario

Martina knows that peer support is invaluable and wants to create a mechanism for staff to support one another in the difficult work they do every day. She created a one-on-one volunteer mentoring program for staff, matching new staff members with a senior staff member in a similar position. Before starting this program, she surveyed all staff to determine what would have been helpful when they were new to their positions. In this survey, she also asked staff to brainstorm reasonable expectations for a mentoring/mentee relationship. She used the feedback gathered to develop the mentoring program's structure. In addition to the new mentoring program, Martina also asked for volunteers for a peer support group for front-line staff and ensured that the schedule allowed for all front-line staff to participate in a biweekly group while the essential functions of the library were covered by others. She contracted with a local social worker to facilitate this group for the first few months, just to get it off the ground and until the group had well-established norms, rules, and structure. This group allows staff to discuss stressful events at work and process their reactions. Martina also found that some group discussions prompt members to reach out when they need to learn new skills or when processing a work-related event has led to a need to revise policy or clarify a practice.

---

In this scenario, Martina clearly demonstrated the importance of staff receiving and giving support to one another. By seeking input from all staff when developing the mentoring program, she helped to reduce the impact of the hierarchy and gave staff at all levels opportunities to provide feedback on services that are ultimately there to help and support them. Notably, she also ensured that time for peer support was incorporated into the schedule so staff did not have to obtain support outside of scheduled work hours. Although this can be difficult to do, depending on the size of the library and the number of individuals on staff, creating opportunities for peer support to take place during the workday is essential for it to occur on a consistent basis. Scheduling time for such groups during work hours conveys the importance of peer support for sustainable library practice.

4. Collaboration and Mutuality: The fourth principle of trauma-informed care is collaboration and mutuality. This means that the library and its staff operate from a framework that "we're all in this together" and a spirit that acknowledges that all people heal, progress, and thrive through the power of genuine human relationships. Applying this principle in action means that library administrators and staff use a relationship-first approach, which is apparent in their day-to-day actions with one another. *People matter most*. This should be clear even when needing to enforce policies that result in painful consequences. Policy enforcement can be done in a caring and sensitive manner, being mindful of how the individual is impacted by the policy or the consequences. In a library that practices collaboration and mutuality, library administrators and staff use solution-focused and

strengths-based language with one another, focusing on developing shared goals and outcomes when possible. Staff understand and acknowledge that patrons often behave in ways that are coping mechanisms for them, considering "what happened to you" rather than "what's wrong with you" when reflecting on incidents that occur in which behavior might appear strange, overly aggressive, or otherwise inappropriate. Library administrators intentionally create mechanisms for shared decision-making at all levels, inviting and welcoming feedback from patrons and staff to make informed decisions, guide policies, and inform needed improvements.

## Scenario

Sam is CEO of a midsize suburban library which has forty-two full-time staff members and many other volunteers and part-time staff. Sam's library experienced a crisis this morning when someone overdosed in the bathroom and a staff person discovered them unconscious and lying on the floor. Staff attempted to revive the person but were unable to do so. When emergency responders arrived they declared the person deceased. Staff were quite distraught, especially the staff member who found the person. After the crisis had ended, Sam talked with this staff person privately and learned that her mother also had a substance abuse problem so this situation had hit her especially hard. Sam asked her what supports she had available to help her cope with the stress of the library situation in addition to her personal situation with her mother, and ensured she knew resources she could contact for counseling and support. Sam told her she could have the rest of the day off and to let Sam know if she needed to take additional time. Sam also checked in with other staff members who had been present that day and offered the same thing for them if needed. Sam decided to work the circulation desk for the rest of the day so an additional staff person who was upset by the incident could leave. Sam also personally contacted the city's HR department to inquire about Employee Assistance Program (EAP) resources or other supports and learned that someone from the EAP provider could come and debrief as needed with staff who were present at the overdose. After getting permission from the board, Sam also reached out to local emergency responders and asked if someone from that program could train staff on administering Narcan in the future.

In this scenario, Sam helped to demonstrate collaboration and mutuality by responding in a "relationship-first" way. Visibly concerned about the mental health and well-being of the library staff, Sam volunteered to cover library responsibilities so staff who had been impacted by the crisis could leave if needed. This sends a loud and clear message that "they are in it together" and that Sam does not feel superior as the CEO, and is willing to do whatever is needed to support staff. Sam actively sought assistance for the mental health of the staff, acknowledging and normalizing that a crisis such as a patron overdose and death has a personal impact on everyone.

5. Empowerment, Voice, and Choice: The fifth principle of trauma-informed practice is empowerment, voice, and choice, which applies to both patrons and staff. For patrons, this principle means that the library intentionally gives everyone a voice in programming, policies, and services, and gives people a choice in activities or outcomes. For example, the library might distribute a survey after a program to ask feedback from participating patrons, with feedback being used to improve the program in the future. The library is intentional about specifically empowering people who may not normally have much power in their lives due to discrimination or oppression and ensures that patrons from oppressed/vulnerable groups have opportunities to share their voices.

    With patrons, this means that the library offers a variety of services or programs whenever possible, using feedback from patrons to make programming decisions. Policies are clearly informed by diverse groups of patrons, with consequences of those policies considered for vulnerable or oppressed groups. The library looks for opportunities to empower people to make choices for themselves or reminds them of choices they have. This principle can be particularly important when someone is violating a policy that will have consequences for their access to the library. For example, rather than telling someone they "can't" do something because it's against the rules, a staff member might be intentional about letting someone know they can choose to continue doing what they are doing but that means they are choosing to leave the library at that time and come back at a later date. See the scenario here for an example of how this works in practice.

## Scenario

Marie is working at the circulation desk and multiple patrons complain that someone is panhandling immediately outside the front door. Marie notices that an elderly woman is seated on the sidewalk in front of the door with a sign asking for money, and some patrons are turning away and leaving rather than pass by her to come into the library. Both panhandling on library property and blocking an entrance are prohibited by library policy. Marie knows she has to ask the woman to stop doing these things but is concerned that the woman might need help or to be connected to resources. Marie walks to where the woman is seated and says, "Hi, I'm Marie and I'm the Circulation Manager here. I couldn't help but notice that you're asking for money. I'm not sure if you know, but we have a resource list we can give you if you need to connect to resources here in town. That list includes places that give financial help as well as food, clothing, shelter, or other things you might need. We also have some snacks and warm coffee inside the library, if you'd like to come in and sit down for a little while?" The woman thanks her but says she doesn't need anything and wants to stay outside for now. Marie responds and says, "Okay, I just wanted you to know those things were available anytime we're open if you decide you need them in the future. However, if you're going to stay outside I have to ask you to please move over to the bench on the sidewalk [points to a bench on the library property] so you're not blocking the entrance. We have to ensure that everyone can come and go from the library without the risk of accidentally hurting you or having difficulty getting through the door. Also, nobody is allowed to ask for money or anything else on library property. If you want to sit on our bench, I have to ask you to please put down your sign. However, I understand that you might really need money right now, so if you want to continue using your sign please move to the corner over there [points to a public bench on the street across the road from the library parking lot] because that's not considered library property."

---

In this example, Marie provided several options for the woman to allow her to have a choice in the outcome. The woman had the option of coming into the library to access resources and have a snack, the option of sitting on the bench by the front door, or the option of moving across the street. Ultimately, her ability to make her own choices was reinforced and respected in this scenario and worded in a way that did not imply judgment.

For staff, the principle of empowerment, voice, and choice means that administration attempts to reduce the hierarchical nature of the library, ensuring that staff at the bottom of the institutional hierarchy have a voice in processes and policies. There is an intentional effort to diversify the board, administration, and all decision-making groups so decisions are made with diverse voices at the table.

## Scenario

Sean became the director of a large, metropolitan library that had operated quite formally until he began his position. The previous director made nearly all of the decisions by herself and led using a top-down approach. Meetings were rarely held unless she wanted to inform people of a decision she had already made; communication was almost always one-directional. Morale at the library was very low when Sean became director, and he noticed that employees rarely voiced their opinions even when asked directly. Sean decided to hold regular staff meetings where he talked openly about important issues impacting the library and asked all staff for their input. Noticing that people did not feel comfortable talking in the meetings or providing their opinions, he created a monthly electronic "check-in" form which allowed staff to offer their opinions and feedback on any library matters that were important to them. After he started collecting these opinions, he discussed themes of the feedback in staff meetings and shared how they informed his decisions. As staff recognized that their opinions mattered and their feedback was being used to shape the future of the library, more of them began speaking up. Sean demonstrated that he not only welcomed their feedback, but that he respected their opinions and experiences.

---

In the foregoing example, Sean was able to intentionally create a work environment where all employees had a voice in many of the decisions being made. The anonymous method he used to solicit feedback also ensured that people with dissenting views would have a safe way to share their opinions without fear of reprimand from others. Of course, not all decisions are appropriate to discuss with all staff, but library administrators should voice what can be safely shared with others and seek as many opportunities as possible to solicit feedback. Not only does a shared decision-making process help with empowering staff to express their opinions, it also enables a director to make well-informed decisions that already have buy-in from their staff.

6. Cultural, Historical, and Gender Issues: The final principle of trauma-informed practice involves cultural, historical, and gender issues. This principle entails that everyone in the organization is aware of specific cultural or historical issues that impact peoples' experiences of the organization, their perceptions of the choices they have to make, or how they might interpret specific interactions within the organization. In the library, this means that administrators and staff understand how contextual factors impact peoples' choices and behaviors and they are cognizant of how demographic factors may impact trauma and resilience. Library policy and practice should reflect this understanding and knowledge.

Library staff and administration should make equity-minded decisions to try to repair or reduce harm for vulnerable, underrepresented, or oppressed demographic groups. Administrators should intentionally invite opinions and respond to the cultural needs of staff and patrons, particularly those from oppressed or marginalized groups. Library leaders and staff should review policies, procedures, and practices for disparate outcomes among specific demographic groups and make changes when needed. The Public Library Association's (PLA) Social Worker Task Force offers a useful guide to help libraries review and reframe existing behavioral policies through a trauma-informed lens.[25] The library should also offer culturally relevant programming and services for the local community and patron groups. Trauma-informed libraries are intentional about creating opportunities for cultural and cross-cultural connections among patrons. The library should ensure there is gender-inclusive signage, bathrooms, and that staff use gender-inclusive language.

Librarian and trauma-informed trainer Karina Hagelin emphasizes the importance of universal design principles to ensure library spaces are accessible for all patrons. It's critical for libraries to regularly assess and prioritize the modification and adaptation of their physical spaces, particularly for individuals with disabilities or health concerns. Karina reminds us that not all disabilities and physical challenges are visible or obvious; therefore, ensuring libraries are accessible benefits everyone.[26]

## Scenario

Marc is a library branch manager and finds himself needing to talk with a patron about her disruptive behavior. The patron is standing in the library lobby and talking loudly to herself, cursing and frightening other patrons nearby. Before Marc approaches her, he pauses to consider how several factors might impact the conversation he needs to have with her. First, as a man approaching a woman, he is aware that his gender might influence how she perceives his comments. He has seen her at the library before and, although he doesn't know details about her life, he thinks she may have been a victim of intimate partner violence based on interactions he's observed of her with other males who are sometimes with her. He is also aware that she's unhoused and he knows that she's had several negative interactions with police and authority figures. He worries that she may perceive him as yet another person who wants to control or harm her, and he knows she may not automatically trust him or feel comfortable with him. He wants to ensure the conversation is successful and knows that asking someone to change their behavior is difficult under any circumstances. Before approaching her, Marc decides to include another staff member, Brenda, who is a soft-spoken and mild-mannered woman. He has noticed that Brenda and this patron had previous conversations and perceives the patron feels comfortable around Brenda. Instead of Marc approaching the patron, he asks Brenda to talk with the woman, to ask her to lower her voice and stop cursing so she can stay in the library.

---

In this scenario, Marc is mindful of how contextual and personal factors might impact the conversation based on the patron's personal experiences. He uses that knowledge to guide his decisions on how to best address the patron's behavioral issue. With an awareness of cultural, historical, and gender issues, Marc decides to involve someone else in the conversation to increase the chances the discussion will be a positive encounter.

Libraries attempting to provide trauma-informed services should consider all six of the aforesaid principles and incorporate them throughout the library's policies and practices. Many libraries are using at least some of these principles without always knowing it or referring to them as "trauma-informed," and they are successfully providing welcoming and comfortable spaces for community members. Librarian, writer, and activist Dr. Julie Ann Winkelstein concurs that many libraries already exhibit practices that involve "patience, a sense of humor, listening, showing respect, examining your policies and procedures, having signage that uses positive language rather than shouting 'no, no, no'—all of these contribute to an environment that feels welcoming and safe."[27] Similarly, Caroline Sharkey, former coordinator of the Trauma Informed Library Transformation (TILT) program and current consultant to public libraries, observes that "libraries are remarkably developed to be safe. They are actually the perfect example—for me as a social worker—of spaces that are designed to be trauma-informed. Their empathic architecture demonstrates thoughtful, safe, and open inclusive spaces."[28] With many libraries already demonstrating at least some of the principles of trauma-informed librarianship, a few modifications and changes to fully implement the framework might be all that is needed.

Trauma-informed approaches create healthier organizations for patrons and library employees alike, prevent re-traumatization for those who have experienced trauma, reduce the number of escalating events or disciplinary actions, and increase overall morale, communication, satisfaction, and shared decision-making for both staff and patrons.[29] For library staff interested in applying a trauma-informed approach directly to common scenarios involving patrons, the PLA Trauma Informed Workbook uses a case-based model to illustrate how library staff can respond in a trauma-informed manner.[30] There also are a number of consultants available to support this work, if expert assistance is needed for assessment and guidance.

## Organizational Change Process

Although many libraries are already incorporating some aspects of trauma-informed services, for others implementing this framework may be more of a stretch. Savvy administrators need to recognize that not all organizations are immediately ready to make a significant change and that the necessary steps required to initiate and sustain change will depend on the readiness of the library. As social workers, we are often trained to apply the Transtheoretical Model of Change[31] to individuals as we work with them to make a life change such as stopping substance use, taking prescribed mental health medication, or making lifestyle changes such as beginning an exercise routine or diet. However, we discuss the Transtheoretical Model in this chapter because it also applies to changes in organizations such as libraries.

The Transtheoretical Model helps one to understand the complex process people go through when attempting to make life changes, and it explains why some are able to make and sustain major changes in their lives while others do not even recognize they have a problem or have difficulty taking small steps to address a significant problem. The stages of change are as follows:

1. Precontemplation
2. Contemplation
3. Preparation
4. Action
5. Maintenance

People making any substantive change to their life typically progress through all five of these stages during the process, sometimes including relapses and returning to earlier stages of change.

In **precontemplation**, the person does not yet recognize that they need to make a change and is not intending to take any type of change-related action. In this stage, we see people that we commonly refer to as being "in denial" of a problem that others can recognize. **Contemplation** is the next stage of change in which the individual can now see that they need to make an adjustment in their life but they're not ready to do so and are not planning any immediate actions. During **preparation**, the person is actively making plans to soon take action, perhaps by exploring the best methods to use or gathering the support they need to make a change. In **action**, the individual is actively making a change in their life, and during the **maintenance** stage, they are working to maintain their new change. Any attempts to place pressure on individuals during the early stages of change will most likely fail, since they are not yet ready. Instead, preferable actions for people early in the change process are ones that draw attention to the consequences of their current actions and create a discrepancy between what they think is not a problem and the reality of their lives. Such strategies can help people progress through contemplation, preparation, and eventually to the action stage.

Let's walk through these stages with a scenario to demonstrate how they tend to look in a real-world case:

## Scenario

Darlene was a woman with a history of alcohol use disorder. She drank heavily for nearly twenty years and developed multiple alcohol-related health problems. Her family and friends tried to talk to her about her drinking and convinced her to go to treatment, but she felt she could control her drinking on her own and attributed her health problems to genetics rather than alcohol. At one point, her mother paid for her to see an alcohol specialist, but Darlene only went once because she did not view herself as an alcoholic or someone in need of such services. *This is what it looks like to be in precontemplation.*

She went to numerous doctors for her health problems, all of whom suggested it was her alcohol use causing her illness. At first, she rejected what the doctors were saying, but after she heard it from five different specialists she began to consider that even if genetics caused her health problems, her alcohol use might be making them worse. She started to consider what life would be like for her if she stopped drinking. Yet after two decades of alcohol use, this was a scary prospect because she no longer knew how to navigate life while sober. She began reading blogs and intentionally seeking out information from people who were in recovery from alcohol use. *This is the contemplation stage.*

After about six months of learning how other people managed a sober life, Darlene began exploring possibilities for treatment. She read reviews about treatment programs in her area, explored what the costs would be, and consulted with human resources at her job about taking medical leave. *This is the preparation stage.*

After exploring her options, Darlene chose a treatment program and made an appointment. She chose to enter a residential program for women, which provided long-term support after the residential component that included peer support, outpatient groups, case management, and individual counseling. When Darlene entered the treatment program, *she moved into the action stage of change.*

She remained in the program until she graduated and then moved back into her own home. While at home, she continued to participate in peer support groups, outpatient counseling, and individual counseling. To minimize the temptation to drink, she formed a new social support group of people abstinent from alcohol. *This is the maintenance stage of change.* People often have to make significant adjustments to their lives to maintain change, which applies not only to sobriety but to all kinds of changes such as weight loss, exercise routines, dietary modifications, smoking cessation, and so forth.

---

Although this model of understanding change is widely used for individually focused services such as substance-use treatment, weight-loss programming, and other services focused on helping people make significant changes to their lives, it has also been applied to the process of organizational change.[32] Understanding and applying this Transtheoretical Model of Change to their own organizations can help library leaders understand barriers to change, reduce staff resistance to change, increase participation and buy-in, and ultimately increase the success of change efforts.

Libraries are comprised of many different individuals and those individuals within the organization need to agree to and be motivated to make the necessary change for it to succeed. If the library attempts a major alteration to its operations, mission, or focus but only a quarter of employees are ready for the shift, it is unsurprising that the change may very well fail. Before initiating any modifications, library leaders should assess the overall organization's readiness for change and adjust their strategies accordingly. Matching actions to the organization's stage of change (discussed further here), rather than pushing forward when it isn't ready, will increase its chances of success.

## Leadership Strategies for Supporting Cultural Change

As we mentioned earlier, burnout, secondary traumatic stress, and trauma responses are complex, interconnected issues in public libraries (and other workplaces) and require broad organizational solutions. Transitioning an entire library to be a trauma-informed organization is no small feat. From our work with numerous libraries, as well as our work in other types of management and administrative roles, it is clear to us that successful library initiatives and trauma-informed responses are dependent primarily on the quality of support from library administrators. In order for a true transformation of library culture to take root and thrive, change must be initiated and instituted from the top. It is critical that library leaders and directors demonstrate a genuine commitment to change and growth, even in the face of inevitable challenges. They need to engender buy-in from their staff and help them understand reasons their library culture needs to transform and how these changes will benefit everyone in their branch's community. No matter the size of the library, organizational and leadership principles and strategies are extremely important for creating sustainable change. Based on our experiences with leaders in libraries of all sizes, we highlight specific strategies that can be utilized in public libraries to demonstrate each of the leadership principles mentioned earlier.

## Lead with a Relationship-First Approach

For a library leader trying to create a person-centered library, one of the most important strategies is to use a *relationship-first approach*. From our perspective, a relationship-first approach means leaders intentionally focus on developing genuine, trusting, and caring relationships with everyone on their team. The health and well-being of people is primary and this is reflected in the leader's actions and behavior. When operating from this approach, staff feel heard and trust that their concerns matter. Staff are more likely to open up about stressors and to voice suggestions for improvement. When traumatic or stressful events happen in the library, staff undoubtedly know their well-being is valued by their supervisor and they feel supported. When modeled from the top down, the expectation is for all staff to operate from a relationship-first approach. This in turn impacts relationships between library staff, workplace satisfaction, and well-being, and also affects relationships between staff and patrons.

## Hire with a Vision in Mind

One of the best strategies for transforming an organization is to hire with an overall vision in mind of what the leader wants the library to look like and what kinds of characteristics or skills are important for team members to possess. Although many leaders inherit a library team they have when they first begin their position, staff vacancies and new positions create opportunities to transform the culture of the organization. Everything from the composition of the hiring team, the creation of interview questions or formats, and how job positions are worded sends a message about the type of organization the library is and wants to be.

Depending on the community, libraries can face challenges with hiring because people lack an accurate understanding of what a modern library entails or the responsibilities of working within one. Although it is important to correct false assumptions or misunderstandings about public libraries, the discrepancy between public perception and reality can mean that people apply for or are hired for library positions without understanding the context in which they will be working. To best prepare new employees for the reality of library work, it is essential to use the hiring process as an opportunity to educate applicants about the role and what to expect. Anne-Maree Pfabe, manager of City of Melbourne Libraries in Victoria, Australia, notes that she intentionally hires front-line staff "who would be comfortable working in a pub."[33] To her, this means that people she hires to work on the front lines of the library have the natural ability to talk to diverse groups of people and are able to make everyone feel welcome, but they are also able to set boundaries when someone crosses a line. Although different libraries have varying expectations about specific jobs, Ms. Pfabe's criteria for hiring applies to many front-line library positions.

## Be Intentionally Inclusive

Person-centered libraries create opportunities for *all* constituents to have a voice and intentionally listen to people who may be marginalized, oppressed, or underrepresented in libraries. Due to societal "-isms" such as racism, sexism, heterosexism, and ableism, individuals from marginalized groups may rarely operate in environments where they feel empowered to speak up and know that their opinions and perspectives matter. Even in a library environment that intentionally invites their opinions, patience, and persistence may be required as it can take time for marginalized persons to become comfortable based on their previous experiences in which their voices were not welcomed.

A leader who intentionally listens, values, and incorporates feedback from diverse voices can generate an inclusive environment where everyone feels welcome and heard, and ultimately usher in better policies, programs, and services. Library director Tonya Garcia speaks about the importance of "egoless decision-making," which entails putting aside one's ego to remain open to feedback from others that you're trying to serve.[34] When receiving difficult feedback, criticism, or acknowledging mistakes she tries to ask herself, "is this for your ego or is this for the betterment of the program?" Tonya's approach is a positive one for fostering an environment that solicits and utilizes feedback from diverse voices.

## Create a Safe and Supportive Environment

Public libraries often serve as a "protective factor"[35] for patrons, which means that offering a safe, welcoming, and supportive environment can actually reduce or mitigate other societal harms for vulnerable or oppressed individuals. Recognizing and being mindful of the ways in which libraries provide safe spaces for patrons can extend the scope to being a *transformational* space instead of merely a *transactional* one. One former library social worker, Patrick Lloyd, found that facilitating a perspective shift of his suburban library's staff to recognize and build upon the protective factor concept was helpful. "Seeing our building and ourselves as protective factors, our goal when interacting with patrons who face substantial challenges is no longer to simply provide helpful customer service but to also consider how we might increase the chances that those patrons return [to our library] again tomorrow."[36] Leaders of person-centered libraries should communicate to their staff that the library operates as a protective factor for many people at risk of harm in the local community, and a goal of the library is to reduce this harm, prevent retraumatization of people who have been victimized, and help bring about good for those individuals and the wider community.

## Use a Strengths Perspective

Transforming into a trauma-informed organization means that we use and demonstrate a strengths perspective in our day-to-day work. The strengths perspective is commonly known and discussed in social work education and practice but, in our experience, is lesser known in the library world as such. Yet we recognize many public libraries are naturally using asset-based approaches in their day-to-day work. What is the strengths perspective? Originally attributed to the work of Dennis Saleebey, the strengths perspective was designed as a social work approach to working with people who had severe mental illness and was later expanded to other populations and areas of practice.[37] Rather than focus on someone's weaknesses, challenges, and barriers, the focus is instead placed on their capacities, talents, resources, and possibilities.[38] This is opposite to the way some of us are oriented since we are socialized to look for the "cracks," the diagnosis, the symptoms, the label, and the problems. It is normative to see the negative in someone, especially someone who might have mental health challenges, be visibly impoverished, or who seems to have a substance abuse issue. In the United States, our culture focuses on one's "deficits," and we're quick to pathologize others for symptoms they may display. Yet even a person with high needs has *some* and often *many* strengths if we look beyond their immediate needs. It is through this recognition and awareness of one's strengths that we may be able to establish rapport with them, build their self-esteem and confidence, empower them to make choices for themselves, and ultimately help them make progress toward their goals.

A considerable body of research provides evidence for using a strengths perspective when working with high-needs individuals as well as the general public. The messages we receive about ourselves often correlate directly with our self-esteem, confidence, self-efficacy, and overall well-being.[39] A supportive environment that emphasizes our strengths can help us function better, have higher achievement in school and at work, feel more satisfied with our lives, and cope better with life stressors.[40] A strengths perspective can also be particularly powerful for people who have interfaced with social services, "welfare" organizations, or the criminal justice system, many of which tend to focus primarily on one's "deficiencies."

It's important to note that, when learning about the strengths perspective, some people misunderstand the concept by erroneously concluding we should ignore challenges, problems, or barriers and disingenuously focus only on the positive. This is untrue. It is possible to assist people while recognizing barriers, challenges, and boundaries and simultaneously capitalize on their existing strengths and resources.

## Assess the Organization's Stage of Change

Based on information earlier in this chapter about the stages of change, it behooves library leaders to analyze their organization's current stage of change before moving forward with a new initiative. How much buy-in does leadership have in regard to change? Is the organization as a whole in a stage of precontemplation or contemplation, or is it ready for action? If the organization is not yet ready to change, strategies to highlight the discrepancy between the library's current state and the type of library that staff desire can be helpful. Some of these strategies are included here.

---

### Strategies for Supporting Organizational Change Using the Transtheoretical Model

To prepare an organization for change, there are overarching strategies leadership can use to help usher staff into the action and maintenance stages of change. Prochaska, Prochaska, and Levesque (2001) suggest the following strategies to facilitate change in an organizational context, and we adapt each one of them here to fit a library context. These strategies include the following:

- *Consciousness-raising*: Increasing motivation for change by bringing awareness of how the library's current practices or policies are problematic.

To do this, library managers might choose a specific problematic policy, ask staff to collect data about the number of times that policy causes a conflict in the library, and allot time in a staff meeting to discuss the data and examples of how the policy generates conflict. For staff who may not have realized or accepted the policy as problematic, this can help raise their awareness and increase motivation to change the policy.

- *Self-reevaluation*: Helping staff to see that the change is important to their own identity, happiness, and success.

   To implement this strategy, a library manager might spend time in a staff retreat or meeting by asking staff to consider why they initially chose library work and to write down how their current work aligns (or does not align) with those initial reasons for selecting librarianship. What did they imagine this work would be like? How is their current work different from how they envisioned it? What kind of library do they want the organization to be? For staff who experience their work in the library as different than what they want it to be, time can be spent discussing what needs to change to align their work with their own happiness and vision of professional success. These conversations can open the door for more conversation about developing a person-centered approach, which often aligns with most staff's images of what library work would be.

- *Self-liberation*: Encouraging staff to visualize success with the change and obtaining a firm commitment from them for the change.

   For this strategy, library managers might spend time in a staff meeting or retreat asking them to consider what success with the desired change will entail or how it will look (i.e., how will the library know it has been successful with change?). Staff may be asked to consider things they or others do that derail or prevent the change from being successful and then think about what is needed from them as individuals to make the change successful. At the end of the exercise, staff can express through words or in writing their commitment to doing their part to ensure a successful change.

- *Environmental reevaluation*: Helping the staff group understand and accept that the change will have a positive impact on their own work and social environments.

Library staff should spend time discussing how they feel about their work and share discrepancies that exist between how they experience their work environment and the way they want the library to be. It can be helpful to walk staff through the process of visualizing the library after the change, perhaps including an exercise where they write descriptors or draw pictures of the enhanced library environment and consider how their experiences of work will be different after the change is made. Envisioning how the change will personally benefit their work and their vision of themselves can be quite powerful to engender widespread support for a new initiative.

- *Counter-conditioning*: Replacing dysfunctional or unproductive ways of working with new behaviors or thoughts.

Rather than simply telling people to stop doing something perceived as negative, counter-conditioning replaces the negative behavior with a new, positive action. When making changes in our lives, it is often hard to break old habits by just telling ourselves to stop doing something unproductive or harmful; this applies with professional, work-related changes as well as personal ones. Change is rarely successful long-term unless we replace a negative behavior with a positive one. If we find that library staff are correcting patron misbehavior through a scolding or condescending manner, we need to help them learn more productive and strengths-based ways for managing patron behavior. Creating a worksheet that clearly demonstrates both unproductive and more productive methods of communicating with patrons to correct patron behavior could be helpful, combined with training or discussion to practice the more productive methods of behavior correction. Replacing unproductive habits with new skills can help maintain the change we are trying to make.

- *Helping relationships*: Creating and implementing mechanisms for social support to facilitate the change.

This strategy for facilitating organizational change is useful when there are internal "champions" of the change that library administrators can intentionally rely on to influence others. When looking at library staff groups, there are always people who are particularly influential, either in a formal way due to their managerial positions, or in an informal way based on their personality types or strong relationships with other staff. Choosing influential staff and intentionally nurturing them as "champions" of the change can help influence the way the rest of the staff group perceives the change.

- *Stimulus control*: Restructuring the overall library to include reminders and prompts of the new behaviors.

  It is difficult for people to learn and sustain new ways of thinking without prompts and reminders. Providing concrete examples of reframing negative behaviors on a handout or small sign and strategically placing these at the circulation desk or other places frequented by staff can help counter-condition them to use strengths-based terminology rather than shaming or blaming language to refer to patrons. Placing cards that say "What happened to this person to make them talk to me this way?" is a reminder to think in a trauma-informed way and helps interrupt the habit of judging behavior as "bad" or thinking, "What is wrong with this person?" We all need prompts and reminders to adopt new behaviors and ways of thinking until the new way of thinking becomes second nature.

Libraries will be most successful with initiating and maintaining change if all of these strategies are incorporated in the overall approach.

## Use Clear and Consistent Communication

Person-centered leaders should focus on consistent communication with all library constituents. This means clearly communicating with staff, especially about decisions made and the reasons for those decisions, as well as ensuring policies, procedures, and practices are well-known and understood by all. Although this unified communication takes effort, it is essential that all library staff are on the same page about expectations and understand the purpose or reasons behind policies. Clear communication is also important for patrons, particularly for ensuring they understand expectations for their behavior and consequences that will occur if they violate behavioral policies.

*How* we communicate policies about behavior at the library is as important as what we say, and the language we use should be clear and fair, without being punitive or negative.[41] For example, optimal phrases such as the *suspension of library privileges* are preferable to *banning* patrons[42] as it communicates an outcome without the disciplinary tone. Public libraries might consider getting help from outside partners to recontextualize behavioral policies in a way that is more trauma-informed. For example, some social work students assist libraries with creating equitable and trauma-informed policies as one of their practicum/ internship tasks. Other libraries might choose to hire a consultant focused on trauma-informed organizations to guide policy changes. Additionally, inviting persons with lived experiences to share their insight on the language of library policies can be a powerful way to gain insight from patrons who may otherwise be overlooked.[43] It's also important to keep in mind that if a patron's actions are in conflict with the stated policies of the library, we must focus on the behavior more than the individual. What may be deemed as odd or strange behavior to some is not necessarily wrong or incorrect. To borrow a phrase from social worker and trainer Patrick Lloyd, we could simply chalk up a patron's way of being in the world as "her normal" even if it is different from our own experiences.[44]

## Recognize and Reward Small Successes

Change is hard and typically takes a long time to adopt. To keep staff motivated (and frankly, to keep themselves motivated!), leaders should intentionally plan on recognizing small "wins" as they occur. Sometimes people look for significant differences to indicate change has taken root, but it can be a bumpy path until a major shift occurs. Even minor changes in the right direction should be acknowledged and celebrated. Rewards and positive reinforcement for staff should also be built into the recognition strategy to help reinforce and maintain small steps in the right direction. Using the Transtheoretical Model of Change described earlier, this strategy is known as *reinforcement management*. It can be particularly helpful for libraries that have already made a significant change (and are in the action stage) and need to sustain it long-term.

In practice, reinforcement management might include attaching something positive to the desired action we want to see. If the library creates a mechanism for ongoing peer support, such as organizing reflective practice groups for staff to process work-related stress and to learn skills for addressing patron challenges, library administrators might consider scheduling these groups over lunch breaks and providing food for those who attend to encourage everyone to participate. Similarly, if the changes made are to make the library a friendlier and more strengths-based environment, library administration might craft a system whereby staff or patrons can nominate one another for an award based on their positive handling of a difficult situation. Incentives do not need to be something expensive; genuine appreciation and recognition can go a long way to sustaining long-term behavioral change.

## Provide Opportunities for Staff Training

A considerable piece of creating a person-centered workplace culture is supporting the development of staff and having them engage in regular and worthwhile training. Training is helpful for ensuring that staff understand and have empathy for high-needs patrons and can also increase their sense of competence and confidence for handling patron needs. Psychosocial education for library staff, including security personnel, is critical for helping them understand the structural barriers many patrons face to care, housing, and other basic needs. From a social work perspective, training on how macro-level societal factors may impact some of our patrons can help us understand a bit more about the micro or individual ways they operate in the world. In doing so, we refrain from blaming our patrons and begin to change an aspect of the library environment.

Community partners can be helpful by providing library staff with training that can bolster their knowledge about the services of local agencies and facilitate a warmer handoff[45] or referral to help address the psychosocial needs of patrons. Many times, community partners will provide such instruction for free. We know of many libraries that have been able to implement staff-wide training on de-escalation, setting boundaries, mental health, substance abuse, poverty-related needs, community resources, serving patrons experiencing homelessness, and other topics at a reduced or zero cost. Persons with lived experiences also have their own expertise to offer that is worth considering, and they may be able to facilitate training on select topics. To help library administrators know where to start, it can be helpful to start with a training needs assessment of library staff (refer back to Chapter 1 for how to conduct a needs assessment and Appendix B for a sample staff needs assessment survey). Winkelstein also provides a *Library Staff Survey* template that can determine what trainings are most desired by staff. Administrators should be wary of requiring too many instructions as staff can indeed experience training fatigue. Educational opportunities should be selected for their relevance, importance, and practicality rather than taking advantage of every opportunity that comes your way.

# Limits to Cultural Change

Although this book has focused on cultural shifts that libraries can make, and we want to empower libraries to take steps to alter their internal cultures when needed, we also want to point out that libraries are just one component of a community and may be limited by the culture of that community. A popular theory in the field of social work is *systems theory*, which posits that human behavior is heavily influenced by the larger systems and environment surrounding an individual. Even when we desire change, sometimes our surroundings act against us and limit the changes we want to make. Similarly, the library is one system in a broader community and is similarly impacted by the context surrounding it.

Sometimes the library's change efforts may be stymied by other organizations and entities that don't operate from a trauma-informed or compassionate point of view. Especially today, when libraries attempting to ensure unbiased and uncensored access to information are being viewed as too "progressive" and are threatened with a loss of funding or even violence, well-intentioned administrators and staff may have their hands tied when it comes to some changes they wish to make. Throughout the rest of this book, we highlight various initiatives libraries can make to provide services to high-needs patrons. But depending on the culture of the wider community, motivated staff may have to adjust their expectations for the types of changes possible or the timeline for those transformations in light of the community in which they are located.

As social workers who maintain a sense of optimism in the face of adversity and challenges, we believe change is always *possible*; however, we want readers to set realistic expectations for their libraries given their community context. Since libraries are central and key components of a healthy community, we believe that even small changes in the library can have a positive ripple effect on other organizations in the community. Just as organizational change can be slow, community-level changes can be even more sluggish. It's important for all libraries to focus on the things within your control that you can change and take whatever steps possible to elicit a healthier environment for your staff and patrons.

# Summary and Key Takeaway Points

- Libraries can inadvertently become toxic workplaces for employees, and cultural shifts are needed to create and sustain positive environments for employees and patrons.

- Due to the high prevalence of trauma among patron populations as well as staff, using a trauma-informed approach is often beneficial.

- Experiences of trauma can impact people's behavior in a variety of ways, including apparent behavioral problems including rudeness, substance use, inappropriate sexual behavior, and difficulty setting or respecting boundaries.

- Trauma-informed libraries use a framework that considers "what happened to this person?" rather than "what's wrong with this person?" when responding to challenging behaviors.

- Trauma-informed libraries incorporate the six principles of trauma-informed care throughout their organization: safety; trustworthiness; peer support; collaboration and mutuality; empowerment, voice, and choice; and cultural, historical, and gender issues.

- Organizational change can be slow and depends on your library's readiness and current stage of change. Libraries at various stages of change need different interventions and programs to move things forward.

- Helpful strategies in preparing your library for change include using intentional hiring practices, creating a safe and supportive environment, using clear communication, empowering staff to set boundaries, applying a strengths perspective, and ensuring consistent space and time for reflective practice and ongoing staff support and development.

## Notes

1  R. Kegan, L. L. Lahey, M. L. Miller, A. Fleming, and D. Helsing, *An Everyone Culture: Becoming a Deliberately Developmental Organization* (New York: Harvard Business Review Press, 2016), 6.

2  P. Lloyd, "The Public Library as a Protective Factor: An Introduction to Library Social Work," *Public Library Quarterly* 39, no. 1 (2020): 50–63, https://doi.org/10.1080/01616846.2019.1581872.

3  K. Hagelin, "Moving Towards Healing: A Trauma-Informed Librarianship Primer," *ACRLog* (blog), June 23, 2020, https://acrlog.org/2020/06/23/moving-towards-healing-a-trauma-informed-librarianship-primer/.

4  A. M. Scheyett, "Trauma-Informed Library Transformation: The Next Step in Library Social Work," *The New Social Worker*, February 9, 2019, https://www.socialworker.com/feature-articles/practice/trauma-informed-library-transformation-next-step-in-library-social-work/.

5   R. C. Kessler et al., "Trauma and PTSD in the WHO World Mental Health Surveys," *European Journal of Psychotraumatology* 8, sup 5 (2017): 1353383, https://doi.org/10.1080/20008198.2017.1353383.

6   Center for Disease Control, "Fast Facts: Preventing Adverse Childhood Experiences," April 6, 2022, https://www.cdc.gov/violenceprevention/aces/fastfact.html.

7   Substance Abuse and Mental Health Services Administration, *SAMHSA's Concept of Trauma and Guidance for a Trauma-Informed Approach*, HHS Publication No. (SMA) 14-4884 (Rockville, MD: Substance Abuse and Mental Health Services Administration, 2014), https://store.samhsa.gov/system/files/sma14-4884.pdf.

8   American Psychiatric Association, "Anxiety Disorders," *Diagnostic and Statistical Manual of Mental Disorders*, March 18, 2022, https://doi.org/10.1176/appi.books.9780890425787.x05_Anxiety_Disorders.

9   S. P. Koury and S. A. Green, *Trauma-Informed Organizational Change Manual,* Institute on Trauma and Trauma-Informed Care, Buffalo Center for Social Research (Buffalo, NY: University of Buffalo, January 2019), https://socialwork.buffalo.edu/social-research/institutes-centers/institute-on-trauma-and-trauma-informed-care/Trauma-Informed-Organizational-Change-Manual0.html.

10   American Psychiatric Association, "Anxiety Disorders."

11   J. Badalamenti and E. Hardy, "Supporting Autonomy While Setting Clear Boundaries," *Public Libraries Online,* February 19, 2019, http://publiclibrariesonline.org/2019/02/supporting-autonomy-while-setting-clear-boundaries/.

12   C. Smith, "The Trauma of Library Work," *American Libraries,* January 20, 2022, https://americanlibrariesmagazine.org/blogs/the-scoop/the-trauma-of-library-work/.

13   Urban Libraries Unite, "Urban Library Trauma Study: Final Report," 2022, https://urbanlibrariansunite.org/ults/.

14   Urban Libraries Unite. "Urban Library Trauma Study," 14.

15   J. J. Freyd, *Institutional Betrayal and Institutional Courage,* February 2023, https://dynamic.uoregon.edu/jjf/institutionalbetrayal/#:~:text=The%20term%20institutional%20betrayal%20refers,the%20context%20of%20the%20institution.

16   The National Child Traumatic Stress Network, "Understanding Who is at Risk," https://www.nctsn.org/trauma-informed-care/secondary-traumatic-stress/introduction.

**17** World Health Organization, "Burn-Out," in *International Statistical Classification of Diseases and Related Health Problems* (11th ed.), February 11, 2022, https://www .who.int/news/item/11-02-2022-icd-11-2022-release.

**18** R. Bianchi, G. Manzano-Garcia, and J. P. Rolland, "Is Burnout Primarily Linked to Work-Situated Factors? A Relative Weight Analytic Study," *Frontiers in Psychology* (2021): 1–14, https://doi.org/10.3389/fpsyg.2020.623912.

**19** Substance Abuse and Mental Health Services Administration, SAMHSA's Concept of Trauma and Guidance for a Trauma-Informed Approach.

**20** Center for Preparedness and Response, "Infographic: 6 Guiding Principles to a Trauma-Informed Approach," U.S. Department of Health & Human Services, September 17, 2020, https://www.cdc.gov/cpr/infographics/6_principles _trauma_info.htm.

**21** Safe Place, "What is a Safe Place?" https://www.nationalsafeplace.org/what-is -safe-place.

**22** A. Stewart, personal communication, August 24, 2022.

**23** Wayne, personal communication, August 28, 2022.

**24** B. Agarwal, S. K. Brooks, and N. Greenberg, "The Role of Peer Support in Managing Occupational Stress: A Qualitative Study of the Sustaining Resilience at Work Intervention," *Workplace Health and Safety* 68, no. 2 (2020): 57–64, https://doi.org/10.1177/2165079919873934.

**25** The Public Library Association Social Worker Task Force, *A Trauma-Informed Framework for Supporting Patrons: The PLA Workbook of Best Practices*, Public Library Association, 2022, https://www.alastore.ala.org/PLAtiframework.

**26** K. Hagelin, personal communication, August 15, 2022.

**27** J. A. Winkelstein, *Libraries and Homelessness: An Action Guide* (Santa Barbara, CA: Libraries Unlimited, 2021), 25.

**28** C. Sharkey, personal communication, February 16, 2022. TILT is a partnership between the University of Georgia School of Social Work and the Athens-Clarke County (GA) Library.

**29** J. Purtle, "Systematic Review of Evaluations of Trauma-Informed Organizational Interventions That Include Staff Trainings," *Trauma, Violence & Abuse* 21, no. 4 (2020): 725–40, https://doi.org/10.1177/1524838018791304.

**30** The Public Library Association Social Worker Task Force, *A Trauma-Informed Framework for Supporting Patrons: The PLA Workbook of Best Practices* (Chicago: American Library Association, 2022), https://www.alastore.ala.org/ PLAtiframework.

**31** C. C. DiClemente, D. Schlundt, and L. Gemmell, "Readiness and Stages of Change in Addiction Treatment," *The American Journal on Addictions / American Academy of Psychiatrists in Alcoholism and Addictions* 13, no. 2 (2004): 103–19, https://doi.org/10.1080/10550490490435777.

**32** J. M. Prochaska, J. O. Prochaska, and D. A. Levesque, "A Transtheoretical Approach to Changing Organizations," *Administration and Policy in Mental Health and Mental Health Services Research* 28, no. 4 (2001): 247–61.

**33** A. M. Pfabe, personal communication, November 1, 2022.

**34** T. Garcia, personal communication, August 25, 2022.

**35** Lloyd, "The Public Library as a Protective Factor," 50–63.

**36** P. Lloyd, "The Public Library as a Protective Factor," Public Libraries Online, December 13, 2018, http://publiclibrariesonline.org/2018/12/the-public-library -as-a-protective-factor/.

**37** D. Saleebey, *The Strengths Perspective in Social Work Practice* (White Plains, NY: Longman, 1992).

**38** D. Saleebey, "The Strengths Perspective in Social Work Practice: Extensions and Cautions," *Social Work* 41, no. 3 (1996): 296–305.

**39** R. P. Douglass and R. D. Duffy, "Strengths Use and Life Satisfaction: A Moderated Mediation Approach," *Journal of Happiness Studies* 16, no. 3 (2015): 619–32, https://doi.org/10.1007/s10902-014-9525-4.

**40** C. Harzer and W. Ruch, "The Application of Signature Character Strengths and Positive Experiences at Work," *Journal of Happiness Studies* 14 (2013): 965–83, https://doi.org/10.1007/s10902-012-9364-0.

**41** Winkelstein, *Libraries and Homelessness*, 46–8.

**42** The Public Library Association Social Worker Task Force, *A Trauma-Informed Framework for Supporting Patrons*, 21–3.

**43** Winkelstein, *Libraries and Homelessness*, 127–9, 247.

**44** Lloyd, "The Public Library as a Protective Factor," 50–63.

**45** Winkelstein, *Libraries and Homelessness*.

# **3** Person-Centered Programming and Services for Patrons' Needs

In this chapter, we present options for libraries to address patrons' various psychosocial needs and promote the overall wellness of high-needs patrons. We focus on general approaches to working with high-needs patrons and discuss specific approaches to serving patrons with needs in eight different areas of wellness. Throughout this chapter, we highlight multiple examples of existing library programming and services that are used to address these needs.

## Consequences of Unaddressed Psychosocial Needs

Both globally and in the United States, there is a severe shortage of healthcare workers.[1] Worsened by the Covid-19 pandemic, aging populations, increasing burnout and numbers of healthcare providers leaving the field, and the inaccessibility of educational and training programs, these shortages lead to many people having difficulty or an inability to access the necessary services for preventive care and treatment of acute or chronic medical issues. Similarly, mental healthcare shortages are worsening in the United States,[2] which is particularly concerning due to the increase in mental health problems that have accompanied the pandemic. Compounding matters are the growing economic inequality, increased cost of living, and lack of affordable housing throughout the country,[3] which contribute to deteriorating health and mental health.

Research on people with mental health problems, chronic health problems, substance use disorders, poverty-related needs, unemployment, and other psychosocial needs has consistently established an inverse relationship between each of these needs and overall wellness. For example, people with chronic illnesses such as cancer, diabetes, or heart disease are more likely to develop mental health problems such as depression.[4] Similarly, those with mental health problems are at a higher risk for developing physical ailments and chronic diseases. Poverty, unemployment, low education levels, food insecurity, and lack of affordable housing are referred to as the "social determinants of health" because these factors predict poor mental and physical health conditions more than healthcare and lifestyle-related factors such as diet and exercise.[5] Any of these conditions or factors, left untreated or unaddressed, leads to worsened health and wellness.

## Libraries and Wellness

With so many individuals falling through the cracks of our social support systems and healthcare networks, community-based efforts for health promotion, disease prevention, and early intervention are essential. Although the general public does not often associate libraries with wellness promotion, they are indeed fitting locations to impact individual and community health and wellness. Public libraries are widely located across the United States and globally, are free and accessible for many demographic groups, and are trusted institutions that welcome everyone. Libraries offer opportunities to promote wellness directly and indirectly in various ways we will discuss in this chapter.

## Dimensions of Wellness

When considering the types of programming and services that might best meet the demands of high-needs patrons, it can be helpful to consider specific aspects of wellness that can be supported or promoted by the library. In this book, we refer to the eight dimensions of wellness promoted by the US Substance Abuse and Mental Health Services Administration (SAMHSA):[6]

1. emotional
2. physical
3. occupational
4. intellectual
5. financial
6. social

**7.** environmental

**8.** spiritual.

Wellness is multidimensional in that all eight of these factors are interconnected and influence one another to comprise an individual's overall wellness. Different people may be well in some dimensions yet unwell in others. Although it cannot be assumed that libraries will address every aspect of patrons' overall wellness, libraries provide many opportunities to incorporate programming and services that can help promote each of these dimensions. In this chapter, we highlight examples of successful library-based wellness services and programming which are key to developing and demonstrating a commitment to a person-centered library for all patrons.

# General Approach to Working with High-Needs Patrons

When faced with patrons who have a variety of needs, library staff are often trained to use an information and referral approach, defined as "the active process of linking a person with a need or problem with a service which will meet the need or solve the problem."[7] This approach is typically transactional, involving a reference interview to determine the patrons' needs and then providing information or resources to try to address those needs. However, people with complex psychosocial needs often have difficulty following through with simple referrals and, as the number of needs increases, so does the difficulty with follow-through.[8] While a transactional information and referral approach works well for connecting patrons to books, electronic resources, and relevant programming, a more integrated and comprehensive approach is required when referring high-needs patrons for services from a social worker, health professional, or other community resource. People with high needs often benefit from techniques such as intentional engagement or rapport building, "warm handoffs," outreach, and service navigation/coordination. Each of these approaches is described here.

## *Intentional Engagement*

Intentional engagement means making efforts to quickly build rapport with people from the very first interaction. Many who experience homelessness, poverty, mental illness, substance use, and legal issues may be slow to trust others. Without trust, they are unlikely to be forthcoming about their needs and receive assistance. Libraries are often generally warm and inviting spaces, although sometimes they are more welcoming to some demographic groups than others. An honest self-assessment is vital to ensure both the library space and its employees are inviting to all. By using intentional engagement strategies, libraries examine their physical space to ensure diverse groups of people see themselves represented in images on the wall and in the collections. Those from marginalized groups, in particular, tend to quickly assess a space to determine if it is not only safe but also welcoming. Sometimes staff inadvertently ignore people who are unhoused or have other obvious psychosocial needs out of fear and anxiety about interacting with them. In addition to being cognizant of messages sent via the physical space, library staff should be intentional about being cordial and welcoming to all. Learn people's names, make conversation with them (if conversation seems welcomed), show interest in helping them find needed resources, and reach out to demonstrate the library is *for* them. Intentional engagement is about purposefully trying to build a genuine relationship with everyone who walks in the door.

## Warm Handoffs

Warm handoffs are a method of connecting people from one organization to another. This can be accomplished by phoning a trusted organization in front of the patron or walking them over to the provider. Rather than handing someone a resource list, giving them a phone number to call, or writing down a web address for them, a warm handoff provides a personal introduction between the patron and the organization. It reduces a patron's anxiety of needing to call on their own, decreases the chances referral information will get lost, and ensures the person gets connected to the necessary contact. Warm handoffs greatly increase first appointment show rates with mental health providers, healthcare organizations, and social services.[9] When conducting a warm handoff, library staff should first ask the patrons' permission to contact the provider. With consent (and preferably in a private location), the library staff can contact the provider, introduce the patron, and explain the reason for the referral. The library staff should then ask the patron if there is additional information they would like to include and allow them to directly communicate with the provider. After which, the library staff member should excuse themselves and allow the patron to privately continue the phone conversation with the provider.

## Outreach

Outreach is an extension of intentional engagement, but rather than only considering how welcoming and inviting is the physical space and the staff working within it, the library is intentional about extending resources and information outside the traditional library walls to reach marginalized or high-needs groups in their own communities. This may involve taking laptops, books, informational pamphlets, or other resources to places like homeless shelters, jails or prisons, mental health facilities, or low-income neighborhoods. The library might consider helping people sign up for library cards, assisting them with creating an email address, or even doing a fun, recreational activity to build rapport and demonstrate that the library cares. When conducting outreach activities to a new neighborhood or facility, it can be helpful to first do a quick survey to determine what people in that location might need from the library. Quickly assessing needs and then trying to address them can send a powerful message that the library is mindful about them and exists to help.

## Service Navigation/Coordination

After initially connecting with a service provider, many high-needs patrons have difficulty following through with keeping appointments. Sometimes their social circumstances, difficulty with meeting basic needs, lack of phone or transportation, or other barriers cause problems with connecting to services even when they are motivated to do so. Plus, social service and healthcare systems are often complicated and difficult to navigate, even for people with high education levels and multiple resources. With service navigation or coordination, assistance is provided for people with psychosocial needs to increase the chances they can schedule and keep appointments and ultimately receive the care or services they need. This assistance may be provided by peers, trained professionals, clinicians, or volunteers and can be provided using phone, in-person conversations, texting, or web applications.[10] Although there are various existing models of service navigation/coordination, they typically offer active and intentional strategies to engage participants long-term, assess their needs and barriers, identify required services, make referrals, monitor progress, and follow up to identify when people are "falling through the cracks" and provide additional referrals and follow-up as needed.[11] Receiving assistance with service navigation and coordination leads to a decrease in overall needs, increases service engagement and follow-up, and improves health for many different populations.[12]

Although the extent a library is able to provide these services depends on its size, budget, and staffing model, without these services in place at the library or elsewhere it can be difficult for high-needs patrons to connect with community resources or obtain assistance. Many libraries are now using social work students, hiring or contracting with social workers, hiring peer navigators (laypeople with lived experiences of poverty, homelessness, mental health problems, or substance abuse problems), or soliciting volunteers to assist with these types of patron services. Each of these approaches has its strengths and challenges, which we'll discuss in Chapter 6.

If your library is unable to utilize the aforesaid strategies due to staffing limitations and volunteer shortages, one simple tactic for increasing patron success with referrals to community organizations is to make the "hidden rules" of navigating services clearer and more transparent. Many libraries create resource lists or "street cards" of commonly used community organizations, including a brief description of their purpose and their contact information. These lists can be easily distributed to patrons or displayed in a common area to be independently picked up as needed. However, community organizations sometimes have "hidden" rules that are not known by someone who has not used their services before. Navigating social services can be complex and often requires multiple phone calls, remembering information, following up, and persistence. Although high-needs patrons can be very resourceful, their needs may interfere with their ability to navigate these services successfully. They may encounter difficulty regularly accessing a phone for repeated calls. They may also have disabilities, substance use, mental health problems, or trauma that impacts their abilities to plan, focus, schedule, and follow through. One strategy for increasing the chances of success with accessing community services is to create a referral sheet to accompany resource lists or agency brochures. This sheet should list prompts about the type of information a patron needs to prepare for the phone call and includes space for them to make notes. Worthwhile tips for navigating services can also be included on the referral sheet. See Appendix D for an example of this type of sheet, created by social work students from the College of Saint Rose during their practicum placement at the Cobleskill Community and Waterford Libraries in New York.

## Library Services and Programming for Addressing Specific Needs and Barriers to Wellness

Depending on specific patron and community needs, many libraries have begun offering a variety of services or programs to address barriers to wellness or specific psychosocial needs. Organized by each dimension of wellness, we discuss examples of these initiatives here. With creativity and ingenuity, the examples can be modified by libraries of all sizes to meet the needs of their patrons while considering available resources and space.

## Emotional Wellness

Emotional wellness pertains to one's ability to effectively cope with stressors, feel a sense of enjoyment about life, adjust to challenges, and identify and express feelings in healthy ways.[13] One who is emotionally healthy is resilient and can manage the ups and downs of their lives. They have methods of self-care and utilize them regularly to avoid feeling overwhelmed or resorting to unhealthy coping mechanisms. In common vernacular, we think of emotional wellness as "mental health."

As overall emotional wellness has worsened in recent years in the United States, an increased awareness of how libraries can support the mental health[14] of their patrons and communities has developed. Mental health is consistently one of the top patron needs identified by many library staff in Beth's needs assessments, and staff frequently comment on patrons who appear to be in emotional distress or in crisis while in the library. Because of this need, many libraries have created initiatives to support the mental health of their patrons,[15] including:

- Offering social work services to conduct assessments and make referrals to mental health–related resources
- Adding bibliographies about well-being and mental health–related materials in the library's collection so patrons can easily locate them on the shelves
- Training staff to identify a mental health problem, prevent or de-escalate a patron crisis, and how or where to refer someone in crisis

- Inviting mental health providers to educate the public on the symptoms of common mental health problems and what to do if you or a loved one experiences a mental health problem
- Offering library facilities and meeting spaces for mental health support groups
- Creating "wellness walls" or spaces in the library with books, pamphlets, and other informational mental health-related content
- Situating a mental health "wellness hub" within a large, urban public library.[16]

Even when libraries across the United States had to temporarily close their buildings at the onset of the Covid-19 pandemic, they developed creative ways to virtually reach their patrons to address emotional wellness. Social work student interns guided children through mindfulness practices[17] and emotional regulation on their libraries' respective YouTube channels.[18] Virtual mental health assessments were provided for the public by both the Oak Park Public Library (IL)[19] and Philadelphia's Central Library (PA).[20] Since many people adjusted to online services and programming during the height of the pandemic, some libraries might want to continue offering online or virtual assistance focused on emotional wellness.

One notable way libraries have addressed emotional wellness on a broad scale is the 2020 California Mental Health Initiative.[21] Supported by funding from the US Institute of Museum and Library Services, the California State Library led an initiative to support library staff with the information and skills they needed to provide services to patrons experiencing mental health problems. This initiative provided staff with training such as Mental Health First Aid,[22] which is an evidence-based training to teach how to identify mental health and substance abuse problems, take action in a mental health crisis, help someone experiencing a mental health or substance use problem, and to boost skills for managing patrons with mental health problems. The California Mental Health Initiative also provided resources to library staff about trauma-informed care, information about how to do outreach with communities outside of the library, and ideas for mental health–related programming in the midst of Covid-19. Lastly, staff from select California libraries were provided mental health books to add to their collections and were supported through the process of planning community engagement action projects. Participating staff were also guided to create collaborative programming with a community partner for Mental Health Awareness Month.

In central Texas, seven public libraries have been piloting a program that focuses on building nonclinical mental health supports within public libraries.[23] Funded by the local St. David's Foundation, this "Libraries for Health" initiative employs trained laypeople to act as library-based peer support specialists, situating them in libraries with communities that lack sufficient mental health care. These peer support specialists are supervised by a licensed mental health provider, who also works directly with patrons experiencing more severe mental health issues than can be addressed by the peer specialists. Overall, this program seeks to supplement existing mental health services and increase emotional wellness in these communities.

Other initiatives that address patron mental health include Rochester Public Library (MN) partnering with a local agency[24] to provide a part-time social worker who maintains a "wellness corner" of resources, available for patrons of all ages. This social worker is able to connect patrons to resources for employment, health, housing, or food. In Missouri, the St. Louis County Library partners with Mental Health America to offer public programming to promote mental wellness and "demystify mental health topics,"[25] which helps reduce the stigma in communities about issues related to mental health. Collaborations with local providers are one way many libraries have been able to address the emotional wellness of their patrons and communities.

Some libraries are tailoring programs to support mental health for children and teen patrons, combining them with components that encourage family engagement and increase caregivers' awareness of how to support their child's mental health. One innovative example is Ericson Public Library's (IA) new initiative in partnership with Iowa State University's Extension and Outreach—Boone County, *Little Engines*, aimed at impacting children's mental health and their social and emotional development while encouraging a love of reading, active learning, sensory engagement, and interaction between caregivers and children.[26] Initially piloting the program with a local preschool and soon expanding to additional sites, Ericson partners with local organizations including the University of Iowa's Scanlan Center for School Mental Health, Iowa PBS, Iowa Child Care Resource and Referral, and the Iowa Association for the Education of Young Children to fund and to carry out the program. Participating families receive a digital library of select activities through a mobile app and receive the materials and supplies to complete them at home. Children earn badges for participating in activities pertaining to social and emotional development, mindfulness, and mental health. Other libraries offer social-emotional learning kits to be checked out by parents and caregivers for use at home with children. The Oak Park (IL) Public Library offers kits for checkout that contain a book along with open-ended questions to guide a discussion between a child and their caregiver about emotions.[27] These kits are available in both Spanish and English and also include information for caregivers about how to adapt them for use with children who have disabilities, speech delays, or other communication-related challenges.

For libraries with difficulty obtaining funding for activities such as Little Engines or social-emotional learning kits, one inexpensive strategy many libraries use is developing specialized webpages focused on mental health for a specific population. For example, the Fairfax County Public Library's (VA) website includes a specific page focused on adolescent mental health, which lists young adult–focused books on mental health–related topics and includes a quick resource guide for finding books pertaining to self-esteem, abuse, alcohol use, depression, anxiety, and eating disorders. This library also created an online resource guide of helplines and offers information about local, regional, and national resources for adolescents experiencing mental health problems or abuse.[28] Libraries can also use storytime to increase children's emotional identification and growth by reading stories about social and emotional health, or books that demonstrate a range of emotions. When staff are reading to children, they can pause and ask children to identify the feeling experienced by a character in the book or stop to name the feeling for the children.[29] Drawing attention to sentiments in this way can help young children begin to understand emotions and identify their own and others' feelings.

## Mental Health Initiatives and Other Rural Community Needs

### Union County Public Library (SC)

Taylor Atkinson, director of Union County Public Library, has a passion for mental health and a dedication to improving resource access and reducing barriers for individuals in need of mental health services in her community.[30] Union County, South Carolina, is a rural area, with a shortage of mental health providers and no public transportation available to access services in the neighboring city (approximately forty-five minutes away). When she was assistant director of the library, Ms. Atkinson attended a Mental Health First Aid (MHFA) training to learn how to respond to mental health concerns of her patrons. She became intrigued by its usefulness in the library setting as well as for other community organizations. Seeing the gaps it could fill in Union County, she pursued training to become a MHFA facilitator and offered training to library staff, local law enforcement officers, emergency medical professionals, school teachers, daycare providers, and clergy. Based on the positive responses she received, Ms. Atkinson determined this training had a tangible impact on her community. It helped her build relationships and trust with community partners, and she soon began looking for other opportunities to positively impact mental health. After becoming director of the library, Ms. Atkinson became involved in a number of Union County groups such as the Mental Health Task Force. She converted the library's assistant director position to require a master of social work (MSW) degree, and hired a social worker in 2021 to fulfill administrative responsibilities, maintain a caseload of clients, and create a food pantry in the library. After the library went through a substantial renovation, space was created to house a number of community agencies from the closest city, Spartanburg. The library took over Union Cancer Services, a previous nonprofit provider, and absorbed the organization so the library's assistant director/social worker could directly provide support and financial assistance to local cancer patients who normally have to commute a long distance for care. Ms. Atkinson says her goal is for the library to be a local one-stop-shop for people in Union County who need services for a variety of needs.

Ms. Atkinson notes many benefits of these initiatives. Community members in Union County can now access services at the library that were previously only available forty-five minutes away. The community is also more equipped to recognize, address, and intervene when someone is experiencing mental health or substance abuse problems. In addition, community involvement in mental health initiatives has helped numerous community partners understand the library's role and how the library can assist with broad, community-wide efforts. These initiatives have helped build communal trust in the library and increased chances that people think of the library when they have an issue or challenge.

When asked about lessons learned from these initiatives, Ms. Atkinson responded, "You have to invite yourself to relevant community initiatives and help others learn what you do and what you can do." Although she wasn't initially invited in the past, the more she is present at these groups, the more community members think of her and the library when planning new initiatives.

## Physical Wellness

Physical wellness focuses on having good health habits, such as regular exercise, sufficient sleep, a balanced diet, screenings and preventive healthcare, and engagement in needed treatment services. To be physically well, one proactively manages their health and has access to the necessary tools and resources for their body to function as well as possible. Although library staff strictly avoid giving medical advice to patrons, libraries are uniquely positioned to offer support and assistance with physical wellness through health-promoting activities, primary prevention of common health problems, and help accessing healthcare. These types of activities are typically offered through collaborations with healthcare providers, public health experts, or educational entities like nursing schools. Because of their placement in different kinds of communities, services can be tailored to address gaps that exist in each specific community or neighborhood.

Although not limited to rural communities, a growing number of rural libraries offer access to healthcare through telehealth technology and designated space in the library to connect virtually with providers in nearby cities.[31] For example, the Richland (SC) Public Library offers virtual health care clinics at their Main Library to facilitate access to medical care for community members. The Charleston County (SC) Public Library created the WISE (Women in the South East) Telehealth Network to provide health education, screenings, referrals, and telehealth-based services specifically for women in rural areas of the county that lack access to healthcare resources, birth control, lactation support, cancer screenings, pregnancy care, and preventive services for sexually transmitted infections.[32] Telehealth initiatives grew in many libraries during the Covid-19 pandemic, especially in rural communities where residents often lack reliable broadband internet. Even small rural libraries without private meeting space are adding freestanding "privacy pods" to provide soundproof space for telehealth or other private conversations.[33] These services directly address the difficulty rural communities encounter accessing healthcare, particularly for under-resourced populations that may lack transportation, sufficient job flexibility to take time off, or other barriers commuting to a different location to see a physician or other provider. One of the most expansive telehealth-related library initiatives is the Delaware Telehealth and Teleservices Initiative, discussed further in the Afterword of this book. Similarly, the New Jersey State Library administers a program called Just for the Health of It![34] This program features a team of certified consumer health librarians at the East Brunswick Public Library who facilitate and train other librarians in the state to implement their own telehealth programs, provide iPads to those libraries for telehealth initiatives, and provide ongoing support to other public libraries in New Jersey seeking to provide health information and access to telehealth and improve access to health information and health literacy.

Libraries also provide access to health and wellness-promoting activities such as exercise programs or health screenings, mostly through collaborations with health-focused educational programs or local healthcare providers. High Point Public Library (NC) partnered with a local university in 2022 to offer body fat, glucose levels, blood pressure, and cholesterol checks free of charge to reach community members who did not have primary care physicians or were reluctant to go to the doctor due to the pandemic.[35] Fremont Public Library (IL) collaborates with a local university to offer free health screenings in both English and Spanish, as well as vaccines, information about community resources, and health education.[36] Bellwood-Antis Public Library (PA) holds an annual Family Health and Safety Fair in collaboration with a healthcare provider and the county's recreation center. [37] This event reaches hundreds of community members in their small town and includes health screenings, informational booths for local healthcare providers, children's exercise programs, demonstrations by local emergency responders about fire safety, and a 5K race.

Exercise or movement-focused programs are inexpensive and relatively easy to integrate into a library. The Let's Move in Libraries[38] initiative, founded by Dr. Noah Lenstra from the University of North Carolina at Greensboro, encourages libraries to support physical health and wellness in their local communities by including physical movement or other health-related efforts. One way many libraries are trying to promote physical activity is through storywalks, which are growing in popularity in the United States. Storywalks involve breaking down a family-friendly story into small parts and placing each section along an outdoor path to encourage families to walk along the path and read the story together. Dr. Lenstra's book *Healthy Living at the Library: Programs for All Ages* provides other ideas of health- and movement-focused programming that can be used by public libraries of all sizes.

Libraries often promote physical wellness by enhancing health literacy and connecting people to reliable health-related information. Earlier research found that over one-third of library computer users use computers to search for information related to health, medical problems, medical providers, or health insurance.[39] Because of this, public libraries have a unique opportunity to ensure their community members have accurate health information. To support their public libraries in meeting the health needs of their communities, the Montana State Library offered a Health Literacy Month Toolkit[40] to prepare for this designated month in October. This toolkit could easily be replicated by other states, including content for library staff about health literacy (what it is and why it is important), statewide health assessment data, a list of potential partners in the state available for on-site health programming, open access webinars and training videos on health literacy, social media graphics, printable flyers, ideas for book displays and book lists, and programming materials.

Other libraries choose different avenues for impacting physical wellness. Some provide assistance with signing up for health insurance, such as the Brooklyn Public Library (NY).[41] The Ericson Public Library (IA) offers programming aimed at improving sleep.[42] Many branches provide vaccination clinics, and this number grew during the pandemic with libraries offering both Covid-19 vaccines and Covid-19 on-site testing or take-home testing supplies. Some libraries combine numerous services to broadly address health and wellness in their libraries. Libraries in rural South Carolina partner with community health workers who offer health information and telehealth services for a wide array of needs.[43] Similarly, the Charlotte Mecklenburg Library (NC) teams up with a local healthcare provider to place community health workers in several branches to offer health screenings, referrals to healthcare providers, and resources to meet basic needs of patrons including housing, food insecurity, and financial assistance. This program also provides additional health-related programming in select branches for health promotion and disease prevention.

**Substance Abuse Initiatives.** Although linked with emotional wellness, we include substance abuse initiatives under the dimension of physical wellness. In Beth's needs assessments, patron substance use is consistently at the top of the list as a staff-identified patron need, and they often express fear and uneasiness about people in the library using substances. A recent study[44] reports that nearly half of public librarians surveyed have witnessed patrons using alcohol on-site and 12 percent had witnessed a patron overdose in their library during the previous year. To address overdoses, some libraries[45] are training their staff on how to administer the drug Naloxone, which reverses potentially lethal overdoses.

Led by the Public Library Association and OCLC and funded by IMLS, a 2021 report from Allen et al. examined the various ways public libraries are responding to the opioid crisis in the United States.[46] Approaches include the following:

- Through partnerships with community organizations and after completing a community needs assessment, Barrington Public Library (RI) led a community discussion on the book, *Dreamland: The True Tale of America's Opiate Epidemic*. They also held film screenings related to substance use disorders for both youth and adults, facilitated Naloxone training by the local health department for both library staff and the public, promoted drug take-back days to collect and properly dispose of unused prescription opiate medication, and facilitated MHFA training for both library staff and the public to identify and respond to signs of both mental illness and substance use. The library director and select staff also participated in the Community Overdose Engagement program, an initiative with the local health department, to design substance use–related resource brochures that would be distributed at the library and throughout town. These efforts increased and improved partnerships between the library and other organizations, led to similar programs expanding to other libraries in the region, and increased community awareness of substance use and mental health problems in the community.

- Everett Public Library (WA), located in an area of the state with high opioid overdose rates, partnered with their local department of behavioral health to offer Naloxone training to library staff and the public, as well as teaching them to recognize the signs and symptoms of substance use disorders. Education also included content aimed at destigmatizing substance use. Sharps containers were placed in bathrooms for safe needle disposal and bathrooms were modified by placing windows in the main bathroom door and lowering the stall height to ensure security could determine if an emergency was occurring. The library hosted monthly resource days where community partners including social services, substance abuse treatment providers, employment agencies, and healthcare organizations hosted informational tables for the public. The library also hosted community events on books related to the opioid crisis. This work helped minimize stigma for substance use disorders, increased partnerships between the library and community partners, and educated the public about substance use disorders and opioid overdose.

- Twinsburg Public Library (OH) conducted a community needs assessment to learn the specific addiction and recovery-related needs of their local area. Based on the results, the library partnered with community organizations and the police department to operate as a safe medication disposal point, offer educational events for the public on topics related to substance use and mental health, and train library staff to identify illicit drugs and respond appropriately if discovered on-site. Finally, the library also began offering SMART (Self-Management and Recovery Training) support groups.

For libraries considering programming or services additions pertaining to substance use, OCLC's 2020 Call to Action[47] encourages taking the following steps:

1. Explore local community data for information about substance use in the region

2. Seek out local assets and collaborate with community partners such as public health departments, substance abuse treatment centers, or prevention- or harm reduction-focused organizations

3. Create opportunities to increase awareness and knowledge, and subsequently reduce stigma, about substance abuse in the community as well as with library staff

4. Anticipate staff stress and compassion fatigue, and develop post-crisis plans for supporting staff after a substance use-related crisis (or other crisis) in the library

5. Team up with community partners to offer programming and training in the library to enhance community awareness of substance use and the opioid crisis, host guest speakers, offer drug take-back events, create informational displays, add resource lists on the library website, and distribute pamphlets about substance use disorders.

## Occupational Wellness

Occupational wellness means that one works or volunteers in ways that align with their personal values, give them a sense of purpose, stimulate their minds, and allow them to use their gifts and talents to help or support others. To be occupationally well, one maintains work-life balance and feels that their work (paid or volunteer) allows them time for other enjoyable activities. Libraries commonly offer initiatives related to occupational wellness, and it is not uncommon to see them posting job listings, videoconferencing or virtual workspaces, or assistance resume development and job applications. The Charlotte Mecklenburg Library (NC) offers assistance to patrons with formatting resumes, searching for careers, and learning computer skills; it also maintains an online job board. [48] The JobNow™ program at Anne Arundel County Public Library (MD) provides resume assistance, career advice, interview coaching, and live job coaching through Brainfuse.[49] Other libraries such as the Daniel Boone (MI) Regional Library, LA County (CA) Library, Ericson (IA) Public Library, Everett (WA) Library, and Milwaukee (WI) Public Library also use Brainfuse for patron career-related support.

Since high-needs patrons often need more intensive services than patrons without significant needs, libraries might consider adding more comprehensive workforce development programs in partnership with local organizations. One example of a program created for high-needs patrons is the Job and Career Help program offered by Columbus Metropolitan Library (OH).[50] It collaborates with Goodwill, Jewish Family Services, and a local healthcare technology company called CoverMyMeds to offer technology-focused curriculum to job seekers, provide mock interview assistance and resume coaching, and support patrons with developing the soft skills necessary for job readiness such as dependability, communication, decision-making, teamwork, time management, and ethics. A similar initiative, the Berkeley Career Express Program,[51] offered by the Berkeley County Library System (SC) in collaboration with their local adult education program and Chamber of Commerce, offers instruction on digital literacy skills, career readiness, adult education, and training in employment-related soft skills.

Another way libraries can address occupational wellness is by offering entrepreneurship programming and services, which can be useful for patrons with or without psychosocial needs. For example, Austin Public Library (TX)[52] partners with a local Small Business Program to offer entrepreneurship-focused programming, networking, and job-related resources to historically underserved communities by using the library's branches. They provide library card holders with information about creating business plans, seeking funding for new businesses, and also provide business-focused training videos. East Baton Rouge Public Library (LA)[53] offers similar services to help community members learn how to start small businesses. Some libraries with makerspaces deliver entrepreneurship training programs; for example, the Eugenia H. Young Memorial Library (NC) is planning an entrepreneurship training program in their makerspace for teens and young adults interested in starting their own creative business. Makerspaces can be especially helpful for improving the occupational wellness of people experiencing homelessness. The St. Paul Public Library's (MN) Innovation Lab—a makerspace containing a recording studio, laser engraver, 3D printers, sewing machines, crafting supplies, and other creative technologies—is used for housed and unhoused patrons alike. In fact, one member of their Innovation Lab Advisory Board was unhoused when she started using the makerspace to start a small craft business.[54] Makerspaces can be particularly beneficial for this group of patrons to provide them a place to develop skills, use creative energy, find social connections with others who have similar interests, and feel a sense of pride in their work and in themselves.

## Intellectual Wellness

Intellectual wellness involves activities that keep our brains active and engaged and our minds continually learning and expanding. To be intellectually well, one knows their own personal interests and looks for opportunities to engage in activities they enjoy. They actively pursue learning, sometimes through classes, language development, or learning how to complete a puzzle or play a new game. Persons who are intellectually well participate in discussions that engage their minds, such as debates, conversations, or activities to learn new things.

Overall, libraries excel at helping patrons expand and improve their intellectual wellness through accessing reading material, computer and language classes, events designed to expand cross-cultural understanding, public art, or informational seminars and workshops. Libraries often focus these programs on patrons using the physical library space, but to reach high-needs patrons it is often necessary to do outreach in marginalized communities. For example, some public libraries reach out to local prisons and jails to teach literacy skills and provide information and resources to inmates. Others, like the Brooklyn Public Library (NY),[55] provide reading material and other resources in homeless shelters to address the intellectual wellness of high-needs populations. Some libraries, such as the High Point Public Library (NC),[56] address multiple areas of wellness by taking bookmobiles along with mobile food pantries and wifi hotspots to neighborhoods known for residents having low incomes, transportation challenges, and/or food insecurity. In Long Branch, New Jersey, the library received a grant from the state's library association to donate children's books to local barbershops with the aim of increasing exposure to culturally relevant stories and enhancing literacy among young boys of color. This award-winning[57] Fade to Books program offered an incentive to children and caretakers alike: for every ten books a child read, they received one free haircut. After starting small as a form of grassroots outreach, this time limited grant helped the program expand to fifty barber shops throughout New Jersey.[58]

One way libraries are addressing the intellectual wellness of high-needs patrons is by focusing on digital equity efforts such as increasing access to wifi, loaning laptops and hotspots, and providing computer classes. Some libraries are taking this a step further, such as the Salt Lake City Public Library (UT), which created a replicable Digital Navigator program. This program pairs individuals trained as Digital Navigators with patrons who need assistance with accessing and navigating the internet, foundational computer skills, and information about online security and safety. The program also connects patrons with low-cost computers and internet service. Based on a successful 2021 pilot of the program, an online Toolkit[59] is available for download so the program can be replicated in other regions. Digital Navigator programs can be particularly successful in rural libraries; Pottsboro Area Public Library (TX) recently received funding from the National Digital Inclusion Alliance to help rural regions of the United States increase access to the internet and computer devices, and to improve digital literacy skills.[60]

## Financial Wellness

Financial wellness involves sufficient income for one's needs, reducing debt, having savings to cover emergencies, and being financially literate. To be financially well, one can provide for their own and their family's basic needs. To address financial wellness, some public libraries offer financial literacy classes. The Patrick Beaver Memorial (NC) Library partners with a local educator from the Society of Financial Awareness to teach a debt reduction course as well as a course on estate planning.[61] Financial literacy classes can be helpful for some high-needs patrons such as immigrants, much like classes offered by the Lakewood (OH) Public Library for Nepali and Burmese-speaking new immigrants[62] to help boost skills needed for financial stability. In Virginia, the Alexandria Library offers a website of financial literacy resources, including books, online tutorials, and links to public information about budgeting, saving, managing credit, planning for retirement, and real estate.[63]

Financial literacy classes are minimally helpful if people do not have financial resources to manage. In December 2021, the average living wage in the United States was $100,498.60 per year for a family of four, yet the minimum wage is $7.25 per hour. Even families with two working adults and more than one job have difficulty making a living wage. There are practical poverty-related challenges for many people that cannot be fixed through a financial literacy course. Thus, many public libraries offer resources or assistance to address poverty-related needs. Libraries such as the Decatur Public Library (IL) offer web pages about financial resources, emergency rental assistance, federal supplemental income programs, and local organizations providing financial help.[64] Others help with basic needs such as connecting patrons to clothing banks and housing assistance, provide referrals for utility assistance or local social service agencies, help applying for jobs or public benefits, and offer bus passes.[65] Many libraries offer free hygiene kits for patrons who have financial limitations and have difficulty affording hygiene supplies. These kits include toothpaste and toothbrushes, deodorant, soap, shampoo, conditioner, and menstrual products. For example, DC Public Library has free hygiene kits available at their front desk and a "no questions asked" policy that means patrons do not have to show proof of financial need or meet qualifications to access the kits. Others provide free menstrual supplies, such as the St. Louis Public Library (MO).[66]

As we can see, libraries are using various, creative strategies to support financial wellness and therefore ease financial strain for many members of their communities. Although not every library can assist with financial needs, at a minimum, libraries can aim to not add to patrons' existing financial strains. An increasing number of libraries, such as Michigan's Kalamazoo Public Library, are eliminating late fees[67] for all patrons, a decision we support for minimizing financial burdens on patrons and ensuring everyone can maintain access to much-needed library resources.

## Social Wellness

Social wellness means that one has healthy relationships and positive social support from family, friends, and others in their communities. They also find ways to connect with others around common needs or interests on a regular basis. People who are socially well have a group of people with whom they feel a sense of belonging and fulfill their needs for interaction, connection, and care. This can be difficult for individuals from marginalized groups, especially in areas that lack diversity. Generally, libraries offer several opportunities to increase social wellness by reducing isolation and increasing interaction and connection to others. With effort and intention, libraries can increase opportunities for social wellness for patrons who may not have other places where they feel welcome and supported.

One model for improving the social wellness of high-needs patrons is "Coffee and Conversations." This program is used in a number of libraries throughout the United States to enhance social connection, compassion, and empathy with and for diverse groups of people, often for people experiencing homelessness in particular. To host a Coffee and Conversation, libraries create intentional spaces for congregating with tables that prompt attendees to sit together. Typically, coffee and sometimes snacks are offered to help encourage participation (people love free snacks and drinks!). Some libraries combine Coffee and Conversation events with crafts or poetry-writing activities, while others focus specifically on discussion topics. There may be thematic conversations related to library services (questions about what kinds of programs participants would like to see offered) or a hobby or interest. At the Multnomah County Library (WA), staff found that Coffee and Conversations created opportunities to talk about behavior "in a way that is less hierarchical and more open than conversations intended to correct or modify patron behavior"[68] and to clarify reasons for the library's rules. The model also creates opportunities for connection and relationship building between staff and patrons. The Dallas Public Library (TX)[69] finds that Coffee and Conversations is an affordable, relatively easy program to implement that helps people find commonalities and develop mutual respect for one another.

Social wellness is poorly impacted by racism, sexism, heterosexism, and other "isms," and libraries have an opportunity to increase understanding between groups of people, reduce bias, and ultimately impact social equity. Another means of accomplishing this is by creating affirming spaces for people from marginalized or socially isolated groups. Some examples include the following:

## Neurodiverse Patrons

Many libraries now offer programming and services aimed at increasing social inclusion for neurodiverse patrons. The Racine Public Library (WI) created a sensory room that can be especially useful for patrons with autism.[70] In Victoria, Australia, Yarra Libraries implement numerous strategies to be inclusive of patrons with sensory needs, as described further in the chapter. Another notable example of a library-based program for increasing social wellness of neurodiverse patrons is the Gamechanger program offered at the Taunton Library in Somerset, England. In collaboration with a community organization called Love Community CIC and funded by a local foundation, Gamechanger makes video gaming equipment available for us during drop-in times at the library and is specifically meant for community members who are neurodivergent or have learning disabilities. Co-led by three autistic individuals who are "experts by experience," the program intentionally offers fewer consoles than the number of attendees to facilitate collaborative play and social interaction. The program initially began with only a few participants and has grown to up to forty weekly visitors from some of the most isolated communities in the area. This innovative program is a great example of a library-based collaboration to address the social wellness of a group of people who can often be quite isolated.

## Sensory-Friendly Initiatives for Neurodiverse Patrons

### Yarra Libraries (Victoria, Australia)

Kylie Carlson, former senior coordinator of Community Engagement and Partnerships at Yarra Libraries, is driven to create sensory-friendly experiences for neurodiverse patrons.[71] Previously noting that patrons who are neurodiverse or have sensory challenges were becoming overstimulated and overwhelmed at some library events, she became concerned that these families and children were unable to fully participate in library programming and did not necessarily feel included or welcomed. As she said, "libraries should be a safe space for all kids and families, including individuals with disabilities." Based on her philosophy that the library should be welcoming to *all* individuals no matter their needs, and her knowledge that neurodiverse individuals or those with sensory integration-related challenges want to be included in activities with neurotypical people rather than segregated, Ms. Carlson collaborated with a local autism-serving organization called Amaze to initiate and lead a number of sensory-friendly initiatives to foster inclusion and belonging. Some of these events at Yarra Libraries include the following:

- Sensitive Storytime: To create inclusive storytimes for families of children with sensory challenges, the Library offered sensory aids such as earmuffs and sensory tents available for anyone who wants to use them. They added schedule boards for children who benefit from a visual schedule during Sensitive Storytime, and a visual clock so children know how much time is remaining. They created a social story about Storytime, so families with kids who need advance preparation to participate can talk with their children prior to the program and help manage expectations. These tools have been added to *all* storytimes, and they now run "Inclusive Storytimes" rather than only having specific times available for families with sensory challenges. Their library ensures all aspects of inclusion are modeled to attendees and that inclusive practices are part of everyday programming, thereby advocating for and creating inclusion spaces to make everyone feel welcome.

- Sensitive Santa: Knowing that many children with sensory challenges are unable to visit with Santa in a shopping mall or other public place, the Library created Sensitive Santa events so all families had the opportunity for their children to visit with Santa. These visits with Santa take place in a quiet and low-stimulation environment, and all of the tools that are available for Sensitive Storytime are also used for these events. In addition, Santa interviews families in advance so he is aware of the children's interests and any specific challenges that could impact the interaction between them. Children are unrushed and have up to 20 minutes to spend with Santa to help foster a sense of relaxation and ease. The Library records these interactions on video for the family to keep as a souvenir of the time their children spent with Santa.

Ms. Carlson also collaborated with Amaze to create online training for library staff about autism and the challenges with sensory integration, which has now expanded for use by library staff across the state of Victoria. All staff are trained in how to make library events inclusive for neurodiverse patrons and develop better skills for working with all patrons. Overall, the library is better able to demonstrate their mission of serving the wider community so families with all types of sensory needs can feel welcome and included in programs.

When asked about lessons learned from Yarra Libraries making this transformation to be inclusive for patrons with sensory needs, Ms. Carlson said, "Libraries have to be willing to use a design thinking approach, to try something, see how it's working, and tweak it as needed. We need to focus on relationships and what changes we can make to make our space more comfortable for all patrons. Rather than expecting them to adapt to us, we should adapt to their needs."

# People with Disabilities

Another group of people who can inadvertently be isolated and have reduced social wellness are people with disabilities. With deliberate planning and intention, libraries can and should ensure their spaces and programming are accessible to a wide group of people who may have limited access and reduced social inclusion. This entails those with physical disabilities such as mobility challenges or vision problems. For example, the Georgia Library Service for the Blind and Print Disabled provides access to a collection of audiobooks, a large print collection, braille materials, telephone support, access to audio-described popular movies, and remote programming such as book clubs, peer support groups, and children's summer reading programs for those with visual disabilities.[72] What is particularly commendable about this program is that it not only focuses on access to print materials but includes events intended to enhance social connections with others. Similarly, the Library for All program at Jefferson County Public Library (CO) provides a monthly interactive art, craft, or game activity specifically for adults with intellectual or developmental disabilities[73] with an aim to increasing their social wellness.

Making the library fully accessible to people with disabilities means ensuring the building and activities can be used by people with a range of needs and barriers to service. The DO-IT (Disabilities, Opportunities, Internetworking, and Technology) Center at the University of Washington provides a useful online checklist to ensure library resources are accessible.[74] This includes physical access to the building and environment, adequate parking, pathways, entrances, and wide aisles for wheelchairs, posting high-contrast and large print directional signage in the library, and ensuring library study rooms (if available) are adaptable for patrons with specific equipment needs such as a screen reader. It also includes making sure staff are aware and trained to communicate with people who have various disabilities and communication needs, to provide accommodations to people with disabilities, and that there are library staff with sign language skills. Library services should be coordinated for persons with disabilities so someone on staff is knowledgeable and designated to respond to accommodation requests, sign language interpretation is available at library-sponsored events, and readers, magnifying glasses, talking books, and large print materials are available. Resources should be delivered for people who are confined to their homes or medical facilities. When possible, there should also be adaptive technology for computers, though this can be cost-prohibitive. Ensuring the physical space and services are fully accessible to patrons with many different types of disabilities enhances their social wellness (and other types of wellness mentioned in this section) and ensures access to the library's valuable resources for all.

# Patrons from Minoritized Groups

Diversity is currently one of the American Library Association's (ALA) Key Action Areas,[75] including a focus on diversifying the field of librarianship and ensuring equitable access to library services, information, and resources for all populations and communities. In fact, the ALA revised Code of Ethics includes a new principle focused on the role of libraries in regard to diversity and social justice. This new ninth principle states, "We affirm the inherent dignity and rights of every person. We work to recognize and dismantle system and individual biases; to confront inequity and oppression; to enhance diversity and inclusion; and to advance racial and social justice in our libraries, communities, profession, and associations through awareness, advocacy, education, collaboration, services, and allocations of resources and spaces."[76] According to ALA, "Libraries can and should play a crucial role in empowering diverse populations for full participation in a democratic society."[77]

Despite this call, there are numerous critiques of public libraries and the inadvertent perpetuation of structural racism and oppression in both the profession and services to local communities, particularly in light of libraries' focus on neutrality.[78] Although unfortunate, anti-racism and diversity-focused efforts are conflated with liberal political ideology in the United States, which complicates libraries' efforts to implement these efforts and sometimes invites negative attention from alt-right activist groups. Yet, neutral attempts to address "diversity" and "tolerance" alone are typically not sufficient to minimize harm to marginalized populations, increase equity, and improve social wellness for minority populations. From our perspective, efforts of anti-racism and equity for marginalized communities are apolitical and are representative of and essential for libraries to offer person-centered services and implement the relationship-first approach discussed throughout this book.

Some examples of library-based initiatives to increase equity and inclusion for racialized populations are the "Coming Together" events at Neuse Regional Libraries (NC), which included facilitated book discussion on *So You Want to Talk About Race* by Ijeoma Oluo, a community presentation on the history of environmental racism, a film screening of *Just Mercy*, and a Juneteenth Celebration.[79] While it is promising that such library-based initiatives have increased in recent years, specifically through advocacy and awareness-raising community efforts, programming, and exhibits, these efforts comprise a small portion of total library initiatives.[80] Libraries are showing their commitment to equity and justice through programming and services, but also through crafting strong anti-racism statements which make their end goals clear, invite opportunities for reflection about the current state of the library, and help hold the library and staff accountable to stakeholders for meaningful steps toward equity.[81] It can also be helpful to highlight resources on your library's website, such as the list maintained by Evanston Public Library (IL).[82] To know where your individual library should start, a comprehensive strategic planning process specifically focused on anti-racist goals and strategies can help uncover current challenges, create and communicate group goals, and identify individual objectives to advance anti-racism with your staff and your patrons. The Oak Park Public Library (IL) provides a useful example of its own anti-racism strategic plan on its website that can serve as a guide and template for other libraries.[83]

In addition to anti-racism efforts, libraries also have an important opportunity to address equity and social wellness for minoritized groups based on sexual orientation or gender identity. Although collections and events centering on inclusion and equity for people of diverse sexual orientations and gender identities have been the focus of a number of recent library protests, including threats of violence made against library administrators and staff, we commend libraries for being on the front lines of the current culture wars and continuing to ensure that all patrons see themselves represented in their local library. Examples of library-based initiatives aimed at inclusion and wellness for LGBTQ+ populations include the many drag queen story hours happening across the country, performances of *Queer Kid Stuff* happening at Brooklyn Public Library (NY) to educate children about LGBTQ+[84] history and issues, and libraries such as the Corvallis-Benton County Public Library (OR) sharing resources on their webpage from the Gay, Lesbian, and Straight Education Network focused on reducing bullying of LGBTQ+ children.[85] For libraries hoping to start specialized programming or resources for this population, an online toolkit is available from ALA for how to better serve people in the LGBTQ+ community.[86] Even for libraries without specialized programming or services for LGBTQ+ patrons, adding materials about gender identity and sexual orientation to your collections, offering at least one gender-neutral bathroom in your library, and including personal pronouns to staff nametags can send powerful messages to patrons that they are seen, heard, and cared about.

ALA also offers other helpful resources for promoting diversity and conducting outreach to many different underserved populations.[87] Programming aimed at connecting with people from marginalized groups can greatly impact overall community and individual well-being.[88] In their recent article, "*Libraries can Unite a Lonely, Divided Nation,*" Richard Florida and Brooks Rainwater argue that libraries are an essential part of the social infrastructure and hold the key to healing our increasing isolation.[89] In a time when we have become more and more disconnected due to the Covid-19 pandemic, an increase in people living alone, a reduction in family size, increased global mobility separating family members by long distances, an increase in remote work, and growing social and economic inequality, the library is one of the few places that can bring us together.

## Environmental Wellness

Environmental wellness means that one's living environment is supportive of their overall well-being, and that they have access to clean air, food, and water, have a safe place to live and learn, and can access to green space and outdoor locations for relaxation and contemplation. Many high-needs patrons do not have safe, stable housing, access to healthy food or clean water, or spaces which encourage their relaxation and prioritize their safety. Although a library is not able to fully provide for someone's environmental wellness, there are a variety of programs and services that libraries offer that address this component of wellness.

In many cases, libraries are comfortable, welcoming spaces that simply being able to enter and stay for a while helps improve one's environmental wellness, albeit temporarily. Libraries serve as refuges for many vulnerable populations, especially those experiencing homelessness or who are unable to afford their utilities. In hot locales, libraries often serve as cooling centers, and alternatively in cold locales where they provide places to warm up. In the earlier subsection on financial wellness, we mentioned how libraries opting to go fine-free are helping ease the financial burdens on patrons. Small changes similar to this that reduce monetary strain can help free up available financial resources for patrons to use on other expenses that contribute to their overall environmental wellness.

Some libraries are taking environmental wellness-focused services a step further by offering assistance signing up for housing programs, and many provide help signing up for emergency utility payments. Tiffany Russell, LCSW, recalls that during her first year as a social worker at Niles District Library (MI), "it became very obvious to me that housing concerns were the number one issue I was assisting patrons with. In addition to helping patrons who needed to find a place to live after being evicted, I was addressing emergency services when their gas was cut off or they couldn't afford their electricity bill."[90] Because of these patron needs, many libraries in the United States are designated enrollment centers for the Low Income Home Energy Assistance Program (LIHEAP) to aid under-resourced households access much-needed heating-related utility assistance during cold winters.

Some libraries are beginning to offer food pantries in their spaces as another dimension aimed at improving environmental wellness. For example, the Dayton Metro Library (OH) recently began a partnership with their local food pantry to create food distribution sites in ten branches. Similarly, North Fitzroy Library in Yarra, Victoria, Australia offers a community pantry with dry and canned goods including packaged, perishable meals in an upright display freezer. These food items are also provided through a partnership with a local food organization and are available to all patrons who need meal assistance. In Yarra, they've observed that meals are often accessed by a range of people including local seniors who may have difficulty cooking nutritious meals for themselves. Although library-based food pantries are a way to expand food access in urban and suburban communities, food pantries may be even more impactful in rural areas that lack other food distribution sites. Union County Carnegie Library (SC) is one example of a small, rural library that decided to create a food pantry on-site due to a lack of other food-related services available in their community. The library stocks perishable and nonperishable items as well as utensils and hygiene products, and unlike the two previous library examples who manage their food sites through collaborations with local food organizations, this library collects their own items to stock their pantry.

In addition to library-based food pantries, many libraries—such as the Saint Louis Public Library (MO)[91]—are distribution sites for the summer months or after school to address hunger and food insecurity for children and families when school is not in session. The US Department of Agriculture funds both the Summer Food Service Program and the At-risk Afterschool Meals Program, administering monies through state agencies to libraries located in areas where 50 percent or more school-aged students are eligible for free or reduced-price school meals. No Kid Hungry[92] provides a variety of resources for libraries interested in becoming summer or afterschool food distribution sites.

## Spiritual Wellness

Spiritual wellness entails having a sense of purpose, meaning, and appreciation for life. For some people, spiritual wellness might connect to personal religious beliefs, while for others it may simply mean having a sense of peace and connection to the universe. To be spiritually well, one understands their own values and beliefs align with their lives. Although public libraries do not promote any particular religion or spiritual belief, they can support the spiritual wellness of patrons in a number of ways. This may involve intentionally offering diverse collections and holding cultural events that allow people of specific spiritual faiths to celebrate together. Some libraries provide lists of books available for specific religious groups or people with shared spiritual beliefs.

Although it's easy to conflate the word "spiritual" with organized religion, creating a space to foster patrons' spiritual wellness includes far more than creeds and shared faiths. Pyati[93] argues that public libraries are "contemplative spaces" by nature and can play an important role in developing the internal spiritual worlds of their patrons. Particularly after the onset of the Covid-19 pandemic and the subsequent anxiety and isolation many patrons experienced (and may still be experiencing), libraries offer programming and online resources for practicing mindfulness and meditation which also foster spiritual wellness. Such programs can be especially impactful on vulnerable and traditionally oppressed groups that may not otherwise have access to fee-based meditation or yoga classes. Some libraries incorporate spiritual wellness classes combined with life skills aimed to promote physical health. For example, social work student interns at Riverhead Free Public Library (NY) provide guidance on developing better sleep habits[94] while the Salt Lake County Library (UT) offered yoga classes to families, adults, and children.[95]

# Summary and Key Takeaway Points

- High-needs patrons often have many barriers to overall wellness that can worsen if left unaddressed.
- Wellness is multidimensional and includes emotional, physical, occupational, intellectual, financial, social, environmental, and spiritual dimensions. Some patrons may be well in some areas but not in others.

- Although libraries cannot address all patron needs and should not be expected to be everything to everyone, there are several examples of successful library-based programming and services to address and promote dimensions of wellness that can be helpful for high-needs patrons.

- Specific programs or services selected by each library should be informed by your local patron and community needs as well as your library resources.

- No matter what programming your library offers, general approaches to working with high-needs patrons include using intentional engagement strategies, warm handoffs, outreach, and service navigation or coordination to increase successful connection to community partners.

## Notes

**1**  World Health Organization, *Health Workforce*, 2022, accessed November 19, 2022, https://www.who.int/health-topics/health-workforce#tab=tab_1.

**2**  L. Kuntz, "Psychiatric Care in the U.S.: Are We Facing a Crisis?" *Psychiatric Times* 39, no. 4 (April 1, 2022), https://www.psychiatrictimes.com/view/psychiatric-care-in-the-us-are-we-facing-a-crisis.

**3**  J. Semega and M. Kollar, *Increase in Income Inequality Driven by Real Declines in Income at the Bottom*, U.S. Census Bureau, September 13, 2022, https://www.census.gov/library/stories/2022/09/income-inequality-increased.html#:~:text=Using%20pretax%20money%20income%2C%20the,index%20had%20increased%20since%202011.

**4**  National Institute of Mental Health, *Chronic Illness and Mental Health: Recognizing and Treating Depression*, 2021, https://www.nimh.nih.gov/sites/default/files/health/publications/chronic-illness-mental-health/recognizing-and-treating-depression.pdf.

**5**  P. Bravemen and L. Gottlieb, "The Social Determinants of Health: It's Time to Consider the Causes of the Causes," *Public Health Reports* 129, no. 2 (2014), https://doi.org/10.1177/00333549141291S2.

**6**  Substance Abuse and Mental Health Services Administration (SAMHSA), *SAMHSA's Concept of Trauma and Guidance for a Trauma-Informed Approach*.

**7**  J. Poe, "Information and Referral Services: A Brief History," *The Southeastern Librarian* 54, no. 1 (Article 8) (2006), https://digitalcommons.kennesaw.edu/seln/vol54/iss1/8.

**8** K. P. Fiori, C. G. Heller, C. D. Rehm, A. Parsons, A. Flattau, S. Braganza, K. Lue, M. Lauria, and A. Racine, "Unmet Social Needs and No-Show Visits in Primary Care in a US Northeastern Urban Health System, 2018–2019," *American Journal of Public Health* 110 (2020): S242_S250, https://doi.org/10.2105/AJPH.2020.305717.

**9** D. Sanderson, S. Braganza, K. Philips, T. Chodon, R. Whiskey, P. Bernard, A. Rich, and K. Fiori, "Increasing Warm Handoffs: Optimizing Community Based Referrals in Primary Care Using QI Methodology," *Journal of Primary Care & Community Health* 12 (2021): 21501327211023883, https://doi.org/10.1177/21501327211023883.

**10** J. Waid, K. Halpin, and R. Donaldson, "Mental Health Service Navigation: A Scoping Review of Programmatic Features and Research Evidence," *Social Work in Mental Health* 19, no. 1 (2021): 60–79, https://doi.org/10.1080/15332985.2020.1870646.

**11** Ibid.

**12** L. M. Gottlieb, D. Hessler, D. Long, E. Laves, A. R. Burns, A. Amaya, P. Sweeney, C. Schedule, and N. E. Adler, "Effects of Social Needs Screening and In-Person Service Navigation on Child Health: A Randomized Clinical Trial," *JAMA Pediatrics* 170, no. 11 (2016), https://doi.org/10.1001/jamapediatrics.2016.2521. Epub 2016 Nov 7. PMID: 27599265.

**13** SAMHSA, *Creating a Healthier Life: A Step-By-Step Guide to Wellness*, 2016, https://store.samhsa.gov/sites/default/files/d7/priv/sma16-4958.pdf.

**14** K. Hall and S. McAlister, "Library Services and Resources in Support of Mental Health: A Survey of Initiatives in Public and Academic Libraries," *Journal of Library Administration* 61, no. 8 (2021): 936–46, https://doi.org/10.1080/01930826.2021.1984137.

**15** Ibid.

**16** A. Oudshoorn, A. Van Berkum, J. Burkell, H. Berman, J. Carswell, and C. Van Loon, "Supporting Mental Health in a Public Library Context: A Mixed Methods Brief Evaluation," *Canadian Journal of Community Mental Health,* e-First https://doi.org/10.7870/cjcmh-2022-013.

**17** *Now and Zen Mindfulness with Samantha, Part 1*, East Brunswick Public Library, October 6, 2020, https://www.youtube.com/watch?v=2zKqxsh6Hsk.

**18** *Dealing with Covid-19 Emotions and Uncertainty*, Baldwin Public Library, May 10, 2020, https://www.youtube.com/watch?v=TyprFooLI2M.

**19** *Free Mental Health Assessment*, Oak Park Public Library, October 11, 2019, https://www.oppl.org/news-events/announcements/free-mental-health-assessments-available/.

**20** *Depression Screening at the Central Library of Philadelphia,* Healthy Philly Minds, 2022, https://healthymindsphilly.org/event/depression-screening-at-the-central -library-of-philadelphia/.

**21** *Mental Health Initiative: Working with Libraries Across California to Create Safe Spaces for Mental Health Knowledge and Access to Resources,* California State Library, n.d., https://www.library.ca.gov/services/to-libraries/mental-health -initiative/#:~:text=The%20Mental%20Health%20Initiative%20works,service%20 to%20all%20community%20members.

**22** *Mental Health First Aid USA*, Mental Health First Aid, October 10, 2013, https:// www.mentalhealthfirstaid.org/.

**23** Reimagining Mental Health Care Delivery Through Public Libraries, St. David's Foundation, February 18, 2022, https://stdavidsfoundation.org/2022/02/18/ reimagining-mental-health-care-delivery-through-public-libraries/.

**24** *Sensory Room*, Racine Public Library, 2022, https://www.racinelibrary.info/use -your-library/social-services/sensory-room/.

**25** *Community Partnerships*, Salt Lake County Library, 2022, https://www.slcl.org/ content/community-partnerships.

**26** *Little Engines*, Ericson Public Library, 2022, https://www.boone.lib.ia.us/about/ little-engines.

**27** *Social-Emotional Learning Kits*, Oak Park Public Library, November 18, 2021, https://www.oppl.org/read-listen-watch/beyond-books/social-emotional -learning-kits/.

**28** *How Can the Library Help Teens with Mental Health?* Fairfax County, Virginia, September 9, 2019, https://www.fairfaxcounty.gov/library/how-can-library-help -teens-mental-health.

**29** L. Purdy, "A Crisis in Youth Mental Health: How the Public Library Can Respond," *ALSC Blog*, December 26, 2021, https://www.alsc.ala.org/blog/2021/12/a-crisis -in-youth-mental-health-how-the-public-library-can-respond/.

**30** T. Atkinson, personal communication, July 28, 2022.

**31** P. DeGuzman, S. Abooali, N. Jain, A. Scicchitano, and Z. C. Siegfried, "Improving Equitable Access to Care Via Telemedicine in Rural Public Libraries," *Public Health Nursing* 39, no. 2 (2021): 431–7, https://doi.org/10.1111/phn.12981.

**32** *CCPL Telehealth Program*, Charleston County Public Library, 2022, https://www .ccpl.org/telehealth.

**33** "Conway Public Library 'Privacy Pod' Now Available for Use," The Conway Daily Sun, March 18, 2022, https://www.conwaydailysun.com/news/local/conway

-public-library-privacy-pod-now-available-for-use/article_ca3d074e-a3e8-11ec
-9c75-1707529ecdc7.html#:~:text=CONWAY%20%E2%80%94%20The%20
Conway%20Public%20Library,glass%20on%20front%20and%20back.

**34**  *NJSL's Telehealth Program,* New Jersey State Library, https://www.njstatelib.org
/services_for_libraries/american-rescue-plan-act-arpa/njhealthconnect-your
-library/.

**35**  S. Yost, *High Point Public Library To Host Free Health Screening,* February 3, 2022,
https://www.rhinotimes.com/news/high-point-public-library-to-host-free
-health-screening/.

**36**  *Free Health Screenings,* Fremont Public Library, n.d., https://fremontlibrary.org/
event/5538000.

**37**  N. Lenstra, *Don't Do It All Yourself: Creating Health Fairs through Partnerships*,
March 20, 2018 [Blog post], https://programminglibrarian.org/blog/don%E2
%80%99t-do-it-all-yourself-creating-health-fairs-through-partnerships.

**38**  *Let's Move in Libraries*, UNC Greensboro School of Education, 2021, https://
letsmovelibraries.org/.

**39**  E. Rubenstein, "Health Information and Health Literacy: Public Library
Practices, Challenges, and Opportunities," *Public Library Quarterly* 35, no. 1
(2016): 49–71.

**40**  *Lifelong Learning: Health Literacy*, Montana.gov, https://msl.mt.gov/libraries/
lifelonglearning/.

**41**  *Brooklyn Supports*, Brooklyn Public Library, March 23, 2022, https://www
.bklynlibrary.org/calendar/brooklyn-supports-bushwick-library-20220323.

**42**  *Mindful Monday: Better Sleep,* Ericson Public Library, December 12, 2022, https://
boone-lib.libcal.com/event/9991588?hs=a.

**43**  N. Lenstra, J. Roberts, and UNCG, *South Carolina Public Libraries & Health: Needs
and Opportunities*, May 2, 2022 [Online white paper], https://libres.uncg.edu/ir/
uncg/listing.aspx?id=37560.

**44**  R. Feuerstein-Simon, M. Lowenstein, R. Dupuis, A. Dolan, X. L. Marti, A. Harvey, H.
Ali, Z. F. Meisel, D. T. Grande, N. Lenstra, and C. C. Cannuscio, "Substance Use and
Overdose in Public Libraries: Results from a Five-State Survey in the US," *Journal
of Community Health*, 2022, https://doi.org/10.1007/s10900-021-01048-2.

**45**  V. Wong, C. C. Cannuscio, M. Lowenstein, R. Feuerstein-Simon, R. Graves, and Z.
F. Meisel, "How Do Public Libraries Respond to Patron Queries about Opioid Use
Disorder? A Secret Shopper Study," *Substance Abuse* 42, no. 4 (2021): 957–61,
https://doi.org/10.1080/08897077.2021.1900980.

**46** S. G. Allen, L. Clark, M. Coleman, L. S. Connaway, C. Cyr, K. Morgan, and M. Procaccini, *Public Libraries Respond to the Opioid Crisis with Their Communities: Case Studies* (Dublin, OH: OCLC, 2021), https://doi.org/10.25333/cx18-1p87.

**47** S. G. Allen, L. Clark, M. Coleman, L. S. Connaway, C. Cyr, K. Morgan, and M. Procaccini, *Call to Action: Public Libraries and the Opioid Crisis* (Dublin, OH: OCLC, 2020), https://doi.org/10.25333/w8sg-8440.

**48** *Job Help*, Charlotte Mecklenburg Library, 2022, https://www.cmlibrary.org/services/job-help.

**49** *Career Center*, Anne Arundel County Public Library, n.d., https://www.aacpl.net/career.

**50** M. Kristakis, "Workforce Development: A Library Partnership Success Story," OCLC, May 31, 2022, https://www.webjunction.org/news/webjunction/workforce-development-a-library-partnership-success-story.html.

**51** K. Morgan, "Library Offers Training to Enhance Job-Readiness in the Community," OCLC, February 15, 2018, https://www.webjunction.org/news/webjunction/career-express-program.html.

**52** Small Business Reference Center, Austin Public Library, n.d., https://library.austintexas.gov/virtual/small-business-reference-center.

**53** "Introducing Small Business Services @Your Library," *East Baton Rouge Parish Library InfoBlog*, May 16, 2018, https://blog.ebrpl.com/2018/05/16/introducing-small-business-services-your-library/.

**54** A. Feist, "Serving Patrons in Your Makerspace Who Are Experiencing Homelessness," *Public Libraries Online*, April 16, 2020, https://publiclibrariesonline.org/2020/04/serving-patrons-in-your-makerspace-who-are-experiencing-homelessness/.

**55** H. Bruinius, "Books on Wheels: When the Library Comes to the Homeless Shelter," *The Christian Science Monitor*, October 31, 2019, https://www.csmonitor.com/USA/Education/2019/1031/Books-on-wheels-When-the-library-comes-to-the-homeless-shelter.

**56** *Partner Spotlight: High Point Public Library,* Ready for School, Ready for Life, n.d., https://www.getreadyguilford.org/partner-spotlight-high-point-public-library/?utm_source=rss&utm_medium=rss&utm_campaign=partner-spotlight-high-point-public-library.

**57** *Books & Barbers,* Bridge of Books Foundation, n.d., https://bridgeofbooksfoundation.org/2017/05/11/bridge-of-books-receives-2017-innovative-partmership-award/.

**58**  *Social Services*, Long Branch Free Public Library, n.d., https://www.longbranchlib
.org/social-work-and-divesity.

**59**  K. Zappie-Ferradino, "Salt Lake City Public Library Publishes Digital Navigator
Toolkit," *National Digital Inclusion Alliance*, September 7, 2021, https://www
.digitalinclusion.org/blog/2021/09/07/salt-lake-city-public-library-publishes
-digital-navigator-toolkit/.

**60**  Y. Scorse, "NDIA Awards 18 National Digital Navigator Corps Grants in Rural
& Tribal Areas," *National Digital Inclusion Alliance*, September 7, 2022, https://
www.digitalinclusion.org/blog/2022/09/07/ndia-awards-18-national-digital
-navigator-corps-grants-in-rural-tribal-areas/.

**61**  *Financial Literacy Classes at Patrick Beaver Memorial Library*, City of Hickory,
November 2, 2022, https://programminglibrarian.org/programs/financial
-literacy-workshops-new-american.

**62**  A. Fisher, *Program Model: Financial Literacy Workshops for New Americans*,
March 7, 2018, https://programminglibrarian.org/programs/financial-literacy
-workshops-new-americans.

**63**  *Financial Literacy,* Alexandria Library, 2021, https://alexlibraryva.org/financial
-literacy.

**64**  *Financial Resources,* Decatur Public Library, 2022, https://www.decaturlibrary.org
/community-resources-financial-assistance.

**65**  T. Thompson, *Van Buren Library Hires Social Work Inter to Facilitate Community
Needs*, August 26, 2021, https://www.swtimes.com/story/news/local/van-buren
/2021/08/26/van-buren-library-hires-social-work-inter-to-facilitate-community
-needs/8171095002/.

**66**  *Period Supplies,* St. Louis County Public Library, 2022, https://www.slcl.org/using
-the-library/period-supplies.

**67**  D. Fallows, "Why Some Libraries are Ending Fines," *The Atlantic*, December 4,
2020, https://www.theatlantic.com/ideas/archive/2020/12/why-some-libraries
-are-ending-fines/621445/.

**68**  A. Honisett, R. Short, and K. Schwab, "Building Community at the Library with
Coffee and Conversation," *OLA Quarterly* 23, no. 4 (2018): 24, https://doi.org/10
.7710/1093-7374.1919.

**69**  J. Africawala, "Program Model: Coffee and Conversation," *Programming
Librarian*, April 25, 2015, https://programminglibrarian.org/programs/coffee
-conversation.

**70**  C. Smith, "Good Vibrations: Libraries Supply Sensory Spaces," *American Libraries*
53, no. 9/10 (2022): 44.

71  K. Carlson, personal communication, November 1, 2022.

72  GLS: Georgia Library Service for the Blind and Print Disabled, Chattahoochee Valley Libraries, n.d., https://www.cvlga.org/gls-georgia-library-service-for-the -blind-and-print-disabled/.

73  S. Douglas, "Program Model: Library for All," *Programming Librarian*, April 19, 2017, https://programminglibrarian.org/programs/library-all.

74  "Disabilities, Opportunities, Internetworking, and Technology. Universal Access: Making Library Resources Accessible to People with Disabilities," University of Washington, 2022, https://www.washington.edu/doit/universal-access-making -library-resources-accessible-people-disabilities.

75  *Key Action Areas*, American Library Association, n.d., https://www.ala.org/ aboutala/missionpriorities/keyactionareas.

76  *Code of Ethics*, American Library Association, 2021, https://www.ala.org/tools/ ethics.

77  *Diversity in Libraries*, American Library Association, n.d., https://www.ala.org/ educationcareers/libcareers/diversity.

78  A. N. Gibson, R. L. Chancellor, N. A. Cooke, S. P. Dahlen, S. A. Lee, and Y. L. Shorish, "Libraries on the Frontlines: Neutrality and Social Justice," *Equality, Diversity, and Inclusion* 36, no. 8 (2017): 751–66.

79  S. J. Sever, "Coming Together at Neuse Regional Libraries," *Neuse News*, May 11, 2021, https://www.neusenews.com/index/2021/5/10/coming-together-at -neuse-regional-libraries.

80  E. P. Jones, N. S. Mani, R. B. Carlson, C. G. Welker, M. Cawley, and F. Yu, "Analysis of Anti-Racism, Equity, Inclusion and Social Justice Initiatives in Library and Information Science Literature," *Reference Services Review* 50, no. 1 (2022): 81–101, https://doi.org/10.1108/RSR-07-2021-0032.

81  "An Anti-Racist Statement in the Library: Working Toward Praxis," American Library Association, October 2, 2020, http://www.ala.org/advocacy/diversity/ odlos-blog/anti-racism-statement.

82  E. Bird, *Antiracist Resources and Reads: Lists for All Ages*, Evanston Public Library, June 1, 2020, https://www.epl.org/antiracist-resources-and-reads-lists-for-all -ages/.

83  *Anti-Racism Strategic Plan*, Oak Park Public Library, April 27, 2021, https://www .oppl.org/about/policies/anti-racism-strategic-plan/.

84  *It's Pride with Queer Kid Stuff*, Brooklyn Public Library, June 23, 2022, https://www .bklynlibrary.org/calendar/its-pride-queer-kid-stuff-virtual-20220623.

85   *Anti-Bullying Resources*, Corvallis-Benton County Public Library, n.d., https://cbcpubliclibrary.net/anti-bullying-resources/.

86   *Open to All: Serving the GLBT Community in Your Library* [Toolkit], American Library Association Gay, Lesbian, Bisexual, and Transgender Round Table (GLBTRT), https://www.ala.org/rt/sites/ala.org.rt/files/content/professionaltools/160309-glbtrt-open-to-all-toolkit-online.pdf.

87   Equity, Diversity, and Inclusion, American Library Association, 2022, https://www.ala.org/advocacy/diversity.

88   M. H. Norton, M. J. Stern, J. Meyers, and E. DeYoung, Understanding the Social Well-Being Impacts of the Nation's Libraries and Museums [Report], *Institute of Museum and Library Services*, 2021, https://www.imls.gov/sites/default/files/2021-10/swi-report-accessible.pdf.

89   R. Florida and B. Rainwater, "Libraries Can Unite a Lonely, Divided Nation," *Bloomberg*, October 26, 2022, https://www.bloomberg.com/news/articles/2022-10-26/in-a-divided-nation-public-libraries-offer-space-to-reconnect.

90   T. Russell, personal communication, August 8, 2022.

91   *Community Partnerships*, St. Louis County Library, 2022, https://www.slcl.org/content/community-partnerships.

92   *Share Our Strength*, No Kid Hungry, 2022, https://www.nokidhungry.org/.

93   A. K. Pyati, "Public Libraries as Contemplative Spaces: A Framework for Action and Research," *Journal of the Australian Library and Information Association* 68, no. 4 (2019): 356–70, https://doi.org/10.1080/24750158.2019.1670773.

94   Riverhead Free Library (@RivFreeLibrary), "Social Work Intern Alanna McCabe Will Teach You Techniques to Help Develop a Nightly Routine for Better Sleep" [Tweet] Twitter, November 22, 2022, https://twitter.com/RivFreeLibrary/status/1595190765550198785?s=20&t=_1zDnOa0Br4L8sfyL5qeBQ.

95   *Yoga with Leslie*, Salt Lake County Library, November 18, 2022, https://slcls.libnet.info/salt-lake-county-library/event/703603.

# 4 Addressing the Needs of Specific Patron Populations

The previous chapter addressed programming and services that libraries can offer to address specific areas of psychosocial need in their general patron populations. However, due to their community context, many libraries have large populations of specific groups or demographics of patrons, such as seniors, youth, immigrants, unhoused patrons, or ex-offenders. Shared characteristics of these patron populations can sometimes inform the types of programming or services that will work well in these communities, and libraries should consider offering broad initiatives to address multiple areas of wellness that might be frequently impacted for the specific population as a whole. Additionally, there are sometimes unique differences in urban and rural libraries regarding patron and staff needs. In this chapter, we aim to cover a wide variety of patron populations and include examples of library programming and services that have been successful at addressing the needs of these specific groups.

## Immigrant Populations / Non-English-Speaking Patrons

More immigrants call the United States home than any other country in the world, with more than 40 million immigrants (approximately one-fifth of all global immigrants) living in this country.[1] Many of these immigrants face multiple barriers to economic and social stability and mobility once they enter the United States, depending on the reason for their resettlement (i.e., refugees versus voluntary immigrants), their immigration status, their country of origin, primary language spoken, amount of positive social support, education level, employment background, and additional factors such as mental health or physical health problems. Immigrants often have a challenging road ahead of them to become stable in their new country of residence. Adding to their challenges are the growing anti-immigrant rhetoric in the United States,[2] increasing immigration enforcement activities,[3] and difficulty accessing healthcare and supportive services when needed.[4] The language barrier is also significant; immigrants who do not speak English experience more stress,[5] struggle to build social networks, access needed care for a variety of needs, and obtain and maintain the employment needed to support themselves and their families. Although all immigrants face challenges due to settling in a new country, refugees are an extra-vulnerable population due to the circumstances surrounding their need to flee their home country and related experiences of physical or psychological trauma.[6]

Public libraries have a long history of providing services to immigrants and non–English-speaking patrons. Andrew Carnegie's own experience as an immigrant fueled his passion to build thousands of public libraries that could embolden new Americans to educate themselves and therefore weave themselves into the fabric of their adopted country.[7] Libraries carry on Carnegie's vision today by providing assistance to patrons seeking citizenship,[8] clearly outlining services on their websites to immigrant populations,[9] and targeting services and programming toward specific ethnic groups that have resettled in their local community. Notably, Zettervall and Nienow's concept of "whole person librarianship" originally stemmed from a book club they began with Somali refugees at Hennepin County Library (MN).[10]

Many libraries offer specialized services to the immigrants in their regions. To help with this, the American Library Association offers a free on-demand webinar for libraries interested in incorporating immigration-focused services.[11] This webinar features the Immigration Advocates Network, which provides resources, news updates, and a legal directory (for directly obtaining immigration-focused legal help for patrons) to organizations throughout the United States wanting to provide services to immigrant populations.[12] For libraries serving large populations of non–English-speaking patrons, seeking volunteers or employees who speak those native languages should be a priority. To be able to adequately determine this population's needs and how the library might be able to help, speaking the language is essential. This can, of course, be a challenge in areas where there are few people fluent in the specific language or where there are so many immigrant groups present that multiple language proficiency is needed.

There are many examples of public libraries offering comprehensive and person-centered immigration-focused services. One example is the Louisville Free Public Library (KY), detailed further here. Another is the Hartford Public Library

(CT), which since 2000 has offered industry-recognized certificate training, GED prep, ESL (English as a Second Language) classes, and a US citizenship program for immigrants through a program called The American Place.[13] This program supports immigrants to achieve US citizenship and become vested citizens. It helps to facilitate resettlement, education, and career transitions for new Americans. The library also runs an "After School English Club" for youth that includes snacks and a bus pass to transport teens to and from the program. The Club seeks to help participating youth improve their English fluency for work or school, achieve their academic and career goals, and build community with others.

## Immigrant-Focused Services and Supports

### Louisville Free Public Library (KY)

Ahmed Farah, immigrant and refugee services coordinator at the Louisville Free Public Library, facilitates special programming and services to support the local immigrant community.[14] Surrounded by a growing immigrant community, the library noted challenges occurring for these individuals due to language barriers, social isolation, employment-related needs, and others' lack of understanding of cultural factors. To address these needs, the library has added a variety of services and focused on the following:

- Adding volunteer-run English classes for participants to practice speaking English with others. These classes have been held both in-person and online, and online class options have had attendees participating from other locations around the globe in addition to Louisville area residents. Online English conversation classes have been found to be most helpful for the local community due to minimizing barriers to participation such as transportation and childcare.
- Adding "English Conversation Club," an informal group that matches immigrants and refugees with native English speakers, provides conversation prompts, and enables participants to have casual conversations to learn about each other as well as practicing conversational English. In this club, the conversation prompts are designed to support cultural exchange between participants to learn about each other's cultural values, beliefs, and traditions. They also include practical information such as how to ride public transportation or other

pieces of relevant information to assist the immigrant community with learning to navigate the Louisville area.

- Hosting citizenship classes to assist immigrants with preparing for the citizenship process and exam
- Increasing the number of bilingual staff and being intentional about hiring staff who speak the most frequently spoken languages in the local community
- Hosting Cultural Showcases, events for immigrants from various countries or different cultural groups to showcase information about their beliefs, values, and traditions
- Hosting native language circles to allow immigrants to interact with other community members in their native language and build social support and community connections
- Hosting an art gallery in the library featuring art created by local immigrant and refugee artists
- Increasing collection materials in the most common languages spoken in the community
- Building relationships with immigrant-serving community resources who can address basic needs for this population, such as providing assistance applying for public benefits and services.

These events and programs help facilitate cultural exchanges which can educate community members about the various cultural groups present in the community, help increase social support and community connections of immigrants and refugees, and improve the ability of immigrants and refugees to communicate in the local language which subsequently impacts employment opportunities, educational possibilities, ability to navigate needed resources, and social connections. These programs and services have helped the library better connect to their local community and meet the needs of their patrons.

When asked the biggest lesson learned from being in his position, Mr. Farah said, "Language is key." If a library has no other resources to initiate any other services or programs for immigrant populations, adding English classes or informal opportunities to practice speaking conversational English are the most important because learning the local language opens up other opportunities for this population and decreases barriers to health, wellness, social support, employment, and education. Also, he added, "don't be afraid to take risks." In his experience, it is helpful to try new initiatives, see how they work, talk to patrons about their perspectives of the initiatives, and learn from them. Sometimes programming or services work as planned, and sometimes planned initiatives need modified or changed. Everything should be viewed as a learning opportunity, and he advises that staff should not be afraid of failure.

To initiate services such as these, Mr. Farah recommends that the library should have a designated staff person to take the lead on immigrant-focused services. The biggest resources needed are time to develop collaborations with community partners, do outreach activities with immigrants to determine their biggest needs, and to solicit and oversee volunteer-run activities to meet these needs such as English conversation clubs. He suggests that it is helpful to access local statistics about the number of immigrants from specific groups living in the local community to identify the most common languages spoken by these groups.

Services may not need to be as broad as the examples mentioned earlier, however, depending on what other resettlement-focused organizations are in the library's local community and the comprehensiveness of their services. In some communities, the library's best way to help immigrant populations is to provide opportunities for enrichment, safe entertainment, and building social connections. Ultimately it is best to communicate with your local immigrant community, talk to resettlement organizations in your region to find the gaps in what they are able to offer, and directly ask how the library can help.

# Teen/Adolescent Patrons

Some libraries have large populations of often unaccompanied adolescents who come to the library after school or over breaks. These patron groups can sometimes get rowdy and disruptive, talking or playing so loudly that they disturb other patrons trying to use the library. They may intentionally ignore staff or break the rules, testing boundaries as any adolescent is likely to do at times. They might be experiencing interpersonal difficulties or struggles with their relationships with one another that affect how they act in the library. Teen patrons might also be having more serious problems that impact their lives inside and outside of the library, including mental health problems, emerging eating disorders, developing substance use problems, experiences of intimate partner violence and abuse, and suicidal ideation.[15] As anyone who has ever been a teenager, parented a teenager, or loved a teenager knows, the adolescent years can be quite turbulent and trying times.

Libraries have the potential to be supportive and particularly freeing spaces for teenagers[16] and can positively impact the trajectory of their lives. Creating opportunities for teens to build healthy social relationships with one another and with adults in their communities can prevent violence and other types of delinquent or criminal behavior in at-risk youth populations.[17] Libraries can offer programming, services, and resources aimed at substance abuse and violence prevention, which can often be facilitated through partnerships with community or regional organizations specializing in evidence-based prevention strategies. Programming focused on early detection of mental health problems or eating disorders, especially programming that has a separate component for concerned parents, can have a substantial impact on a teen's life, since early detection and treatment of these challenges is predictive of improved outcomes and a better long-term prognosis.[18] Depending on the biggest issues facing the library's specific adolescent patron population, the library holds the potential to significantly impact overall health, wellness, and social support for these teens.

Many libraries already offer incredible services and programs for adolescent patrons and are fortunate to have dedicated spaces for teens to be active and talkative while minimizing disruption to other patron groups, such as the Bloomington (IN) Public Library's Teen Zone.[19] This area of the library is separated from the other spaces and contains movable furniture, video games, a cafe area, a graphic design studio space, and collaborative/active learning areas to serve as a place for teens to socialize, study, and play. Dedicated staff offer regular programming and support to the teens who use the space to try to keep them engaged and active. A space such as this is a luxury that many libraries can't afford, though, or is a space that is simply unavailable given the age and square footage of some libraries.

Even in libraries unable to create or maintain separate spaces, strategies can be used to make teens feel welcome and heard. Successful examples of this are the teen advisory groups at Ericson Public Library (IA)[20] and Elmhurst Public Library (IL).[21] These groups are comprised of teen patron volunteers who work collaboratively with the Children's or Teen Librarian to make recommendations for programming and services to be offered at the library, including social activities, exercise-related programming, and mental health informational sessions. Creating a teen advisory board does not have to be time-consuming or expensive and is a relatively easy strategy for ensuring the relevance of your teen programming and engaging adolescent patrons.

When considering the needs of adolescent patrons, it's important to be mindful that some of them are experiencing serious psychosocial challenges above and beyond the normal stressors of adolescence, including many who experience severe poverty and/or homelessness. An estimated one out of thirty US teens between the ages of thirteen and seventeen experience homelessness every year.[22] Of these teens, there are often additional risk factors or challenges such as having a mental health problem, substance use disorder, experiencing physical or sexual abuse in their home, dropping out of school before graduation, or having been in the foster care system. All of these needs compound the barriers for adolescent patrons, but also create opportunities for impactful programming and supportive services. We caution libraries to be realistic about what they can do for this population; however; complex barriers such as these require equally complex interventions that are beyond the training of most library staff or the scope or mission of the library. Nevertheless, there are many opportunities to connect these youth to needed resources, involve these patrons in positive social activities, provide enrichment services and assistance preparing for employment or increasing education, or invite community partners in for outreach.

Because libraries often have their finger on the pulse of their community and can detect gaps in services due to the unmet needs they see in their patron population, they can also use their knowledge and influence to initiate change in their local communities. Detroit Public Library (MI) is a great example of how a single library staff member initiated and eventually helped create a new community organization to serve the needs of homeless youth in their area.

## Community Collaboration to Improve Services for Homeless Youth

### Detroit Public Library (MI)

Mary Jo Vortkamp, manager and children's librarian at the Franklin Branch of Detroit Public Library, demonstrates that libraries and library staff can utilize their skills and collaborative relationships to impact not just library services, but even community services for specific groups of patrons.[23] Noting a lack of services for homeless youth in Detroit and a high number of youth who appeared to be homeless visiting the library, Ms. Vortkamp initially volunteered to be part of a Detroit Task Force for the National Association for the Education of Homeless Children and Youth as soon as she heard of this group forming in her area in 2013. She proceeded to use her role at the library to help promote awareness of the issue, including promoting the National Runaway Prevention Month. She developed a resource list for librarians focused on youth homelessness, added programs in collaboration with Matrix Human Services and their "off the streets" program, and even curated a special Hoopla Digital list focused on homeless youth. As awareness of the issue of youth homelessness continued to grow in Detroit, Ms. Vortkamp connected with her local university to provide information and resources to them, and to bring awareness to them about the lack of research on the topic.

Due in large part due to her persistence, her knowledge of available resources and data, and her relationships with people in the local area working toward local solutions, what started as a single staff person hired by the Task Force to address youth homelessness in her community was able to grow to a full-fledged nonprofit organization now called the Detroit Phoenix Center. As Ms. Vortkamp says, "From resume writing workshops to grant writing to cleaning tables and chasing toddlers at events, I have assisted in many aspects of changing the Detroit Phoenix Center from one woman with a dream to a nationally recognized organization supporting young people in Detroit." She continues to advocate for homeless patrons with library policies, to develop educational materials and resources for young people experiencing homelessness, and to promote events such as the National Runaway Prevention Month and National Hunger and Homelessness Awareness Week, and she also now serves as board chair of the Detroit Phoenix Center. She notes that libraries often sell themselves short when it comes to bringing about community-level change, but library staff have skills, information, resources, and community connections that are needed to keep the momentum going as new groups try to form and gain community buy-in. As she said, "Other groups come and go, organizations get funding and lose funding, but the library is the one constant that is always there. I may not be able to house anybody, and

I can't feed anyone, but I can be at the table and *stay at the table* to see things through to the end." Her persistence, dedication to making a difference, and community collaborations helped not only improve services for homeless youth at the library but also to add a new service provider for this population in the Detroit community.

Recent research has found that of the 700,000 unaccompanied or homeless youth in the United States,[24] nearly 40 percent of them identify as LGBTQ+,[25] with LGBTQ+ youth being twice as likely to experience homelessness than their heterosexual or cisgender peers.[26] Libraries serving large numbers of homeless youth should be mindful of this and take extra care to make this group of adolescents feel comfortable and welcome in the space. According to Dr. Julie Ann Winkelstein, libraries can work to create "welcoming, anticipatory, and supportive environments" (2020, p.67) for this population. Sachem Public Library (NY) is an example of a library who is aiming to do just that by encouraging their social work student intern to run support groups specifically for queer teens.[27]

Another significant concern for unhoused youth is the risk of human trafficking, with approximately 20 percent of homeless youth being trafficking victims.[28] Teens who have experienced childhood sexual abuse are at particularly high risk for being involved in human trafficking. The US Department of Justice Office for Victims of Crime provides national resources for education about and response to human trafficking throughout the United States that can be shared in libraries or used to locate community or state partners to offer library training or programming on the topic.[29] In San Diego, staff at the Central Library developed a program to generate awareness about how to identify teens who may have been trafficked.[30] The latter has discovered some of their best advocates to educate staff and the wider public about factors pertaining to youth homelessness are in fact teenagers who are formerly unhoused.

# Senior Patrons

Libraries are one of the few public spaces in society that naturally promote an intergenerational matrix in which people of all ages come together in a shared space. This can be especially important for aging patrons, who are at increased risk for loneliness and social isolation, which notably impact their subsequent risks for dementia and other serious medical problems.[31] Eric Klinenberg highlights the ways public libraries provide a regular means of social connection for seniors through reading groups and bowling clubs. He describes libraries as providing a "social infrastructure" that can help ward off social isolation, something that the elderly are prone to facing.[32] Libraries can help senior patrons maintain quality social connectivity as such supports correlate to higher life expectancy, resilience to stress, reduction in disease morbidity and mortality, and greater overall health and well-being.[33]

The American Library Association offers online tips and tools for assisting older adult patrons[34] and there are a variety of online webinars, resources, and toolkits available for download on WebJunction to guide programming and services for senior patrons.[35] The Reference and User Services Association also developed an online set of guidelines and best practices for providing library services to seniors, including recommendations for staff training, how to best develop helpful information services and collections, programming, technology, and outreach and support for homebound populations.[36] Libraries serving a high number of senior patrons should be mindful that many have accessibility challenges using the physical space and collections as well as the electronic resources.

Examples of libraries working to meet the needs of their aged patrons include branches in Columbus (OH), Denver (CO), and Fort Worth (TX) that offer dementia-friendly services. [37] In some affluent areas, libraries find the elderly are the primary age group seeking assistance from on-site social workers. At the Elmhurst Public Library (IL), former library social worker Tracey Orick noted many of their senior citizens were the ones seeking her help the most with employment-related questions. Libraries such as the New York Public Library and Salinas Public Library (CA) offer retirement planning and assistance exploring second careers and entrepreneurship.[38] Many libraries are specifically focusing digital literacy efforts on senior populations who need assistance with computer skills and internet safety.

One area of opportunity for libraries trying to meet the needs of senior patron populations is in the area of physical mobility and movement-related programming to help keep this patron group as mobile and strong as possible. Lenstra's Let's Move in Libraries[39] initiative mentioned in Chapter 3 offers a number of resources and activities that can be used to help increase physical mobility specifically for senior patrons. Since these activities can be inexpensive and relatively easy to conduct in libraries, this opens the door for many small and rural public libraries to offer movement-based groups to promote healthy physical activity among senior patrons.[40] In fact, one nationwide study of older adults from forty-nine mostly rural and small libraries across the United States found that a library-based strength-training program was associated with increased physical, mental, and social health and well-being for participants,[41] demonstrating that these types of initiatives are well worth the time and energy to help senior patron populations.

## Age-Friendly and Dementia-Friendly Initiatives

### Fort Worth Public Library (TX)

The Fort Worth Public Library (FWPL) offers special programs and services to meet the needs of seniors, community members experiencing dementia, and their caregivers.[42] According to Jana Hill, Adult Services Manager, FWPL began an initiative several years ago to become certified as a "Dementia-Friendly" and "Age-Friendly" business. Partnering with two community partners, the James L. West Center for Dementia Care and Dementia-Friendly Fort Worth, all eighteen library locations underwent a transformation to ensure physical spaces, staff, and programming/services are accessible and supportive for seniors and individuals experiencing dementia. Several specific changes were made:

- Ensuring the library space is accessible and welcoming for people with age-related or other physical limitations
- Training all staff, including non-programming staff, on dementia, including how to recognize signs that someone may be experiencing dementia and the best ways to talk with individuals experiencing dementia without making them feel bad for memory loss.
- Offering memory kits to patrons. Memory kits contain a variety of multisensory and tactile items to serve as conversation starts between people experiencing memory loss and their loved ones. They were designed to be in circulation between multiple library locations and to withstand heavy use.
- Adding programming focused on senior patrons and their caregivers, including programs such as how to use the available memory kits, how to create your own personalized memory kit for a family member, intergenerational music therapy programming, and "La Hora de los Abuelos" to address social isolation and community-building needs of local Spanish-speaking seniors.

According to Ms. Hill, these initiatives did not take a lot of library resources. The largest resource needed for these types of initiatives was knowledge of available community partners in the state or region that specialized in serving aging populations or populations experiencing dementia. She notes that other libraries may find some options for national collaborators if there are none in their local area, although contracts between libraries and national organizations may often be difficult to negotiate. For the Fort Worth partnership, their local Junior League funded the memory kits, which cost less than $5,000 to create.

The Library notes a number of benefits of these initiatives. In Fort Worth, the collaborating community partners had a mission to raise awareness and serve the aging community but had limited reach outside of their single office locations. Ms. Hill stated that these initiatives were win-win situations for the partnering organizations, community members, and the library because, "They [community partners] bring the expertise, we bring the reach, and we bring the trust." With multiple locations of the library, these initiatives helped boost the capacity of the library to meet local community needs while also expanding the reach of the community partners and raising awareness of dementia-related needs throughout the Fort Worth area. These initiatives and programs also helped raise awareness of staff to recognize and better serve vulnerable community members and made the library more accessible to people who are aging or experiencing dementia.

"You don't have to be an expert to launch this kind of initiative," stated Ms. Hill. By locating experts in the community and inviting them to partner, similar types of collaborations are doable in many communities and libraries to improve library services, meet the needs of the community, improve the reach of community partners, and ensure service quality and library accessibility for vulnerable populations.

## Gender-Diverse Patrons

Public libraries are experiencing a paradigm shift in support of gender diversity, recognizing that the promotion of trans- and all-gender-inclusive organizational cultures can serve to better address a range of psychosocial issues among both patrons and staff.[43] There are many people who do not identify with the gender binary of male/female and instead may identify as genderqueer, gender fluid, nonbinary, transgender, or other gender categories. Often it is not possible to identify someone's gender identity by external appearance alone, and library staff should be sensitive to this and never assume to know someone's gender.

This is why it is becoming more common to add pronouns to name tags, email signature lines, or the way one introduces themselves. This is important even when someone is cisgender, meaning they identify as a gender in alignment with the sex they were assigned at birth, because it helps to normalize stating pronouns and creates a culture where people who are gender diverse feel welcome and not singled out.

Gender-diverse individuals experience a great deal of discrimination and bias and have significant barriers to healthcare and other services because of these biases.[44] This contributes to the high rates of mental health problems, suicidal ideation, low social support, and isolation seen in this population. In Beth's needs assessments of patron populations across the United States, she has found that although the number of gender-diverse patrons is low in each sample, the needs experienced by gender-diverse patrons are significantly higher than patrons who identify as male or female. For example, in a broad study of over 5,000 patrons, only 44 identified as gender diverse. Yet, these forty-four patrons had significantly higher needs in nearly every area of unmet need surveyed. They were more likely to self-report mental health problems, substance abuse, employment-related needs, educational needs, social isolation, medical problems, dental problems, transportation challenges, financial challenges, and unsafe/unstable housing than patrons who identified as male or female. Libraries should be aware of these needs and ensure that programming or services designed to address these needs are intentionally designed to be welcoming to people who are gender diverse. When designing welcoming spaces and programs, libraries should also remember that gender-diverse patrons with additional identities that are marginalized, such as minoritized racial or ethnic groups or people with disabilities, may experience additional discrimination, bias, isolation, and subsequent wellness-related challenges.

Examples of libraries intentionally welcoming this population include the Fairmount Heights Branch Library (MD), where a group of librarians partners with their local Trans Coalition to offer The Butterfly Project.[45] This initiative provides assistance with job preparation and connections to an array of local resources for trans and nonbinary people of color.[46] The branch's wider Prince George County Library System also regularly produces videos and online exhibits highlighting awareness and local resources pertaining to LGBTQ+ Pride.[47] Other libraries provide educational resources by way of online panel discussions to help create a greater understanding about patrons who identify as gender diverse. In New

Hampshire, the Jaffrey Public Library hosted a highly attended online panel discussion about gender identity to educate their community about individuals who identify as nonbinary.[48]

Even if libraries do not offer specific projects or initiatives on behalf of gender-diverse patrons, small yet significant choices can be made by libraries to communicate support for all patrons. Including gender-inclusive signage for bathrooms and encouraging staff to note their preferred pronouns on their library name tags or identification badges are two steps libraries can take to foster a safe and inclusive environment for gender-diverse patrons.

## Justice-Involved Patrons

A growing number of public libraries are addressing the needs of justice-involved patrons through prison/jail-based programs or reentry initiatives. The United States has the highest incarceration rate in the entire world, with nearly two million people incarcerated at any given time in this country and over 600,000 people returning annually to their communities post-incarceration.[49] Because of changes in sentencing laws and an increase in drug-related convictions, there has been a 500 percent increase in the number of people incarcerated over the past four decades.[50] Notably, there are significant racial/ethnic and socioeconomic disparities in who gets incarcerated and for how long, with people who are living in poverty and people of color more likely to be incarcerated and for longer periods of time than their White, higher-income counterparts. There are also a disproportionate number of people with severe mental illnesses and cognitive disabilities who become incarcerated.[51] To improve access to resources and information, some libraries offer services to incarcerated populations, such as the Charleston County Public Library's (SC) branch providing services to the local juvenile detention center or the Auckland (New Zealand) Library's branch in their local correctional facility.[52]

People reentering their communities after incarceration often face many challenges,[53] some of which can relatively easily be addressed by public libraries. Incarceration rarely reduces the risk of criminal behavior, and in some cases actually increases the likelihood that someone will re-offend.[54] Re-offending is more likely for ex-offenders who lack positive social or family support, have difficulty obtaining or maintaining employment and a living wage, face housing challenges, or have co-occurring substance abuse problems.[55] Overall, there is a shortage of reentry support programs to help people successfully integrate back into their communities and reduce the likelihood of re-offending, but programs focused on health and wellness, skill development and employment, building positive social support, and building mentorship relationships can be helpful.[56] These align well with programming and services offered by many public libraries. Many ex-offenders do not have a stable work history, so work-focused interventions can especially help increase their chances of post-prison employment.[57] Although all ex-offenders face challenges to community reentry, people in rural communities often have additional challenges due to a more severe lack of available housing, fewer employment opportunities, and inadequate mental health and substance abuse treatment options.[58] Ex-offenders with disabilities understandably face additional challenges with obtaining needed care, maintaining employment, and attaining safe and secure housing.

Although libraries may be hesitant to actively serve ex-offenders, these individuals are living in local communities everywhere, are most likely already part of the library's patron population, and can benefit from the many supportive services libraries can offer. In Tennessee, the Blount County Public Library works in tandem with their local Recovery Court to develop and provide a curriculum to help individuals in recovery develop life skills including finance, career development, and nutrition.[59] Targeted programming for the justice-involved is also underway at libraries in Denver, Brooklyn, and South Carolina.[60] In California, the Ready Access[61] initiative is a coordinated effort to provide library staff with "the tools they need to successfully provide programming to individuals affected by incarceration" and provides a toolkit for library staff including how to initiate partnerships and develop programming to support patrons reentering communities after incarceration.[62] San Francisco Public Library's staff partner with the local sheriff's office to offer services such as reference assistance by mail and book recommendations to incarcerated adults.[63] Some libraries are partnering with professional or student social workers to assist individuals transitioning back into society following incarceration. With guidance from library social worker David Perez and his team of social work students from Rutgers University, the Long Branch Free Public Library (NJ) expanded its Fresh Start reentry program to six branches throughout the state of New Jersey.[6465] Libraries have opportunities to assist this population, contribute to their overall health and well-being, social support, and employment prospects, and therefore potentially decrease the chances of these patrons re-offending in the future.

## Services for Justice-Involved Patrons

### Long Branch (NJ) Free Public Library

Noticing many community members, especially men of color, return-ing to prison because of a lack of opportunities in the local community, Long Branch Free Public Library Director Tonya Garcia[66] was determined to do what she could to help prevent this. Since the library had the tools to help with literacy, digital skills, and connecting people to resources, she decided to use these assets to create a program specifically for the reentry population. The Fresh Start Program was created in 2009, initially starting with group workshops focused on computer skills, resume creation, and job searching skills. She notes that the group "bombed" at first and had trouble attracting participants. To learn why people weren't showing up, she started an advisory group of people who had been incarcerated and directly asked them what needed to be improved. The advisory group informed her that their privacy was important, and they did not feel com-fortable talking about their needs in a group. After changing the program to provide individually focused services, participation increased. Now all Fresh Start participants begin the program with a private conversation about their experiences, their needs, and how the library can help. This one-on-one strategy helps to build a trusting relationship between the participant and the library staff and enables the creation of an individual-ized plan to meet the person's needs.

When asked about lessons learned from Fresh Start, Ms. Garcia stated, "We have to take risks. The library is the most trusted place in the city and people naturally come here for information and support. People trust their library. If we're going to be the most relevant, most recognized, and most vital department in the city then we have to really put our money where our mouth is and take risks to address voids in our local communities and make a difference."

Although the program was initially hard to sell to her superiors out of fear of drawing "criminals" to the library, Ms. Garcia was able to demon-strate that community members reentering her local area from jail and prison were *already* at the library and a reentry program could actually help improve their long-term trajectories and decrease costs to the city. She encourages other libraries to consider making an economic argument for reentry programs with their local officials, since a social justice argument often does not sway them to allow a library-based program for ex-offend-ers. The program has now been in existence for thirteen years, and she notes that they have never had an incident with a Fresh Start participant causing any difficulty at the library. Notably, what began as a local initiative in Long Branch Free Public Library has recently expanded to seven addi-tional New Jersey libraries through the State Library and an IMLS National Leadership Grant.

## Unhoused Patrons

Libraries, especially in urban areas, are visited by large numbers of unhoused patrons on a daily basis. Depending on their location, suburban and rural libraries can also have significant numbers of unhoused patrons, especially if they are located near a bus or train line. Library staff are often unclear about how to best serve homeless patrons, and at times they can be fearful of or anxious about this population.[67] Other patrons may also have concerns about the unhoused due to stereotypes that they are dangerous or violent. However, homeless individuals are more likely to be victimized than they are to victimize someone else.[68] Integrating social workers into public libraries can help tremendously with training library staff to better understand the broader topic of homelessness and, at a micro level, modeling how to engage with unhoused patrons through one-on-one interactions. Yet hiring social workers is not necessary to develop more humanizing ways of engaging marginalized patrons. Many libraries already open their doors to unhoused patrons through inclusive programming by nature of allowing anyone to participate. As discussed earlier in the section on social wellness, *Coffee and Conversations* is a popular event that several libraries around the country offer.[69] Anyone is welcome to gather for coffee or donuts, and socialize on a regular basis. Such forms of engagement can help ensure the library remains a neutral, non-stigmatizing, and welcoming space for unhoused patrons. Other libraries partner with community organizations to provide services that extend beyond what a typical branch offers. San Francisco Public Library has teamed up with LavaMae in recent years as a location site for its free mobile hygiene services.[70] Similar initiatives to bring mobile showers and mobile laundry trucks to library branches exist in Charlotte, NC, and other locations across the country. In Kentucky, the Campbell County Public Library organizes an annual donation drive to provide thousands of clean socks and underwear for children in PreK through high school.[71]

Although libraries serving large groups of unhoused patrons are using innovative ways of doing outreach and connection to resources for this population, sometimes it is particularly powerful to offer opportunities for creative outlets and entertainment rather than focus solely on hygiene, mental health, housing, food, or similar types of needs. People who are homeless want to be treated similarly to everyone else, and the library has an opportunity to create a fully inclusive environment that helps these patrons feel equal to others, something they may rarely experience in often highly segregated communities outside of the library. In Auckland (New Zealand), Daren Kamali facilitates a poetry group for unhoused individuals called *Rough Lives Speak* in collaboration with the library and the Auckland City Mission.[72] Starting in 2021 as an open poet's collective group for people sleeping on the streets, this group includes workshops on poetry along with check-ins about other needs the unhoused patrons might have. Combining education, community awareness, and the arts, the group (now all formerly homeless) published a book of poetry by the participants and held a public poetry reading and art exhibition in conjunction with a panel discussion about housing challenges, homelessness, and local policy. Auckland City Library also has sponsored ceramics and other art classes for City Mission residents to provide opportunities for social gathering, creative outlets, safe entertainment, and to allow unhoused individuals a chance to express themselves and give voice to their experiences. Many of the poems written as part of the Rough Lives Speak project address themes related to mental health, incarceration, intimate partner violence, substance abuse, and suicide, and many participants expressed how healing the experience of writing poetry has been for them.

Though many libraries around the country are offering quality forms of outreach and inclusion toward unhoused patrons, stated behavioral policies and codes of conduct often inadvertently target people experiencing homelessness in punitive and stigmatizing ways. For example, many libraries have policies about sleeping and odors which are often enforced with people who appear to be homeless but not necessarily other patrons. If libraries have these policies, it is important that they are enforced equitably across all patrons (i.e., if your library has a "no strong odor" policy, then that needs to be enforced for the presumably housed patron wearing strong perfume in the library the same as it is for the person who appears to be homeless with a noticeable body or clothing odor). Similarly, behavioral rules directed at homeless patrons are often unclear or inconsistently implemented which can generate frustration and confusion for staff about providing services to this population.[73] Yet despite unfamiliarity and uncertainty with protocols, staff regularly express a desire to help patrons experiencing homelessness. While social workers can help libraries refine policies that are trauma informed and bring nuance to how policies are applied,[74] Dr. Julie Ann Winkelstein encourages libraries to seek feedback from unhoused and marginalized patrons for the feedback on existing policies. Furthermore, including unhoused individuals to share their stories and provide training can "have a huge impact on library staff and the speakers, by creating connections and addressing the built-in power imbalance between staff members and unhoused library users."[75] It's important to note that while they may opt to not participate in targeted programming due to lack of interest or a desire to be left alone, it's essential that libraries treat unhoused patrons equally.[76] In doing so, we provide them with the dignity to make their own choices just like any other patron.

## Initiatives to Improve Services to Unhoused Patrons

### Hoboken Public Library (NJ)

The Hoboken Public Library (HPL) has recently focused on improving services for unhoused patrons, according to Emily Dalton, community service worker, and Ally Blumenfeld, outreach coordinator.[77] Like many urban libraries, HPL has a significant number of unhoused patrons visiting their library. Early in 2022, they began to actively seek input from this population and used feedback to improve services. After forming a relationship with a local homeless shelter, outreach staff met with both shelter guests and staff to understand barriers for this population that could be addressed by the library. Feedback from unhoused individuals has led to policy changes and special programming to reduce barriers, including:

- Regular outreach visits to homeless shelters and food-serving organizations to sign patrons up for library cards, provide free books, and promote other local resources for this population

- The creation of "Project ID," an initiative that includes a monthly program, resource hand-out, and partnership with local agencies, through which HPL has already assisted over thirty individuals in obtaining their state IDs
- Changes in the requirements for a library card to increase opportunities for unhoused individuals to obtain a card
- Networking with local government officials to increase funding for initiatives that better help unhoused individuals
- Aligning practices, procedures, and policies to ensure equitable application to all patron groups

Overall, these collaborations and outreach have brought in more patrons, created a more inclusive library environment, and gained positive attention from the city and other officials who want to assist the library with this process. As Ms. Dalton says, "This is how we build community. If we weren't doing this [outreach to unhoused patrons], there's a whole population that would not feel included at the library." The unhoused population is often ignored and underserved in many communities, and "just because a person is homeless does not mean that they are incapable of understanding information. A lot of them need many different services and information that they would love to access independently from a social service agency, and the library can help with that."

When asked about advice for other libraries considering similar initiatives, they have some advice. "Consistency is the most important aspect of outreach," says Ms. Blumenfeld, learning from experience that it helps to facilitate relationships with unhoused individuals in the area and open avenues of communication for the library to understand barriers to access experienced by individuals who are unhoused. Although the library had been serving unhoused individuals for many years, "we had to leave the building to find out what was really happening for this population" and it was through the regular visits to the shelter that unhoused individuals became comfortable with staff and disclosed information about their experiences. Although all libraries do not have dedicated outreach staff to be able to do visits as often as HPL does, to build relationships with vulnerable populations they recommend that it is essential that libraries do outreach in the community with the same staff members and at specific times, even if it is just once a month or less.

# Large Metropolitan/Urban Libraries

Urban libraries have distinct challenges that have become the focus of recent research and scholarship. Large, urban areas often have more concentrated areas of immigrant populations, higher numbers of people who are unhoused, and may have more problems with gangs or other types of organized crime and violence when compared to rural libraries. Because urban areas have more concentrated populations, large urban libraries often see higher numbers of patrons in all of the various groups mentioned in this chapter so far. In fact, the first library-based social work positions began in large urban libraries due to challenges with high numbers of unhoused patrons and the prevalence of patrons with serious psychosocial needs. Urban libraries also often have city ordinances and/or unions that may inhibit the library's decision-making and flexibility when it comes to adding new programs or services.[78]

The recent Urban Library Trauma Study[79] highlights the stress and strain experienced by many urban library staff from serving high numbers of high-needs patrons. Participants in this study revealed many experiences with library-based violence or threats of violence, frequent and unpredictable physical and mental health-related emergency situations, and patron behavioral challenges that impact their overall sense of well-being and ease in their jobs. They reported experiencing both firsthand and secondary/vicarious trauma from these crises and described feeling burned out in their work. They reported frustration about not being able to help or make a difference in many of the patron crises they witnessed. In addition, they reported additional stress from existing conflict over when and why they were allowed to call for emergency assistance or how to otherwise handle patron emergencies. In this report, there were a number of recommendations for better supporting urban library staff, including having leadership openly acknowledge the stress of the work on staff, adding training such as Mental Health First Aid, trauma-informed approaches, and de-escalation strategies, and exploring the addition of mental health supports for staff. There were also recommendations for how the profession could better support urban library staff, which ranged from changing master's in library science (MLIS) educational programs to adding national or statewide crisis lines and support networks for staff. In our line of work, we are supportive of the recommendations that came from this report and are exploring ways we can help advocate for broad changes to both library education and training programs as well as supportive structures and systems to protect the overall well-being and resilience of library staff (not only for urban libraries, but for *all* public libraries).

Because of the patron populations of urban libraries, focus groups of urban library leaders led to recommendations for specific competencies, traits, and characteristics needed for urban library staff. These include having an understanding of poverty (including its causes and its impacts), easiness among and with diverse groups of people, passion for advocating for marginalized communities, high emotional intelligence, strong leadership skills, good social and self-awareness, and an ability to form and maintain relationships with others.[80] Although these characteristics were derived from responses of urban library leaders when asked what urban library staff needed in order to successfully do the work, we note that these same traits and characteristics are equally as important for staff serving rural libraries, which we will discuss further here.

Although urban libraries face many demands, they sometimes have advantages when compared to their rural counterparts. For example, due to higher numbers of staff, they can create "specialty" positions so staff become experts in a particular area of librarianship or a specific need of the library. A challenge of this approach is that sometimes services can be siloed, though, creating difficulties with acting quickly when a service or program needs to be created that crosses multiple areas. Urban libraries also often have larger spaces, which can be beneficial because the space can sometimes be physically divided into specific zones for different patron groups (children, teens, etc.) or different library-based activities (i.e., makerspaces, art galleries, cafes, wellness areas, social services, etc.) which can prevent tension between groups. Urban libraries also often have many community partners to invite for programming, outreach to patrons, or to provide training or possible self-care support to staff. Keep in mind, though, that more community partners does not necessarily mean more *willing* partners with the library. Although there may be more community partners in the immediate vicinity of the library, these organizations may also have high demands on their time due to the needs of urban communities and may not have the resources to spend time at the library. Everything mentioned here as a potential advantage for urban libraries can sometimes also bring additional challenges.

## Small Communities/Rural Libraries

Although much of the media attention on library worker trauma and library patrons' needs has been focused largely on urban libraries, Beth's needs assessments have found that rural libraries are experiencing similar patron and staff challenges. In fact, rural populations tend to have higher rates of poverty,[81] un- or underemployment,[82] lower levels of education, and have lower access to healthcare[83] when compared to urban populations. The Covid pandemic brought added challenges to rural areas, since workplaces and schools went remote/virtual; many in rural areas had slower or no access to the internet, which caused barriers to both employment and education. Rural counties in the United States with the most persistent poverty rates also are counties that have lower numbers of households with internet access.[84] In addition, fewer rural residents were vaccinated against the virus due to increased vaccine hesitancy, poorer availability of the vaccine, and/or difficulty traveling the distance required to a vaccination site.[85] The pandemic overall had more severe impacts on rural populations than urban ones, negatively affecting physical health, mental health, overall well-being, employment, income, and life satisfaction for people living in rural areas.[86]

Although rural libraries may serve lower numbers of patrons on a daily basis, the patrons who visit these libraries have similar needs and challenges as those in urban areas. Rural libraries can be particularly impacted by the lack of services and barriers to accessing services (such as unavailable transportation), including poor "access to technology and connectivity, and a corresponding lack of skills and training in using that technology."[87] Limited availability of resources can lead to greater impacts of unaddressed mental health issues on rural communities.[88] In many rural communities, the library is the only place to turn for information, social connections, entertainment, resources, and help for a variety of needs. Libraries in rural communities tend to be "one stop shops" and may feel extra pressure to try to be all things to all people. Many rural library staff feel isolated in their jobs, wanting to help their patrons, yet with few community partners to assist. We have met many rural library staff who are going way above and beyond the call of duty in their jobs, sometimes driving far out of their way to deliver library materials to homebound patrons, delivering meals, or transporting patrons across town due to a lack of transportation options. In small and rural libraries, staff may get to know their frequent patrons better than in larger, urban libraries, which can contribute to situations where it is harder to set boundaries or take care of themselves.

Smaller libraries—many which tend to be remote or in rural areas—present unique challenges for public libraries attempting to meet their patrons' needs. Accessing services such as public transportation and limited internet access can be particularly cumbersome. Tiffany Russell, a former library social worker at Niles District Library (MI), found that accessibility issues were certainly a challenge at her smaller, rural branch. She also discovered that working at a smaller branch required her to operate as a true "generalist" in order to address the variety of needs for which her patrons' sought help.[89] *Generalist* social work means the social worker is able to work with diverse populations, all age groups, and many different kinds of psychosocial problems, rather than specializing in a specific service or need. Unlike social workers hired to address specific needs at larger branches (i.e. focusing on patrons experiencing homelessness), Tiffany discovered "everyday was different and I never knew what I was going to get. It's important for libraries that are considering hiring social workers to keep a desired skill set in mind for what is needed at the branch. In my case, I tapped into my generalist knowledge based and broad range of skills to address a variety of patrons' needs." The same challenge exists for rural library staff who are not social workers; with fewer staff employed by small libraries, and some libraries having only a single staff person, the people who are working have to be trained to serve patrons in broad and varied ways. Although large and urban libraries can often hire staff who specialize in specific areas of library work, rural staff have increased demands to know at least a little bit about everything.

Although small and rural libraries often have unique challenges when compared to urban ones, they also have strengths and advantages compared to their urban counterparts. After a levee broke in Caseyville, Illinois due to a 2022 flood, Library Director Ashley Stewart witnessed her small community turn to the library as it became an operating point for FEMA resources and hub of community support. Stewart highlights a strength of smaller libraries is that it can be easier to generate and maintain community connections. "Everyone looks to the library during times of natural disaster. I think the community saw us stepping up in response and it elevates us as an equally important community partner. I think since we are a small town, it does help make generating connections easier."[90] Even though there are fewer community partners in rural areas, it can sometimes be easier to build connections with the ones that are there.

For libraries in areas that lack any close community partners, libraries often have to be creative about how to connect patrons with help and get support for themselves as well. To address the lack of access to mental health providers or medical care, many rural libraries are beginning to offer telehealth partnerships. For small rural libraries with little space for private conversations, privacy pods are often being used to create spaces for patrons to have confidential conversations with providers. Virtual programming increased greatly during the pandemic and continues to be an option in areas with limited local services. Some small, rural libraries have also found that there are organizations in distant towns willing to come regularly to the library for outreach or services in the local area. Many may be physically located in a city but be responsible for covering a broad geographic area; in these cases, a small, rural library often becomes a perfect partner for that agency as well as helping the library fulfill its mission to the community.

## Summary and Key Takeaway Points

- Because of the community context, some libraries have large groups of patrons with some shared needs and challenges.

- Although no group is homogenous, there are common needs observed for libraries serving large groups of immigrants, adolescents, seniors, gender diverse, justice-involved, or unhoused patrons.

- Urban and rural libraries serve patrons with similar types of needs, with library staff experiencing similar challenges from high-needs patrons, although urban libraries often see higher numbers of patrons with psychosocial needs due to higher patron numbers overall.

- Although rural libraries have received less media attention for patron needs and library worker trauma, staff in these libraries face similar challenges as urban libraries.

- Programming or services designed to address common needs of a specific population have the opportunity to impact multiple dimensions of wellness to substantially and positively impact people who may have barriers to health and well-being.

## Notes

1  P. Connor and G. Lopez, "5 Facts about the U.S. Rank in Worldwide Migration," *Pew Research Center*, May 18, 2016, https://www.pewresearch.org/fact-tank /2016/05/18/5-facts-about-the-u-s-rank-in-worldwide-migration/.

2  Anti-defamation League, *Mainstreaming Hate: The Anti-Immigrant Movement in the U.S.*, A report from the Center on Extremism, November 2018, https://www .adl.org/sites/default/files/mainstreaming-hate-anti-immigrant-report-2018-v3 .pdf.

**3** United States Customs and Border Protection, "CBP Enforcement Statistics Fiscal Year 2023," *U.S. Department of Homeland Security,* https://www.cbp.gov/newsroom/stats/cbp-enforcement-statistics.

**4** D. Khullar and D. A. Chokshi, "Challenges for Immigrant Health in the USA: The Road to Crisis," *The Lancet* 393, no. 10186 (2019): 2168–74, https://doi.org/10.1016/S0140-6736(19)30035-2.

**5** H. Ding and L. Hargreaves, "Stress-associated Poor Health among Adult Immigrants with a Language Barrier in the United States," *Journal of Immigrant and Minority Health* 11 (2008): 446–52, https://doi.org/10.1007/s10903-008-9200-0.

**6** A. Kamimura, S. Weaver, K. Sin, M. Pye, and S. Panahi, "Immigration Stress among Refugees Resettled in the United States," *International Journal of Social Psychiatry* 67, no. 2 (2020): 144–9, https://doi.org/10.1177/0020764020939.

**7** "Carnegie's philanthropy brought to the doorstep of citizens and immigrants alike not only the means for self-education and enlightenment, but also the opportunity to understand the history and purpose of our nation's democracy, to study English, to be taught new skills, to exercise the imagination, and to experience the pleasures of contemplation and solitude." "Can Libraries Save America?" Carnegie Corporation of New York, September 27, 2019, https://www.carnegie.org/news/articles/can-libraries-save-america/.

**8** Central Islip Public Library (@cipubliclibrary), "Starting September 1st, They Will Be At the Central Islip Public Library on Wednesdays and Thursdays from 5-9pm, Fridays from 9:30am-1pm, and on Saturdays from 12:30pm-4pm," [Tweet] Twitter, August 30, 2021, https://twitter.com/cipubliclibrary/status/1432334883095973888.

**9** *Immigrant Services at the Library*, Louisville Free Public Library, December 7, 2021, https://www.lfpl.org/ImmigrantServices/.

**10** Zettervall and Nienow, *Whole Person Librarianship*, 12, 14, 23.

**11** *Starting Immigration Services at Your Library*, American Library Association, 2022, https://www.ala.org/pla/education/onlinelearning/webinars/ondemand/immigration.

**12** *Resources*, Immigration Advocates Network, 2022, https://www.immigrationadvocates.org/nonprofit/.

**13** *The American Place: Adult Education, Careers, and Immigrant Services,* Hartford Public Library, n.d., https://tap.hplct.org/.

**14** A. Farah, personal communication, August 30, 2022.

15  *Adolescent Mental Health*, World Health Organization, November 17, 2021, https://www.who.int/news-room/fact-sheets/detail/adolescent-mental-health.

16  Klinenberg, *Palaces for the People*.

17  C. D. Maxwell, J. H. Garner, and W. G. Skogan, "Collective Efficacy and Violence in Chicago Neighborhoods: A Reproduction," *Journal of Contemporary Criminal Justice* 34, no. 3 (2018): 245–65, https://doi.org/10.1177/1043986218769988.

18  N. Kalindjian, F. Hirot, A. C. Stona, C. Huas, and N. Godart, "Early Detection of Eating Disorders: A Scoping Review," *Eating and Weight Disorders- Studies on Anorexia, Bulimia, and Obesity* 27 (2021): 21–68, https://doi.org/10.1007/s40519-021-01164-x.

19  *TeenZone*, Bloomington Public Library, 2021, https://www.bloomingtonlibrary.org/teenzone.

20  Teen Programs: Teen Advisory Group, Ericson Public Library, 2022, https://www.boone.lib.ia.us/services/teens.

21  *Teens*, SPILL! Passive Programming for Teens, Elmhurst Public Library, 2022, https://elmhurstpubliclibrary.org/teens/the-teen-advisory-board-recommends/.

22  *Youth Homelessness Overview*, National Conference of State Legislatures, 2022, https://www.ncsl.org/research/human-services/homeless-and-runaway-youth.aspx.

23  M. J. Vortkamp, personal communication, August 3, 2022.

24  M. H. Morton, A. Dworsky, and G. M. Samuels, "Missed Opportunities: Youth Homelessness in America. National Estimates," Chicago, IL: Chapin Hall at the University of Chicago, 2017, https://voicesofyouthcount.org/brief/national-estimates-of-youth-homelessness/.

25  *The Cost of Coming Out: LGBT Youth Homelessness*, Lesley University, n.d., https://lesley.edu/article/the-cost-of-coming-out-lgbt-youth-homelessness#:~:text=According%20to%20the%20True%20Colors,of%20them%20identify%20as%20LGBT.

26  M. H. Morton, G. M. Samuels, A. Dworsky, and S. Patel, "Missed Opportunities: LGBTQ Youth Homelessness in America," Chicago, IL: Chapin Hall at the University of Chicago, 2018, https://www.chapinhall.org/wp-content/uploads/VoYC-LGBTQ-Brief-FINAL.pdf.

27  Sachem Library (@sachemlibrary), "To Join, Contact Our Social Work Intern at sw.intern@sachemlibrary.org 5:00pm-6:00pm Friday, May 6 For more information email:sw.intern@sachemlibrary.org" [Tweet] Twitter, April 2, 2022.

28  *Human Trafficking*, National Network for Youth, 2022, https://nn4youth.org/learn/human-trafficking/.

29  *Human Trafficking*, US Department of Justice Office for Victims of Crime, n.d., https://ovc.ojp.gov/program/human-trafficking/overview.

30  Urada et al., "Homelessness at the San Diego Central Library," 8449.

31  *Loneliness and Social Isolation Linked to Serious Health Conditions*, Centers for Disease Control, April 29, 2021, https://www.cdc.gov/aging/publications/features/lonely-older-adults.html.

32  "For many seniors, the library is the main place they interact with people from other generations." Klinenberg, *Palaces for the People*, 38.

33  National Academies of Sciences, Engineering, and Medicine, *Social Isolation and Loneliness in Older Adults: Opportunities for the Health Care System* (Washington, DC: The National Academies Press, 2020), https://doi.org/10.17226/25663.

34  Keys to engaging older adults at your library. Office for Literacy and Outreach Services, 2010, https://www.ala.org/aboutala/sites/ala.org.aboutala/files/content/olos/toolkits/olderadults/oat.sequential.pdf.

35  *Older Adults & Seniors*, OCLC, 2022, https://www.webjunction.org/explore-topics/older-adults.html.

36  Reference and User Services Association, "Guidelines for Library Services with 60+ Audience: Best Practices," *American Library Association*, September 2017, https://www.ala.org/rusa/sites/ala.org.rusa/files/content/resources/guidelines/60plusGuidelines2017.pdf.

37  Timothy Dickey (Adult Services) from Columbus Metropolitan Library, Amy DelPo (Admin of Older Adult Services) at Denver Public Library, Mary Beth Riedner (Retired Academic Librarian/Volunteer (Library Services for Dementia/Alzheimer's with ALA-ODLOS Interest Group).

38  *JSL Retirement Planning Workshop*, Salinas Public Library, n.d., https://salinaspubliclibrary.org/learn-explore/adult-learning/events/jsl-retirement-planning-workshop.

39  *Let's Move in Libraries*, UNC Greensboro School of Education, 2021.

40  N. Lenstra and F. Fisher, *Geri-Fit® at the Library: Studying Small and Rural Public Libraries as Venues for Active Living Among Older Adults* (Greensboro: Let's Move in Libraries, February 12, 2020), https://letsmovelibraries.org/geri-fit.

41  N. Lenstra, F. Oguz, C. D'Arpa, and L. S. Wilson, "Exercising at the Library: Small and Rural Public Libraries in the Lives of Older Adults," *The Library Quarterly*,

Information, Community, Policy 92, no. 1 (2022): 5–23, https://doi.org/10.1086/717232.

42  J. Hill, personal communication, July 28, 2022.

43  ALA Statement Affirming the Rights of Transgender People, American Library Association, June 23, 2020, https://www.ala.org/news/press-releases/2020/06/ala-statement-affirming-rights-transgender-people.

44  B. A. Rood, S. L. Reisner, F. I. Surace, J. A. Puckett, M. R. Maroney, and D. W. Pantalone, "Expecting Rejection: Understanding the Minority Stress Experiences of Transgender and Gender Nonconforming Individuals," Transgender Health 1, no. 1 (2016): 151–64, https://doi.org/10.1089/trgh.2016.0012.

45  The Butterfly Project: Resources for Trans/Non-binary Folx, Prince George's County Memorial Library System, n.d., https://www.pgcmls.info/butterflyproject.

46  S. SinhaRoy, "'We Are Not Okay': Supporting the LGBTQ+ Community at the Library," American Libraries Magazine, June 27, 2022, https://americanlibrariesmagazine.org/blogs/the-scoop/we-are-not-okay/.

47  LGBTQ+ Pride, Prince George's County Memorial Library System, n.d., https://pgcmls.info/pride.

48  H. Arata, "News: More than a Pronoun: Small-Town Library Hosts Illuminating Discussion on Gender Identity," Programming Librarian, June 23, 2021.

49  United States Profile, Prison Policy Initiative, n.d., https://www.prisonpolicy.org/profiles/US.html.

50  Growth in Mass Incarceration, The Sentencing Project, 2022, https://www.sentencingproject.org/research/.

51  L. Bixby, S. Bevan, and C. Boen, "The Links between Disability, Incarceration, and Social Exclusion," Health Affairs 41, no. 10 (2022): 1460–9, https://doi.org/10.1377/hlthaff.2022.00495.

52  J. Brewster, personal communication, October 25, 2022.

53  C. L. Jonson and F. T. Cullen, "Prisoner Reentry Programs," Crime and Justice 44, no. 1 (2015): 517–75, https://doi.org/10.1086/681554.

54  G. D. Walters, "Are the Criminogenic Effects of Incarceration Mediated by a Change in Criminal Thinking or a Change in Perceived Certainty?" The Prison Journal 101, no. 1 (2020): 21–40, https://doi.org/10.1177/0032885520978374.

55  Ibid.

56  A. Goger, D. J. Harding, and H. Henderson, A Better Path Forward for Criminal Justice: Prisoner Reentry, The Brookings Institution, April 2021, https://www

.brookings.edu/research/a-better-path-forward-for-criminal-justice-prisoner-reentry/.

**57** G. Duwe and V. A. Clark, "Nothing Will Work Unless You Did: The Predictors of Post Prison Employment," *Criminal Justice and Behavior* 44, no. 5 (2017): 657–77, https://doi.org/10.1177/0093854816689104.

**58** E. J. Wodahl, "The Challenges of Prisoner Reentry from a Rural Perspective," *Western Criminology Review* 7, no. 2 (2006): 32–47.

**59** Blount County Recovery Court Life Skills Program, http://bcpl.populr.me/life-skills.

**60** S. C. Johnson and M. A. Paauw, "Partners in Libraries: Social Work Students and the Justice-Involved," *Public Libraries* 61, no. 3 (2022): 28–36.

**61** A. M. Mills, J. Rogers, L. Mayelian, and G. Mason, *Ready Access*, 2021, https://www.reentryservice.org/home.

**62** Social Justice Team of the 2021 CLA Leadership Challenge, Ready Access: Reentry Services for Decarcerated Populations, *Ready Access*, 2021, https://sites.google.com/view/ready-access/toolkit-for-libraries/programming-workflow.

**63** Jail and Reentry Services (JARS), San Francisco Public Library, 2021, https://sfpl.org/services/jail-and-reentry-services.

**64** L. Kelly and T. McClary, "'Fresh Start' Program Grows from Local Outreach to Statewide Media, ad Blitz," *New Jersey State Library*, August 6, 2021, https://www.njstatelib.org/mediamentions/fresh-start-program-grows-from-local-outreach-to-statewide-media-ad-blitz/.

**65** J. Giantomasi, "Mini-Documentary Celebrates Fresh Start @ Your Library Successes," *New Jersey State Library*, November 21, 2022.

**66** T. Garcia, personal communication, August 25, 2022.

**67** M. A. Provence, "Encouraging the Humanization of Patrons Experiencing Homelessness: A Case Study of the Role of the US Public Library Social Worker," *The Library Quarterly* 90, no. 4 (2020): 431–46, https://doi.org/10.1086/710258.

**68** S. Shortt, "Op-Ed: We Don't Need Protection from the Homeless. They Need Protection from Us," *Los Angeles Times*, October 15, 2018, https://www.latimes.com/opinion/op-ed/la-oe-shortt-homeless-victims-20181015-story.html.

**69** Winkelstein, *Libraries and Homelessness*.

**70** Wellness: Lava Mae Free Mobile Showers, San Francisco Public Library, February 18, 2020, https://sfpl.org/events/2020/02/18/wellness-lava-mae-free-mobile-showers.

71  *Drop Your Drawers*. Campbell County Public Library, n.d., https://www.cc-pl.org/drop-your-drawers.

72  D. Kamali, personal communication, October 25, 2022.

73  M. A. Giesler, "A Place to Call Home?: A Qualitative Exploration of Public Librarians' Response to Homelessness," *Journal of Access Services* 14, no. 4 (2017): 188–214, https://doi.org/10.1080/15367967.2017.1395704.

74  Provence, "Encouraging the Humanization of Patrons Experiencing Homelessness," 431–46.

75  Winkelstein, *Libraries and Homelessness*, 127.

76  C. Adams and M. Krtalić, "I Feel at Home: Perspectives of Homeless Library Customers on Public Library Services and Social Inclusion," *Journal of Librarianship and Information Science* 54, no. 4 (2022): 779–90, https://doi.org/10.1177/09610006211053045.

77  A. Blumenfeld and E. Dalton, personal communication, July 28, 2022.

78  M. E. Gonzalez, "Workforce Competencies: Focus on Urban Public Libraries," *Library Trends* 59, no. 1–2 (2010): 269–87, https://muse.jhu.edu/pub/1/article/407818.

79  Urban Libraries Unite, "Urban Library Trauma Study: Final Report."

80  Gonzalez, "Workforce Competencies," 269–87.

81  B. C. Thiede, D. T. Lichter, and T. Slack, "Working, but Poor: The Good Life in Rural America?" *Journal of Rural Studies* 59 (2018): 183–93, https://doi.org/10.1016/j.jrurstud.2016.02.007.

82  T. Slack, B. C. Thiede, and L. Jensen, "Race, Residence, and Underemployment: Fifty Years in Comparative Perspective, 1968–2017," *Rural Sociology* 85, no. 2 (2020): 275–315, https://doi.org/10.1111/ruso.12290.

83  G. Gong, S. G. Phillips, C. Hudson, D. Curti, and B. U. Phillips, "Higher U.S. Rural Mortality Rates Linked to Socioeconomic Status, Physician Shortages, and Lack of Health Insurance," *Health Affairs* 38, no. 12 (2019): 2003–10, https://doi.org/10.1377/hlthaff.2019.00722.

84  E. A. Dobis, T. P. Krumel, J. Cromartie, K. Conley, A. Sanders, and R. Ortiz, "Rural America at a Glance: 2021 Edition," USDA Economic Research Service: U.S. Department of Agriculture, https://www.ers.usda.gov/webdocs/publications/102576/eib-230.pdf?v=8546.4.

85  Y. Sun and S. M. Monnat, "Rural-urban and within-rural Differences in Covid-19 Vaccination Rates," *The Journal of Rural Health* 38, no. 4 (2022): 916–22, https://doi.org/10.1111/jrh.12625.

**86** J. T. Mueller, K. McConnell, P. B. Burow, K. Pofahl, A. A. Merdjanoff, and J. Farrell, "Impacts of the Covid-19 Pandemic on Rural America," *PNAS* 118, no. 1 (2020), https://doi.org/10.1073/pnas.2019378118.

**87** K. Riggs, "Telehealth and Public Libraries: Bridging Multiple Divides for Healthier Communities," *Public Libraries* 61, no. 1 (2022): 17.

**88** L. Carey, "Texas Rural Libraries Will Help with Mental Health Access," Dailey Yonder, March 24, 2022, https://dailyyonder.com/texas-rural-libraries-will-help-with-mental-health-access/2022/03/24/.

**89** T. Russell, personal communication, August 8, 2022.

**90** A. Stewart, personal communication, August 24, 2022.

# 5 Library Collaborations for Addressing Patrons' Needs

*Success comes when librarians, library workers, and library administrators see the potential of library participation in health-supporting systems. They also recognize that this is work that libraries cannot do by themselves. Librarianship is not a solo enterprise, but a collective enterprise.*

— **NOAH LENSTRA**[1]

Few of the initiatives mentioned in previous chapters have been solely initiated, planned, and led by libraries on their own, and many of them required and relied on some type of collaboration to make them successful. In recent years, as demands have increased for libraries to address many different types of patron and community needs, libraries have found themselves needing to branch out (no pun intended) and partner with a wide variety of organizations. These collaborations might be with service providers in their communities focused on specific areas of patron needs (i.e., dementia, diabetes prevention, homelessness), or broad fields such as social work, public health, or nursing that might be able to address a wide variety of patron needs. Despite the frequency of libraries developing partnerships with external organizations, most library staff have no specialized training in effective collaboration techniques. These skills are also not typically included in library and information science programs despite interdisciplinary collaborations requiring specific competencies to effectively develop and maintain. In this chapter, we start by talking about important principles to consider for successful interdisciplinary collaborations, and then include some of the most common library collaborations to address the types of psychosocial needs we have mentioned throughout this book. We end the chapter by focusing on challenges to collaboration, and how to best position your collaboration for success.

# Interdisciplinary Collaborations

Every discipline brings its own values, priorities, mission, and lens to the people it serves and the role it fills in a community. Because many of the problems modern societies face are complex and interwoven, it often makes sense for multiple disciplines and professions to collaborate to try to make an impact. Although successful models of interdisciplinary collaborations can be found in many different segments of a community, the most research about effective interdisciplinary collaborations comes from the healthcare realm. Although the large and growing body of research coming from interdisciplinary healthcare teams was created specifically for these interprofessional medical environments, we think much of it is also applicable to libraries and library collaborations. For example, the "Core Competencies for Interprofessional Collaborative Practice," developed by the Interprofessional Education Collaborative,[2] provides a number of guidelines for successful interdisciplinary collaborations and describes these guidelines in terms of four domains:

1. Values/Ethics for Interprofessional Practice- Collaborating professionals should center the needs of the people and populations served, embrace the diversity and differences of everyone on the team as well as the people served, respect the expertise of all collaborators, work collaboratively with the team and the people receiving services, focus on developing and maintaining trusting relationships between the team and the people served, act with integrity, and maintain professional competence.

2. Roles/Responsibilities for Interprofessional Practice- Working in an interdisciplinary fashion requires a focus on each discipline's roles and responsibilities and how they complement one another to meet the needs of the individuals and communities being served. All participating professionals try to understand one another's missions and values, recognizing what each one brings to the table. To successfully do this, the collaborating partners must determine and communicate their own roles and responsibilities clearly to each other as well as to the people they serve. They recognize the limits to their expertise and competence and intentionally choose partnerships with other professionals that complement what they can offer. The team focuses on communicating with one another, seeking clarity when needed, to ensure they understand each other's roles and how the roles of all partners interface with one another.

3. Interprofessional Communication- For interprofessional practice to be successful, communication is essential. In this domain, the partnering professionals create effective ongoing tools for communication and ensure frequent opportunities for discussions to enhance the overall function of the team. The partners must practice active listening, demonstrate respect for each other, and seek and encourage the sharing of ideas and opinions. Communication should be regular and consistent to ensure quality care for the individuals and families served and to problem-solve or negotiate differences or challenges in a timely manner.

4. Teams and Teamwork- In this domain, the collaborating partners focus on being a team, agreeing to work together to meet the needs of the people and communities served. This means that all partners value the contributions of all team members and recognize that different people contribute to an end goal in diverse ways. The team focuses on consensus building, shared accountability, collaborative problem-solving, and shared decision-making, and each participating member gives up some independence and autonomy to help the group function as a whole.

With intentional efforts from library staff to focus on all four of these domains, interdisciplinary collaborations with a number of professionals can be successfully used to meet patron and community needs. The library is not expected to be all things to all people, so to meet expectations and address the challenges of high-needs patrons, library staff may need to partner with social workers, peer navigators, health advocates, or other individuals and organizations who bring a variety of skills and expertise to the table. Here, we discuss the most common library collaborations used to address the needs included in this book.

## Social Work Collaborations

Since 2009, a growing number of libraries have partnered with professional social workers to address patrons' psychosocial needs, and this has quickly become one of the most common library collaborations we see to address high-needs patrons. Since both of us are social workers, this is also the collaboration about which we most frequently get consulted. In general, library staff seem open and willing to partner with social workers and feel hopeful that social workers can help to address their needs. For example, a 2022 study found that over 90 percent of library staff would like to hire a permanent social worker in their branch.[3] Another recent study by Baum et al. surveyed library branch managers and found—whether they had a social worker or not at their library—most held positive attitudes about collaborating with social workers.[4] At the time of this writing, approximately 100 branches in the United States partner with full-time, part-time, or volunteer social workers.[5] Some are hired as library employees while others are contracted through local social service agencies. Arrangements vary from social workers dedicated to a specific branch to part-timers that float between various locations within a library system. They may operate under titles such as "community resources coordinator," "community navigator," or "social services specialist." Not all social workers are licensed, though all have either undergraduate or graduate level degrees in the field.

Social workers are trained to work across a continuum of micro (individual), mezzo (group), and macro (organizational and community) level services and bring a systemic perspective that considers multiple levels or factors that may influence how an individual functions or thrives in society. In libraries, this may include considering how a patron's health (micro-level), education (mezzo-level), and the impact of Covid-19 (macro-level) may contribute to how one functions on a particular day. While social workers can assist with macro-level programming and mezzo-level services such as training library staff on trauma-informed approaches, most are hired to address micro-level needs such as outreach and referrals. Patrick Lloyd, a former library social worker, found that "questions regarding Medicare benefits, legal help, emergency shelter, or financial assistance are common in many libraries. I was hired to help answer these questions."[6]

In some communities, hiring a social worker is still controversial for a library, despite the national growth in these positions. Long Branch (NJ) Free Public Library director, Tonya Garcia, states that she was able to obtain buy-in from stakeholders for a full-time library-based social worker by using a number of strategies.[7] First, she initially started with hosting library-based social work interns from Monmouth University, which allowed the library to begin developing their social work program and helped to provide data to demonstrate the need for the position. She notes that starting with interns is a helpful strategy for many libraries wishing to house a social worker, but especially for smaller and/or underfunded ones, since hosting interns does not typically require funding. Second, she was able to encourage stakeholders to take a risk and be the first library in the state to hire a social worker by clearly connecting the role of a library-based social worker to the library's mission so they could see how it aligned with the overall purpose and role of the library. Third, she was able to garner support by explaining to her city officials and board that "The library is serving anyone and everyone, and it is unfair to expect library staff to deal with these issues. It is actually traumatic for our staff and is doing a disservice to the community." She says that even staff who were initially not in support of a library-based social worker now have no idea how they would be able to do their jobs without one.

## Social Work Students

In conjunction with or as an alternative to hiring professional social workers, a growing number of public libraries opt to host social work students. For many libraries, this is a low-cost or free way to add social work services. Since the first known collaboration between San Jose Public Library and the San Jose State University's School of Social Work in 2009,[8] the number of public libraries hosting social work interns has steadily increased to over 170 branches across the country.[9] Often placements are initiated by libraries who desire assistance with needs that fall outside the training and scope of traditional public librarianship.

In order to adhere to educational competencies and standards, social work students are required to complete 400 to 900 hours per academic year "in the field" at a practicum site. Typically, social work internships are unpaid learning experiences conducted under the supervision of a social work professional. Since public libraries are considered non-traditional social work practicum sites, it's imperative that university internship coordinators collaborate with an assigned library-based "task supervisor" to be the point person for the student at the branch. As most public libraries do not have professional social workers on-site, most students arrange off-site social work supervision either through their university or with a social worker that is contracted by the library to provide weekly supervision. Creative supervisory arrangements include hiring retired social workers, locating a volunteer social work supervisor, or partnering with local social services agencies such as the local Department of Health and Human Services to oversee the student. For example, Allen County Public Library (IN) partnered with the Carriage House, a nonprofit organization in Fort Wayne that works with people with severe mental illness, for supervision of their social work practicum student. The social work student primarily served the library but also worked a few hours per week at the Carriage House. The library has many patrons from the same population served by the Carriage House, so it made sense for them to provide the required supervision.

Supervision of social work students is essential for the success of a social work placement. The student, their social work supervisor, and the designated library task supervisor must come to an agreed-upon understanding about the expectations of the student: their learning goals, responsibilities (including what they are not expected to do), and the tasks they will work on. Open and regular communication among all three parties is essential. Necessary documentation such as an affiliation agreement[10] and a learning contract needs to be agreed upon by all. Such agreements should be openly communicated to all library staff, including security.

Based on her extensive research on this topic, Sarah advises it is ideal for a professional social worker to be employed and stationed at the library full time in order to provide on-site supervision to library-based social work students. Unless a quality arrangement can be made with an external social work professional prior to students commencing placement, we advise against hosting student interns. Most successful arrangements ensure ample support is planned and established by the time a student begins their fieldwork. This is especially crucial for interns at non-traditional social work placements—such as a library—where they may experience isolation or struggle to see how their growing social work knowledge, skills, and values apply to public library settings.

One definition of a successful social work internship is when the library extends an offer of employment to hire the student upon graduation from their social work studies. This seamless transition typically occurs when, due to the trial period of hosting a fitting social work student, the library experiences the value of having a student social worker as part of their library. Committed library administrators and boards then choose to hire a social worker as a permanent line item in their annual budget. Examples of libraries that have hired previous social work student interns include Elmhurst (IL), Carbondale (IL), and Long Branch Free (NJ) public libraries.

## Social Work Student/Library Partnerships: Small, Rural Town

### Carbondale Public Library (IL)

Diana Brawley Sussman is director of the Carbondale Public Library (CPL) in Illinois where collaboration with community partners is strong. "We are dependent on them; partnerships are key to all that we have been able to do. We do a lot of networking outside the library's walls."[11] Within one of those networks, a social work professor at Southern Illinois University in Carbondale (SIU) suggested that the library consider hosting student interns working toward a master's degree in social work. Sussman estimates that, when their collaboration started in 2015, CPL may have been the smallest library in the country to offer social work services. Since that time, CPL has hosted one or two master's level social worker students every year, for approximately nine months at a time (a full academic year).

Sussman posits that one of the reasons they were working with a great number of patrons in need is in part due to Carbondale's orientation as a progressive, university town: "In general, we have more social services available than neighboring rural areas, so sometimes I think that leads to people in need being dropped off here from other communities. We were constantly making referrals to local providers, and so the need for outside help was evident. My board (members) were resistant at first to hiring a professional social worker, but they didn't push back on the idea of us partnering with students from SIU."

Sussman says it was not difficult to generate buy-in from her library staff about hosting social work students. "They were excited about this idea. Staff viewed the students as a new, additional resource that could help patrons in need, particularly those experiencing homelessness. I concede that initially the program was more work for me as I opted to be the point person for students when they were at the library. I didn't want to add extra work for my staff." Under the supervision of social work educators and field advisors at SIU, Sussman says the students mostly work with patrons who are currently unhoused and/or are experiencing poverty. Tasks may include working with patrons who seek assistance, such as paying utility bills, transportation, start-up costs to obtain housing, and landlord mediation.

Sussman describes the ideal social work student as someone who is experienced, often a non-traditional student who can apply previous professional and life experiences to their placement. "This work demands patience with some high-need patrons." She finds that students tend to do well in a library placement when they are independent, assertive, and confident. Based on their consistent partnership with SIU, Sussman further determines that the suitability of the student correlates with the number of referrals. In other words, the better suited a student is to work independently and assertively at the library the more patrons they attract, and the more help they can provide to those patrons.

Another challenge is the library's physical space. CPL is the only public library in Carbondale, a medium-sized university town of about 22,000 residents. While the physical space is small, the library is vibrant and dynamic. It's also not a quiet space. The library hosts hundreds of programs every year, but its only meeting room holds just forty-four people. A lot of programs have to be held in the common area in the middle of the building because it's not uncommon for 150 people to attend a program. The building's open floor plan is useful for maintaining a safe space because employees can see almost everyone in the building from the circulation desk's central vantage point. Yet, private spaces are almost nonexistent. Sussman's office is the only private office in the library, which means her social work interns have no confidential area for serving patrons, and unfortunately there are no spaces in the building that can feasibly be converted into offices. A lack of adequate and private space is a common challenge for libraries seeking to provide social work services.

Despite these challenges, in August 2022, CPL was able to hire one of their social work interns upon completion of their graduate studies, using grant monies obtained through the American Rescue Plan Act (ARPA), which will provide one year of funding for the new, professional position. Sussman says the ability to maintain consistency by hiring this student will be enormously helpful for the library's current patrons, and the overall quality of the program. The library aims to look for additional funding sources to continue the social worker's position once the ARPA funds end.

## Social Work Student/Library Partnerships: Large, Urban City

### New York University and New York Public Library

One example of a successful urban partnership is between the New York University (NYU) Silver School of Social Work and the New York Public Library (NYPL). In 2018, the program started small with two NYU students stationed at two NYPL branches. In 2021, twelve students from three different graduate social work programs were placed at ten branches throughout

New York City. Based on simple, anonymized data recorded over the partnership's first four years, the library recognized the value of the work students were doing with library patrons. At the time of this writing, NYPL has hired a full-time Manager of Community Wellness Programs who will oversee the social work student intern program and university/library partnerships as well as grow the library's health and wellness programs.

Anita Favretto has been involved in the program since its inception. As NYPL's associate director of Outreach and Adult Programming, she credits the pace and intentionality of the library's expansion of the program as key factors that led the Library to decide hiring a full-time social worker was worthwhile. Anita explains that "starting small with this program was one factor of our success in building a solid base to expand this program. Even with Covid hitting this program early on, the pandemic forced us to consider how we wanted the partnership to grow. It allowed us time to think through the next stage. Together with a small working group of librarians, dedicated to the framework of whole person librarianship, we focused on building the program. It turns out that persistence really pays off."[12]

The basic data social work students collected anonymously indicated the number of patrons who sought assistance from interns, how much time students spent with each patron, whether they were one-time or repeat visits, and the general topics of help sought (i.e., housing, job applications). This information, in conjunction with a survey of branch managers who overwhelmingly voiced desire to continue the social work program, provided some of the rationale for hiring a social worker. Anita believes the library also recognized the unavoidable struggles highlighted by the pandemic for so many patrons and therefore agreed that a full-time position was warranted.

## Challenges of Collaborating with Social Workers

For all the benefits social workers bring to their collaborations with public libraries, it's worth noting that there are some challenges commonly experienced by libraries adding social work services for the first time. These challenges apply to both paid social workers or practicum students, and primarily pertain to:

1) Confusion about the social work profession and what social workers can offer in a library setting

**2)** Conflicts or lack of clarity about the social worker's role

**3)** Logistical challenges including liability issues, confidentiality, and record-keeping requirements

**4)** Feelings of isolation experienced by the library social worker.

For libraries considering a partnership with social workers, we think it's critical for libraries to first come to a basic, foundational understanding about what social workers actually do and to conceptualize what a collaboration could feasibly entail. Having this baseline understanding of the social work profession will help manage expectations of library staff and put less, unnecessary strain on the library-based social worker to repeatedly define what their role at the branch is. This foundational understanding helps to lay the foundation for clear, well-defined roles and ensures that the library choosing a social work collaboration is ready for the philosophical "lens" that a social worker brings to the library. The social work "lens" is focused on reducing social inequities, addressing the needs of marginalized or oppressed groups, and increasing access for disadvantaged populations. Social workers are also trained to look at individuals' functioning in light of environmental factors; this is the micro (individual) to macro (community and organizational) focus in which all social workers are trained. Libraries choosing to hire or host a social worker should be prepared for this lens to impact the social worker's overall work in the library, recommendations they may make for their library, and training they may offer to library staff.

It can be a challenge for librarianship to grapple with what partnership looks like with a different profession, though. Generally speaking, librarians are mostly in control of their environments versus social workers, who are often trained in interprofessional practice and familiar collaborating with professions different from their own. We like Zettervall's analogy of relationships that she uses when talking with libraries considering adding social work services: "What does it mean to have a long-term relationship with a partner? What does this mean when you (libraries) are used to living by yourself?"[13] Anytime two unique partners come together, there are challenges that arise and issues that need worked out through commitment, communication, and shared goals; this applies whether we are talking about an intimate relationship between two people or a relationship between two disciplines like social work and librarianship.

The scenario here provides an example to demonstrate some of the challenges frequently happening when social work collaborations are first added to a library.

As you read this example, consider the four challenges we mentioned earlier as they play out in this library:

## Scenario

Smith Public Library (not the library's real name) is situated in a midsize metropolitan area and is located across from a large public park. Because of the location of the library, they serve a large number of patrons who appear to be homeless. Since the library has had many overdoses, mental health crises, and patrons who need to be connected to social services, they sought funding for a social worker and recently received a grant to pay for those services. The staff are excited to have the social worker on board and plan to let that person handle all patron crises. They hope to see a dramatic decrease in patrons who are homeless or having behavioral problems in the library because of adding the on-staff social worker.

The library's social worker, Melissa, began her position six months ago. The library provided her with an office that is located on the third floor and gave her a phone extension to use, a locking file cabinet for her records, and a computer. Staff are trying to be mindful of her job duties and provide her with the equipment they think she needs to be successful. For her office, they specifically chose an area of the library that was rather secluded so she would have privacy when meeting with patrons. Even though Melissa is a library staff member, library administration does not think she needs to come to most staff meetings since her job duties are significantly different from other library staff, so she typically does not come unless invited for a specific reason (for example, when staff have questions about what services she is providing). Since beginning her full-time library-based job, she is usually busy from morning until night with individual patrons. Many times, staff walk patrons to Melissa's office when they seem upset about something and they have also asked her to walk the floors and do outreach when not meeting individually with people in her office. They want her to see as many patrons as possible to try to "make a dent in" the patron challenges they face.

After six months of having a full-time social worker, the library is getting frustrated because they have not seen any tangible benefits. Melissa is not able to keep up with the demand and the library still has a lot of patrons who seem to be in crisis. There are people waiting all day to see her and sometimes she is not able to meet with everyone who wants her services. The library has not noticed a decrease in patrons experiencing homelessness or mental health problems, and staff are becoming concerned that having a social worker might actually start attracting more high-needs patrons to the library. Staff are also annoyed that she does not let them know the outcome of her work with specific patrons after they walk someone over to her office. After all, how do they know if she's helping if she doesn't report back to them about what she did?

Library administration has noticed that the social worker seems frustrated often and already "looks burned out." She keeps asking to meet with administration and wants to talk about other job duties she could do besides just meeting individually with patrons. She mentions wanting to revise her job description, but they think that's inappropriate. After all, they wrote the job description from talking with another library who had also recently hired an on-staff social worker. She has also repeatedly brought up concerns about the library's security officers' approach to handling patrons and they think she needs to "worry about social work and not security." They have heard from their friends at a peer library that they are having similar struggles with their new social worker. Melissa has expressed that she feels isolated and "out of the loop" with library business, but administration does not know how to supervise a social worker and are unsure how to help. They are starting to feel like having her in the library is a "hassle" and are concerned that they have made a mistake by hiring a full-time on-staff social worker.

---

As we work with libraries that have added on-site social workers or other collaborations, the aforesaid scenario has unfortunately played out in several different locations. In fact, a number of libraries that were once excited to have on-staff social workers have since allowed those positions to end and the programs to be terminated. Although some of these positions have ended due to funding difficulties, others have also ended due to a number of other difficulties that arise when bringing a new partner into a library. Let's deconstruct and analyze the scenario to help other libraries avoid the same mistakes and challenges.

### Challenge 1: Confusion about the social work profession and what social workers can offer in a library setting

The library did the best they could to connect with another library hiring a social worker to get a job description, and this is a common approach when trying to add a new position that hasn't previously existed. However, without deep knowledge of the profession of social work, the job description might fall short. In this case, it would be best to talk with existing library social workers to get assistance writing a job description that thoroughly captures the essence of the job. If it's not possible to connect with library social workers in a similar kind of library, then reaching out to other social workers in your community or at a local university can also be helpful strategies. Sometimes it is difficult to understand the nuances of a job without involving people from that profession. This strategy is also helpful throughout the hiring process, and we encourage libraries hiring a social worker to invite partners from that profession to sit on the hiring committee and give feedback on job applications and interviewees. This doesn't apply to just social work, either, and applies anytime a new job is being created in the library for someone from a different discipline or field. There are important parts of the job and characteristics of potential employees that will be missed by library staff who do not have intimate knowledge of the profession and what is needed to do the job well.

### Challenge 2: Conflicts or lack of clarity about the social worker's role

Without a clear understanding of the profession of social work, many libraries add social workers without clarity about that person's role other than asking them to address patron needs. Because social workers often work at the community and organizational level in addition to the individual level, most social workers anticipate having work-related tasks related to helping the library as an organization as well as helping individual patrons. This organizational-level approach can include helping the library analyze policies for disparities or changes needed to improve equity or social justice, increasing collaborations with other community organizations, developing strategies to improve staff capacity to address patron needs through training, or helping administration develop revised procedures for addressing patron crises. However, when staff have a limited view of social work, they may want the person to be limited to serving individual patrons. When social workers only work at the individual level, they have less of an impact than when they can operate at the community and organizational levels as well. Without clarity of roles for everyone, sometimes the social worker tries to do things that are not necessarily welcome or anticipated by library staff, or vice versa.

Although social work and librarianship share many core values, social workers have a professional mission to serve people who are marginalized and oppressed and to impact equity and social justice to reduce oppression and marginalization,[14] while librarians have a professional mission to serve the entire public equally and neutrally. Because of this lens, a library-based social worker often will expect to work at the organizational level to identify and try to address library policies and practices that may perpetuate inequity. They often will also expect to work at the community level and participate in local task forces or advisory groups to impact community-level change. If there are no active community-focused task forces or advisory groups, the library social worker may try to start one. Related to our aforesaid point, without the library understanding and inviting this perspective, social workers can sometimes "step on toes" when they work in a library. In Melissa's situation mentioned earlier, her request to discuss security-related issues is a demonstration of her using her macro-focused lens to try to identify and address practices that may be impacting patrons in disparate ways. However, the library did not expect that from her role and seemed to be upset or caught off guard by her focus on other aspects of the library outside of individual patron needs.

Staff may also have unrealistic expectations for what the social worker can accomplish with individual patrons. Although social workers can engage with patrons, assess their needs, connect them with resources, and provide service navigation assistance, they cannot fix existing "problematic" patrons or situations. Patrons have a right to self-determination, and sometimes they don't want assistance with things that staff might identify as problems. Earlier in this book we mentioned the stages of change; many people may be in precontemplation or early stages of change and may not yet be ready to address things that are viewed as problems by others. Also, even when they do want help with specific problems in their lives, there are other barriers that prevent progress. For example, sometimes there are not enough services in the community to meet the needs, or existing services may have requirements for participation that the person cannot meet.

Even if there is a mutual understanding of the role of the social worker, and that role reflects the whole continuum of social work responsibilities, sometimes library staff anticipate that they will collaborate with the social worker in a "reference and referral" type of approach, which we can see demonstrated in the aforesaid scenario. In Smith Library, they placed Melissa in an office by herself, did not involve her as part of the overall library team, and wanted to send all patron challenges to her. This is not best practice for interprofessional collaboration or for addressing high-needs patrons.

### Challenge 3: Logistical challenges including liability issues, confidentiality, and record-keeping requirements

There are many logistical challenges to be negotiated when a library hires a social worker for the first time. Where to place their office, how much time they spend in the office versus walking the floor or participating in outreach activities, how much detail they will keep in records and where those records will be stored, and when and how they can share information with others are all details that need to be discussed and planned. Social workers will need a private office or space to meet with patrons; however, this space should not be removed from the rest of the library, due to safety concerns. The social worker should be able to have private conversations with patrons while also being able to easily call for help or assistance in an emergency situation. In the preceding scenario, the library chose a secluded location of the library for her office to try to allow Melissa privacy. Doing this places her at potential risk of harm, however, and it would be better to have an office space closer to other staff so she can get help if needed. If Melissa's office needs to be in a secluded location due to the layout of the library, then she needs an emergency call button or some way to quickly get help if needed.

Both social work and librarianship value privacy and confidentiality, but sometimes differences in how this is handled can cause concerns or challenges with a library-based social worker. In Melissa's situation, the staff expected to be updated about what she did with individual patrons; however, Melissa could not share that information because of her obligation to protect the confidentiality of patrons who seek her services. On the opposite end of the spectrum, some libraries do not want to know what the social worker is doing with individual patrons and become concerned about any records being kept at all due to privacy concerns. Libraries and their legal representation are sometimes hesitant to have any private records kept at the library pertaining to mental health, substance use, or other psychosocial needs out of fear that these records could accidentally wind up in the wrong hands. When libraries hire their first social worker, there needs to be discussion about record-keeping because social workers have an obligation to keep some records on patrons in order to track referrals, etc. Libraries should rest assured that most library-based social workers keep as minimal records as possible and often do not include identifying information about patrons such as social security numbers. To ensure confidentiality and compliance with legal regulations around record privacy, some libraries with on-staff social workers purchase specialized case management software such as Charity Tracker or UniteUs to reduce the need to keep physical records in the library space.[15]

### Challenge 4: Feelings of isolation experienced by the library social worker

A single social worker in a library can be quite isolated. The social worker needs to be embedded into the library as an essential component of the wider team, participating in staff meetings, retreats, celebrations, or any event in which other library staff would participate. Not only will this decrease isolation of the library social worker, but it will also help ensure the library staff understand the role of the social worker and consider the social worker "one of them." Being integrated into the library team will deepen relationships between the social worker and other staff, which facilitates development of rapport and trust and provides opportunities for problem-solving and discussion when needed. One example of successful integration is former library social worker Tracey Orick's role at the Elmhurst Public

Library (IL). When she completed her undergraduate social work internship at Elmhurst, the library hired Tracey as their first, full-time professional social worker. Tracey credited her positive collaboration to Elmhurst's intentional integration of her role as part of their wider library team. As a library employee, she attended staff meetings and participated in overall library decision-making processes.

Outside of the library team, the social worker also needs to connect with the network of other library social workers. It is extremely isolating being the only person in a library who has a separate function than most library staff, and there are unique experiences of library-based social workers that are helpful to be shared with others in the same field. The library should support the social worker connecting with other library social workers and attending library/social work professional development opportunities. Participating in these activities will help protect the social worker's own well-being and resilience as well as support their continued skill development as professional social workers.

In our discussions with former library-based social workers whose roles did not extend past their initial grant-funded timelines, our interviewees spoke to a few key factors as to why their library collaborations did not continue. One cited changes in library leadership and the subsequent loss of support from the library's board of directors. Another discussed their library's failure to secure permanent funding for a social work position well in advance of the grant monies running out. Another former library social worker bemoaned the disparate reality of their library leadership's unwillingness to change its culture in response to the needs of patrons that the social worker helped to highlight. They reflect that, "the library liked the idea of having a social worker in the library but when I held up a mirror to the changes that were needed, they did away with my position when the grant ended."

## Peer Navigators

Another option for bringing in outside partners is hiring individuals with lived experiences to help address the psychosocial library patrons. These "peers," "peer navigators" or "health and safety advocates" (HASAs) typically have faced their own challenges with homelessness, mental health, or substance abuse or come from a marginalized population. Such backgrounds are not required to be a peer, yet often these advocates have shared experiences which position them to establish trust and rapport with patrons in need. For example, library social worker

Jean Badalamenti notes, "Lived experience like this gives peers an immediate connection with customers and an insight into the struggles people are facing. This experience, connection, and insight are invaluable for customers who are looking for support as they navigate the complicated terrain of assessing next steps they want to take in their lives and finding services to support those steps."[16] Similarly, Tiffinee Scott with the Maryland Peer Advisory Council says, "Introducing peers in the library reduces the stigma and provides an inclusive, trauma-informed space for individuals or family members to engage in conversation, be supported, and connect to support and services."[17]

Peer navigators are sometimes used to supplement the services provided by a library-based social worker, and such peer navigators can serve as a much-needed supportive role and balance to the clinical approach some social workers bring to libraries. Peers are also used separately from library-based social work programs and can be a stand-alone intervention in a library. Peer navigators can assist library staff and security in de-escalating potentially volatile situations, or they may simply check in with patrons to ensure they are getting their needs met. A recent study by Urada et al. found that surveyed unhoused patrons as well as library staff support the idea of more peer navigators in libraries.[18]

For libraries interested in having a peer navigator program, there are several points to consider:

1) If considering hiring peers that have their own experiences with substance use, mental health, or similar psychosocial needs, how long will you require that they be in recovery, or how will you know they have progressed far enough in their own journeys to support others? People in peer navigator roles will be responsible for helping to support patrons who are in crisis, actively using substances, or experiencing other symptoms of their psychosocial need that can be triggering to others, especially other individuals in early stages of their own recovery. Without stability in their own lives and security in their own recovery process, they can be inadvertently placed at risk of relapse. Some peer navigator programs require one to two years of personal recovery in order to serve as a peer navigator for others.

2) What training will you require of the peer navigators? Lived experience with substance use, mental health, poverty, or other psychosocial needs is not sufficient by itself to ensure that someone knows how

to adequately support others. Peer navigators need training in active listening, community resources, outreach strategies, how to build rapport with others, and need to be knowledgeable about basic interventions for addressing substance use, mental health, homelessness, or any other specific need the program is designed to target. There is currently no known publicly available peer navigator training specifically for library-based navigators; however, there are several online peer navigator handbooks for those working in HIV support, healthcare, child welfare, and other settings that could potentially serve as a template for adaptation by a library. There are also formal peer navigator certification and training programs offered in many states, although the requirements for each one vary by state. For the library to develop adequate training for these navigators, we encourage you to reach out to local community partners serving the populations you wish to target with the peer navigation program for assistance with training. For example, if your peer navigators are designed primarily to assist people with navigating services and resources for persons experiencing homelessness, then approach your local homelessness-serving organization to ask for help designing the peer navigation program and creating the training protocol.

**3)** How will you ensure they receive adequate supervision and support in their role? Peer navigators need ongoing support for their own health and wellness as well as supervision to know how to handle difficult situations that arise in this work. Similar to our preceding point about needing adequate training, these navigators also need ongoing oversight to ensure they are providing ethical and appropriate services to others. For libraries with an on-site social worker, that person often supervises peer navigators. For libraries without on-site social workers, the library often develops and relies upon a partnership with a community organization to provide supervision. In areas with formal training programs or long-established peer navigation programs, there may be a senior peer navigator that can supervise others. Supervision does not necessarily have to be done by someone who has different training or education than peer navigators, but it needs to be provided by someone experienced to provide oversight and support to others.

In order to provide guidance and bolster the sustainability of a peer navigator program, it is essential that quality training and supervision be readily available for such advocates. While libraries in Washington DC and San Francisco employ peer navigators supervised by their on-staff social workers, others operate successful peer navigator programs by collaborating with external agencies to certify and supervise peers. Read the following to learn more about how Kalamazoo Public Library (MI) has structured its peer navigator program in collaboration with a community partner.

## Peer Navigators through Community Partners

### Kalamazoo Public Library (MI)

Since 2018, Kalamazoo Public Library (KPL) has successfully contracted with the Recovery Institute of Southwest Michigan (RISM) to provide certified peer navigators to assist and connect with high-needs patrons. Kevin King, head of Community Engagement at KPL, built on an existing connection with Sean at the RISM. What started with just a few hours per week has expanded to RISM peers covering 50 hours per week in the library.

Mr. King explains that peers are integral to the purpose of the library. "We want our library to be that safe place where everyone can participate in lifelong learning. Peer navigators are integral in our mission of helping all patrons to succeed in life."[19]

He finds that not only is contracting peer navigators a more affordable option than professional social workers, peers also tend to establish more immediate rapport and trust with library patrons. KPL was the first library in the country to bring on peer navigators without also employing a social worker. RISM provides weekly supervision to the peer navigators. Additionally, Mr. King provides on-site support supervision to peers. He asserts that establishing a solid partnership on a peer navigators program is especially important when there is not a social worker on-site at the library to provide the necessary supervision.

Since the program's inception in 2018, Mr. King has received overwhelming support of the peers program from both his library administrators and staff. They find the presence of peer navigators has mitigated the number of violent incidences and challenging behavior from patrons. For libraries interested in creating a peer navigators program, he encourages allowing sufficient time to garner buy-in from staff. By framing peer navigators as a means of supporting library staff to help make their job easier, he found it to be an easy sell to his staff.

Sean Harris is the executive director of RISM where he helps supervise peer navigators who are contracted to work four days a week at the KPL.[20] Peers are trained to walk alongside and offer hope to library patrons with needs that fall outside either the scope, training, or availability of KPL's staff. Peers work closely with librarians at KPL to ensure the peer navigators program is working smoothly. Mr. Harris meets regularly with the peers' direct supervisor, Shay Pounds, and the library's outreach coordinator (Mr. King), to ensure open communication and continuity between the library and the RISM.

KPL is one of a handful of libraries employing peer navigators that does not have a social worker on-site to provide supervision. When we asked Mr. Harris about this, he cautioned that while a social worker may very well provide quality supervision to peers, they must do so from a recovery-oriented perspective rather than a clinical perspective. In his observation, social workers tend to struggle with how to relate to peers who are not social workers in training. The Recovery Institute finds that peers—such as Ms. Pounds—are better suited to supervise other peers. This egalitarian approach to supervision allows for mutual learning and side steps a hierarchy that doesn't need to exist: "Peers are not a rung below social workers in the supervisory order, they are simply different disciplines."

At its core, the peer navigator program offers hope to patrons in need. Mr. Harris finds that often patrons approached by peers simply want another human to talk to; they may not be interested in finding permanent housing or be ready to hear about services pertaining to recovery or mental health support.

Shay Pounds is a peer support specialist (or peer navigator) and peer recovery coach at the RISM.[21] In her case, being a peer means that she has lived experience with mental health challenges and recovering from substance abuse. In 2019 she began working as a peer at the KPL. Ms. Pounds is the team leader for her peers that work four days a week at the library. She works one shift per week at the library which helps her remain familiar with the ongoing events at the library and scenarios her peers may encounter.

In her role as a team leader to her peers, Ms. Pounds meets one-on-one with her team members each week in addition to meeting with a group every other week. Both during these set times and informally, she provides supervision to other peers as they discuss their experiences working at KPL. This may simply involve touching base to see how work is going as well as exploring potential solutions to existing challenges. She also regularly meets with Mr. Harris and Mr. King. She concurs with them that since the inception of the Peers program at KPL in 2018, the number of behavioral incidents and patrons who are "put out" or removed from the premises has decreased.

Part of the approach toward minimizing the number of potentially volatile incidents at the library is establishing a solid working relationship with security at KPL. All three assert that peers aim not to openly converse with security in the presence of patrons, lest patrons develop the incorrect impression that peers are "in cahoots" with security and therefore cannot be trusted. Rather, together with Mr. King and Mr. Harris, peers touch base with security behind closed doors to ensure all parties are aware and on the same page about the goings on of the library and any issues that all need to be aware of. On the floor of the library, peers can communicate with other parties by walkie talkies if necessary. Peers may intervene when appropriate, utilizing the rapport they've established with patrons.

Otherwise, Ms. Pounds states that the main focus of the work for peers at KPL is to "walk alongside patrons and offer them hope. They trust us. I love doing outreach at the library. I can provide help to people in the way that I needed when I had nowhere to live. I can help them find resources that I'm already aware of." Having peers at the library undoubtedly helps patrons that may otherwise be overlooked to have a trusted person they can connect with. When we asked her how *she* benefits from this work, she describes an indicator of the program's success that gives her joy and love of her job: "When I see patrons *outside* of the library—maybe on the street or at a store—and they recognize me. They wave and smile! Maybe they will come talk to me and ask me how I'm doing. This shows me that there is progress. They feel seen and heard. This matters."

# Health Advocates

In addition to social work partnerships and peer navigators, many libraries are partnering with healthcare providers to meet the psychosocial needs of patrons. Although these collaborations with community health workers, public health officials, and registered nurses have distinct purposes and are not homogenous groups of healthcare providers, we group them under the title of "health advocates" for this book since the primary purpose of all of these partnerships is to promote health and wellness for disadvantaged populations.

Examples of successful health-related partnerships include Pima County (AZ) Public Library's award-winning Library Nurses Project that employs a nurse full time alongside volunteer nurses to address the health needs of its library patrons. In fact, the library determined that hiring a nurse was a better fit for their system than employing a social worker. Nurses conduct blood pressure screenings, educate library patrons about health and nutrition, and meet with patrons experiencing behavioral issues.[22]

In North Carolina, a new partnership is underway between Novant Health and Charlotte Mecklenburg Library to offer "wellness hubs" in select branches.[23] Services focus on providing patrons with nutritional guidance, information about well-being at different life stages, health services navigation, health screenings, and current information about medical diagnoses and diseases. Novant provides a dedicated on-site community health worker one to two times per week to connect patrons directly to health and social services including housing, food, and primary care, and hosts a monthly speaker series to provide health-related information to the community. A mobile unit visits the library to provide health screenings and immunizations for underinsured or uninsured children. Finally, this health partnership provides access to Novant's digital resource library and to the MyCommunity (Find Help) platform. As part of this partnership, the University of North Carolina at Charlotte is planning to provide and coordinate social work practicum students and public health interns to assist with community outreach, service coordination, follow-up, health and mental health screening, and wellness-focused programming.

Noah Lenstra, associate professor of library and information science at the University of North Carolina at Greensboro, studies public library and wellness-focused collaborations and highlights for us the primary challenges of healthcare/public library partnerships.[24] Even with sufficient funding to support ongoing collaborations, relationships with healthcare providers often take time and energy to develop and sustain. Libraries are often the ones that have to initiate the partnership with the health provider rather than the health provider actively pursuing a collaboration with the library. In a research study of how public health partners perceive public librarians, Lenstra and McGehee[25] found that in some cases even when public libraries work closely with local health partners, those partners do not understand that all (or most) library staff value such health partnerships. In other words, national work is needed to prepare those in the health sector to see public librarians as critical community-based partners. Additionally, because wellness is multidimensional, healthcare is also often siloed, and it can take a coalition-building effort on behalf of the library to bring multiple sectors of health and wellness-focused programs together to impact change. All of these things can be difficult for most libraries, especially small, rural libraries that are often quite overwhelmed and lack capacity to do more. Lenstra advises that relationships with health providers can often take years to build and develop, yet they are essential to the success of these partnerships.

## Setting Your Collaboration Up for Success

Although social workers, peer navigators, and health advocates tend to be the most common types of collaborations currently used to meet the needs of high-needs patrons, some libraries are developing collaborations with other disciplines as well. For example, many libraries are directly partnering with city parks and recreation departments, retirement communities, homeless shelters, schools, and rehabilitation facilities to address specific patron needs or reach underserved populations. No matter what type of collaboration your library is planning to develop, there can be challenges. Without specialized knowledge about interdisciplinary practice and the skills needed to work collaboratively to meet patron and community needs, library collaborations may be less likely to be successful. In this section, we focus on identifying common challenges to collaboration and listing strategies library staff can use to increase chances of successful partnerships.

## Collaboration-Related Challenges

### Scenario

A midsize suburban public library has wanted for many years to create regularly scheduled "resource fairs." Such events would invite local, community agencies focusing on housing, financial assistance, mental health, substance abuse, and food insecurity to set up tables in the library's foyer. This fair would allow community members to meet and ask questions of agency representatives about the services they provide. Community Partnerships manager Lynn takes the lead on this initiative by starting conversations with five partners open to participating. Lynn confirms and schedules the events for various dates through the upcoming year and the library advertises them to the community. At the first event, all five community partners show up, but only three patrons attend. At the second event, only three community partners return, but this time there are twenty patrons. Most of the attendees are interested in housing and do not spend much time talking to the other two community partners there. At the third event, over forty patrons attend, but only one community partner is present. Many of these patrons are disappointed and agitated that the list of resources promised for the event are absent. Lynn is also dismayed that community partners who promised to attend did not show up. She is concerned about the event acquiring a negative reputation in the community and she is unsure what to do.

---

Even in libraries where there is widespread agreement about strategies for addressing high-needs patrons and support from all library decision-makers, other things can often go awry. Many initiatives depend on collaboration between the library and community partners, yet sometimes the latter are unreliable due to challenges of their own. For example, community partners often have their own struggles with staff turnover and such changes might alter the motivation for or commitment to the library partnership. Changes to funding sources (i.e., a grant that ends and requires the organization to seek funding from a different organization with different priorities), eligibility criteria, or structural alterations may impact who is eligible to seek an organization's services. It can be difficult for the library to keep up with these changes and inform patrons accordingly.

Other challenges include limited operational hours; namely, most nonprofit organizations are stretched thin and may have minimal availability to come to the library to meet with patrons or staff. Some nonprofit organizations have productivity requirements that require providers to meet with a specific number of clients each day. These stipulations can preclude any agency representative from coming to the library for even a brief amount of time. Similarly, the timeframe a provider is able to come to the library may not sync with a time the library has the most foot traffic. Communication may also be difficult with an external agency which makes problem-solving extra challenging when difficulties arise.

In some libraries, working with community partners is complicated by the lack of "ownership" library staff feel over the services provided. Occasionally staff worry they cannot openly discuss challenges with providers and opt to keep challenges to themselves; reasoning they should be grateful for any service provided. As mentioned earlier, many library staff come into their roles with little training or experience working interprofessionally or collaborating with other disciplines. There is no question that there is occasional difficulty arising from collaborating with community partners or depending on them for a service.

## Strategies to Prevent and Overcome Collaborator-Related Challenges

To try to prevent or overcome collaborator-related challenges, there are several strategies that can be used by the library:

*Have one point person in charge of partnerships.* Although midsize and large libraries often have at least one outreach position dedicated to community collaborations, it can be a helpful strategy in libraries of all sizes to have one person primarily responsible for partnerships. This dedicated role can focus on building, developing, and maintaining relationships with community organizations. Designating one library staff member to keep current with collaborators' changes is often more successful than having such responsibilities shared among multiple persons. It's useful for the external community partners as well to have a single library contact so it is clear who they can communicate with about changes to their services or their personnel. The preceding scenario illustrates this strategy by focusing Lynn in her position as community partnerships manager. Libraries may also consider rotating this role every year or two so multiple library staff can be familiar with community resources.

*Ensure the library and community partners understand each other's roles and missions.* When first collaborating with a non-library professional, it is essential to clearly explain and understand the respective professions' mission and role to ensure both partners have a solid foundation for working together. Different disciplines often use different terms for the same concept, or they may use the same terms for different concepts; therefore, developing a shared language is important for clear communication. In many cases, people assume they understand the other's position and role when, in reality, their comprehension is limited or flawed. Without a shared understanding, collaborations can struggle from the very beginning.

As part of the aforementioned strategy, it's important to *seek understanding of the collaborator's needs and determine shared priorities*. Although there will be differences in professional missions, values, and obligations, libraries and potential partners need to be cognizant of shared values and ethics. Focusing and building on overlapping priorities between partners establishes a strong foundation for collaborative projects. When differences arise, revisiting similar goals can help sustain the motivation of both parties to navigate challenges. In the foregoing scenario, it is unclear whether Lynn spoke with her community partners to see if the library event aligned with their professional goals and priorities. It's also unclear if Lynn had any information about this to draw upon when the challenges started to arise with participation. Had there been a preliminary conversation about this, the partnering organizations could be assured their best interest was considered and the planned event kept with mutual benefits in mind. If partners perceive their wants and needs are not considered, they are less likely to work through challenges and continue partnering with the library.

One important strategy for collaboration is *creating avenues for consistent communication and between the library and the community partner*. Typically, both the library and partner organization are extremely busy, so it's easy for long periods of time to pass with minimal conversation between partners if communication is not prioritized. Regular check-ins allow partners to observe how the collaboration is unfolding, if it's meeting the needs of the library and the community partner, and if problem-solving is required. In the beginning of a partnership, such as Lynn's scenario, communication should be open and frequent to unearth and address existing challenges. Communication may understandably become less frequent as the partnership continues, depending on its success and the strength of the relationship among both parties.

## Summary and Key Takeaway Points

- Libraries often rely on collaborations with other service providers to address unmet or undermet needs of high-needs patrons.

- Interprofessional or interdisciplinary collaborations can have challenges at times, and without specific strategies for fostering and maintaining collaboration they can unintentionally fail.

- Core competencies for interprofessional collaborative practice include sharing values/ethics, clearly defining roles and responsibilities, intentionally communicating across disciplinary lines, and focusing on the goals and contributions of the team rather than individual efforts.
- Common collaborations to help libraries serve high-needs patrons include social work collaborations (either paid social workers, volunteers, or social work students), peer navigators, and health advocates, among others.
- Best practices for initiating and sustaining productive collaborations with other professions or disciplines include identifying a single library staff member to oversee the specific collaboration, ensuring all collaborating partners understand one another's missions, roles, needs, and priorities, and how the collaboration aligns with those aspects, and creating avenues for regular and consistent communication throughout the partnership.

## Notes

**1**  N. Lenstra, personal communication, August 3, 2022.

**2**  Interprofessional Education Collaborative Expert Panel, *Core Competencies for Interprofessional Collaborative Practice: Report of an Expert Panel* (Washington, DC: Interprofessional Education Collaborative, 2011), https://ipec.memberclicks.net/assets/2011-Original.pdf.

**3**  "The greatest perceived policy change need was a permanent social worker in the library (69% of patrons, 93% of library staff)." Urada et al., "Homelessness at the San Diego Central Library," 12.

**4**  B. Baum, M. Gross, D. Latham, L. Crabtree, and K. Randolph, "Bridging the Service Gap: Branch Managers Talk about Social Workers in Public Libraries," *Public Library Quarterly*, 2022, https://doi.org/10.1080/01616846.2022.2113696.

**5**  Map, Whole Person Librarianship, accessed December 4, 2022, https://wholepersonlibrarianship.com/map/.

**6**  Lloyd, "The Public Library as a Protective Factor."

**7**  T. Garcia, personal communication, August 25, 2022.

**8**  D. Estreicher, "A Brief History of the Social Workers in the Library Program," *Whole Person Librarianship*, May 5, 2013, https://wholepersonlibrarianship.com/2013/05/05/a-brief-history-of-the-social-workers-in-the-library-program/.

**9**  Zettervall and Nienow, *Whole Person Librarianship*.

**10** To see an example of an affiliation agreement from the University of Michigan's School of Social Work, visit https://ssw.umich.edu/sites/default/files/documents /ofe/field-affiliation-agreement.pdf.

**11** D. Brawley Sussman, personal communication, August 17, 2022.

**12** A. Favretto, personal communication, August 9, 2022.

**13** S. Zettervall, personal communication, September 26, 2022.

**14** *Code of Ethics*, National Association of Social Workers, https://www .socialworkers.org/About/Ethics/Code-of-Ethics/Code-of-Ethics-English.

**15** See https://www.charitytracker.net/ or https://uniteus.com/ for more information about these case management programs.

**16** J. Badalamenti, "Peers—In their Own Words," *Public Libraries Online*, August 7, 2019, http://publiclibrariesonline.org/2019/08/peers-in-their-own-words/.

**17** "Pratt Library Launches Peer Navigators Service Promoting Overall Well-being at Pennsylvania Ave. Branch," CBS Baltimore, March 1, 2022, https://baltimore .cbslocal.com/2022/03/01/pratt-library-launches-peer-navigators-service -promoting-overall-well-being-at-pennsylvania-ave-branch/.

**18** Urada et al., "Homelessness at the San Diego Central Library."

**19** K. King, personal communication, August 16, 2022.

**20** S. Harris, personal communication, October 27, 2022.

**21** S. Pounds, personal communication, November 11, 2022.

**22** *Health Department Public Health Nursing Recognized*, Pima County, December 15, 2014, https://webcms.pima.gov/cms/One.aspx?portalId=169&pageId =178365.

**23** "Novant Health and Charlotte Mecklenburg Library Announce $1 million Investment, Community Well-Being Partnership," Charlotte Mecklenburg Library Foundation, June 29, 2022, https://www.novanthealth.org/home/about-us/ newsroom/press-releases/newsid33987/2658/novant-health-and-charlotte -mecklenburg-library-announce-1-million-investment-community-well-being -partnership.aspx.

**24** N. Lenstra, personal communication, August 3, 2022.

**25** N. Lenstra and M. McGehee, "Public Librarians and Public Health: How Do Partners Perceive Them?" *Journal of Library Outreach and Engagement* 2, no. 1 (2022): 66–80, https://iopn.library.illinois.edu/journals/jloe/article/view/883.

# 6 Organizational Approaches for Best Supporting Staff

As we've acknowledged throughout this book, public library work can be very difficult, especially for staff working in libraries with many high-needs patrons. The current political climate and the resultant external challenges and protests from alt-right activist groups, especially for libraries situated in conservative states or communities, only adds to this stress. In addition, the Covid pandemic has brought increasing behavioral problems from patrons, even for individuals without psychosocial needs. As a society, we have generally become more volatile, more disconnected, less compassionate, and more demanding of others in recent years. All of these factors contribute to the high rates of trauma and burnout we are witnessing in library staff today. Libraries are nothing without the people working in them, and to ensure they can provide needed services, resources, and access to information for centuries to come we need to prioritize the well-being of library staff. Libraries should work to create and nurture an overall *culture of care*, which reflects a person-centered and relationship-focused approach. There are steps library administrators and supervisors can take to demonstrate this approach, support staff through the cultural transformations mentioned earlier, encourage the creativity and energy needed to develop and sustain programming and collaborations we've mentioned in this book, and create healthy and supportive work environments where their employees can thrive.

## Strategies for Supporting Staff
### Ensure the Library Is Welcoming and Accessible for All

People who have disabilities, mental health problems, and other psychosocial needs are not only represented in library patron populations but are also on staff at libraries everywhere. As libraries seek to create welcoming and inclusive environments for their patrons, they should not neglect their staff in this regard.

As a librarian and consultant to libraries and library associations, activist Karina Hagelin, MLIS, offers recommendations to library leaders for employees with physical challenges and chronic health conditions.[1] They encourage leaders to be proactive by ensuring there is regular and open dialogue with and among library staff about accessibility, rather than merely responding to issues once they arise. In other words, it's important for libraries to examine what they mean when they talk about or say that they value accessibility. Hagelin specifies that library leaders need to proactively "reach out" to staff about ensuring a welcome and accessible workspace versus waiting for ("reaching in") employees with disabilities and chronic health conditions to notify them of their needs. Initiating conversations with staff by seeking out their perspectives and trying to understand their needs can help create and maintain a work environment that helps everyone to thrive. This approach exemplifies operating from a strengths perspective and trusting that your staff know what they need. The ALA also provides online tips for supporting library staff with disabilities that are important to ensure an inclusive environment for your employees.[2] If we expect libraries to be welcoming and accessible to patrons with disabilities, we have to ensure first and foremost that we are accessible to and supportive of employees with disabilities. Libraries should intentionally cultivate a culture that normalizes differing abilities and makes accommodations as needed to insure inclusion.

## Demonstrate and Expect Cultural Humility

Another way library administrators can create safe, healthy, and inclusive working environments for staff is to demonstrate and expect cultural humility from all staff. Cultural humility entails the use of self-reflection to understand our own background and cultural beliefs, the application of a lifelong learning framework to explore and learn about others' cultures (i.e., we never "know" or are fully competent when talking about another culture), the humility to understand our personal experiences are not universal, a willingness to acknowledge differences between us and others, and an overall acceptance of others for who they are. Demonstrating cultural humility also means we recognize how cultural differences impact power and privilege in our communities and that we are committed to trying to correct those power imbalances.

In a library environment, demonstrating cultural humility often starts with a racial equity or diversity audit to assess or take a snapshot of the current way the library is operating with diverse employees and patrons. Such reviews can proactively help shape an anti-racist environment among library staff and its patrons and can be a way of intentionally incorporating diverse voices and perspectives from all employees. Questions can also be used to prompt staff discussion about cultural humility, help them reflect on their own cultural beliefs and assumptions, and guide conversations about diversity and culture in the workplace. In her article "Cultural Humility in the LIS Profession," Getgen suggests asking staff to respond to specific prompts to reflect on their own individual cultural beliefs and experiences, cultural beliefs and assumptions about coworkers, and their cultural biases and beliefs about patrons as part of a cultural humility evaluation.[3]

Training on cultural humility is also important for creating trauma-informed library cultures, and psychotherapist Caroline Sharkey finds one of the easiest ways to "ensure that cultural, historical and gender issues (one of the trauma-informed principles mentioned earlier) are being attended to . . . is to make sure that library staff have effective and updated cultural humility and anti-racism training, which can be implemented on a regular basis." She notes that "library spaces tend to be significantly more progressive as far as equity and inclusion than a lot of other spaces that I do work with. I think libraries are a kind of logical partnership to embed anti-racist and anti-oppression trainings."[4] Such cultural humility trainings—when imbued with a trauma-informed approach—can influence the ways that libraries frame and understand patron behavior as well as being useful to create inclusive working environments for diverse staff. As Zettervall and Nienow state, "there are many factors influencing a person's life, and we can't know them all, but we can listen, trust, and understand that different experiences may lead people to different beliefs and behaviors from our own."[5]

## Clearly Define Roles

In Beth's needs assessments, library staff frequently comment on a lack of clarity in their role when it comes to addressing patron needs. Without clarification of their responsibilities, some are doing too much for these patrons while others are not doing enough. Some are crossing boundaries and potentially putting themselves at risk of harm, and others are doing tasks outside the scope of someone untrained to deal with mental health or substance abuse and are potentially putting patrons at risk. Additionally, when we talk with library social workers and library administrators who have hired social workers, we hear again about lack of role clarity and how it causes frustration for both the social worker and the library administrators. As mentioned in Chapter 5, lack of clarity causes misunderstanding, tension, and times when the on-staff social worker "steps on toes." These observations are in line with literature on organizational structure and supporting employees, which clearly emphasizes the importance of role clarity for creating healthy, well-functioning workplaces. In fact, lack of role clarity is a known predictor of workplace stress, burnout, and turnover in various helping fields. On the contrary, having well-defined roles is predictive of increased work productivity and satisfaction.[6] Regardless of whether the library employs two staff or 200, library administrators should deliberately and clearly define roles and responsibilities and adjust them as needed as teams change and jobs are added or removed.

## Invest in Staff Development

Although we focused earlier in the book on offering training for staff about addressing patrons' psychosocial needs and changing organizational culture, we want to highlight here how training can be used to support staff. Training on topics related to patron needs, de-escalation, and handling patron crises can increase staff confidence and competence and therefore reduce work-related strain and increase staff well-being. Some libraries wisely include staff training as part of their strategic plan to cement it as a priority for supporting their employees. At Evansville Vanderburgh Public Library (IN), one of their plan's objectives seeks to "provide training and support opportunities for all staff, including in-service learning days, webinars, conferences, coaching" in order that "staff feel empowered and are trained, developed, and prepared professionally to understand community needs and interests."[7]

Though library staff are requesting practical training[8] to feel more empowered helping patrons while also keeping themselves safe, there are limitations to psychosocial education.[9] Resentment toward library administrators can develop when such activities are undefined or considered busy work. Intentional training should be provided to staff while also being mindful of its limitations and avoiding training fatigue. Training should be incorporated as part of a holistic staff development and support program. For example, as director of Carbondale Public Library (IL), Diana Brawley Sussman provides professional development opportunities through an annual staff day and an ongoing Niche Academy subscription. The library pays for staff to attend library conferences and external training opportunities, including Mental Health First Aid. The library also offers partial tuition reimbursement for college courses. Sussman acknowledges that strong support from her library board allows her to encourage library staff to run with their creative ideas. "I don't micromanage," she says, also noting that her library offers additional perks to support employees, including a flexible work schedule and good benefits. "Since COVID hit in 2020, we haven't had one employee quit. Perhaps we're doing something right."[10] Libraries are encouraged to consider comprehensive plans for supporting the well-being of their employees using a combination of approaches mentioned in this chapter.

---

## Developing Future Library Leaders
### Cincinnati & Hamilton County (OH) Public Library

In addition to training topics related to patron needs, professional development opportunities should also be selected to prepare staff for career advancement or develop leadership skills among current employees. One of the strengths of the Cincinnati & Hamilton County Public Library (CHPL) is how it fosters new leaders within its forty branches and Main Library. CHPL encourages every employee to take opportunities to participate in professional development, including involvement in organization-wide committees, to enhance the diversity and equity of its library leaders.[11] One component of this is encouraging leadership roles for staff who do not have MLIS. While they do require branch managers to have a MLIS degree, the library offers partial funding to other staff toward their pursuit of this degree.[12] CHPL also runs a *Tomorrow's Leaders* program in which every twelve to eighteen months a new cohort of library employees undergo structured training to become leaders within the system. As part of their formal onboarding process, each new manager is paired with a mentor while new youth supervisors are paired with a "Welcome Wagon." Both formal and informal mentoring, support, and professional development opportunities can help transform the library into a positive working environment for staff and a welcoming place for patrons.

---

## *Develop Comprehensive Incident Reporting Processes*

In many libraries, incident reports are kept according to city or county requirements. These tend to be limited to reporting injuries or incidents in which emergency responders are called to the library. However, this doesn't capture the other types of incidents experienced at the library. Without capturing the variations of all incidents, there is little data to justify adding services or to ensure that the powers-that-be understand the realities of the library. Anne-Maree Pfabe, from City of Melbourne Libraries in Australia, changed their libraries' incident reporting process to better understand all types of library incidents; creating a system to not only track incidents but also to problem-solve and develop processes to better address each type of incident in the future.[13] She notes that changing the incident reporting system from physical injuries and emergencies to a broader tracking system demanded training and clear communication for staff to understand and adjust to the new requirements. Initially, upon opening up the incident reporting system to non-emergency events, staff sometimes wrote an *excess* into the reporting system, using a log similar to a journal to help them process their feelings about the incident that occurred. To keep the purpose of the incident reporting system, City of Melbourne Libraries has since modified their system so only specific staff have access to the log and have provided clarification about what types of incidents are logged along with directions for what types of details need to be included. Libraries should aim to strike a balance between accurately reporting the various crises that occur while limiting the information that is logged so the incident report does not lose its purpose. As we've indicated in other sections of this book, creating a process for staff to reflect and process their emotional reactions is essential to supporting long-term sustainable library practice; however, the incident reporting log is not the place to do this.

Incident reporting processes cannot stand alone and must connect directly to planned incident response processes which we describe further here. In fact, the recent Urban Library Trauma Study calls out incident reporting processes as traumatic when there is not a response that correlates with the report.[14] The study rightfully notes that requesting staff to log incidents can cause added emotional stress and should only be required when the information is used to guide a response to the staff involved or responses to the patrons' behavior. As a regular part of his role as a former public librarian, "Bryan" (pseudonym used for privacy purposes) compiled critical incident reports pertaining to patron behaviors and used these to inform the library's next steps. He acknowledges a trauma-informed perspective helped him consider various factors that may have influenced a patron's actions at his mid-sized, Midwest library location. During his role, Bryan strove to ensure that his fellow librarians clearly communicated behavioral expectations to patrons through a trauma-informed lens and that every staff member—no matter their role at the library—had a shared understanding of the policies, practices, and procedures for responding to patrons' challenging behaviors. As a result, staff who were initially reluctant to establish necessary boundaries developed the confidence to ask for help when needed. For example, Bryan encouraged his coworkers to feel empowered to call 911 when they sensed their safety was threatened, without fear of reprimand from coworkers or library leadership. Thus, the incident reporting process can be beneficial when combined with clear strategies to empower staff to act when needed alongside a planned response by the library.

## Develop Detailed Crisis Response Plans

As we started discussing earlier, the incident reporting system should clearly inform the library's development of detailed crisis response plans, with the latter developed for every type or category of incident anticipated and reported in the system. Dr. Rachel D. Williams, a professor at Simmons University's School of Library and Information Science, teaches a course on crisis management and rapid response in libraries. She cautions that while the rapid responses of public libraries to macro-level events such as natural disasters is gaining momentum, micro-level crisis management responses are no less important.[15] One way to do this is to create detailed crisis response plans for both patrons and library staff during and following significant incidents that occur inside the branch. This may involve planning for hostile or aggressive patrons, handling bomb threats, responding to "first amendment audits," or addressing protesters during library programming. Crisis response plans should allocate adequate time and space for library staff to debrief after a particularly stressful or potentially violent interaction with a patron.

Charles Sutton, acting assistant professor of library and information science at Indiana University-Indianapolis, believes it's the responsibility of library leaders to thoroughly examine their environment: policies, codes of conduct, the incident review process, how and if staff decompress from highly stressful interactions with patrons, and ensuring benefits such as Employee Assistance Programs and personal leave (i.e., vacation, sick leave) provide ample support. He told us that because leaders set the tone in work environments, it's important they remain inquisitive and commit to understanding the real challenges library workers face.[16] Using information gained from staff about the work environment, challenges experienced during and after a crisis, and available resources can inform crisis response plans to increase preparation for future incidents. Hamburg (NY) Public Library maintains their emergency preparedness and disaster plan on their public-facing website, which can serve as a template for other libraries.[17] Their comprehensive plan includes responding to an active shooter, handling unruly patrons, responding to medical emergencies, evacuating a special needs patron, and responding to weather-related events, explosions, and bomb threats, among other types of emergencies. Their plan also details the directors' role and informs all staff how to report an emergency.

## Clearly Communicate Expectations for Patron Behavior and Ensure Staff Know How to Respond

Libraries should have well-established, clear codes of conduct for patron behavior and ensure their staff are trained on behavioral expectations and how they should respond to infractions. Ideally, behavioral expectations will allow for exceptions based on patron disabilities. For example, Charleston County (SC) Public Library qualifies in their code of conduct that "the age of the patron and any disabilities that play a role in the inappropriate behavior will be considered."[18] Although most libraries have existing codes of conduct, staff are not always trained on how to respond when someone violates its code. Without clear expectations about their behavior, staff can be hesitant to respond or do so unfairly, with some staff implementing harsher consequences for behavioral violations than others. Creating a detailed behavioral policy guide for staff not only establishes clear expectations about patron behavior, but also empowers staff to act. For example, Beth assists public libraries in crafting their behavioral response guides so staff remember to use a trauma-informed lens when viewing disruptive or inappropriate patron behavior, while also reminding staff of applicable policies, clarifying expectations about staff behavior, and empowering them to take action when needed. See Appendix E for an example. Similarly, staff at the Johnston Public Library (JPL) in Iowa utilize their behavioral policies and guidelines to document scenarios, consider reasons for a patron's behavior, and demonstrate suggested staff responses.[19] JPL uses a number of strategies to ensure consistent and equitable responses to patron behavioral violations while empowering staff to take action when needed.

# Behavior Response Processes
## Johnston Public Library (IA)

To ensure a consistent, trauma-informed response to patron behavior from all library staff, encourage staff to set boundaries when needed and create a patron-centered re-entry process. Eric Melton (Director), Megan Sockness (Youth Services Librarian), and Elizabeth Stevens (Public Services Librarian) from Johnston Public Library collaborated to implement the following strategies:

1. They created a behavior response guide that includes general guidelines for staff to be kind, have empathy, allow a patron to be heard, provide rationale when explaining a policy or rule, and to offer accommodations to a patron when possible. The response guide lists common patron behavior issues such as noise disruptions, defensiveness, aggressive behavior, solicitation, or verbal harassment. For each behavior, the guide includes at least one scenario, an explanation of the reasons why patrons might exhibit this particular behavior, a reminder of applicable library policies, and a script for a possible response from staff. For serious and dangerous behavior violations such as aggression or violence, there are statements reminding staff of techniques to potentially de-escalate the situation and specific instructions reminding staff they have permission to do what is necessary to enforce physical boundaries, call for help, and protect their personal safety.

2. They created a patron-focused behavior form that is provided to the patron at the time of suspending their library privileges. This form clearly explains what behavior the patron engaged in that violated the library code of conduct and identifies the date their library access will be restored. The form also communicates the length of suspension applied for specific conduct violations and ensures that patrons are treated consistently alongside others who have previously violated the same behavioral code. The form includes check-boxes listing the types of behavior codes violated to allow staff to quickly complete the form and provide it to the patron. See an example of this form in Appendix E.

3. JPL includes on their form the appeal and re-entry process for patrons whose library privileges have been suspended. Patrons can have their privileges reinstated after meeting with the library director or

department head to ensure the patron understands the reasons for their suspension and are clear about the library's conduct policies. If the patron believes they have been unfairly suspended, the appeal process is described on the form they receive.

## Encourage Staff Boundary Setting

Encouraging boundary setting is another useful strategy for supporting library staff. Boundaries are verbal limits set with someone who is saying or doing something inappropriate. Since staff often want to serve patrons and be perceived as kind and helpful, they are sometimes uncomfortable setting boundaries when patrons cross a line. They may fear that establishing a boundary will escalate a potentially volatile situation. However, necessary boundaries can often prevent situations from escalating. In our experience with public library staff, we've noticed that staff tend to be more lenient or permissive with patrons after being trained in a trauma-informed approach, out of empathy for the patrons' circumstances or concerns about a history of trauma. Most public library staff are compassionate, kind individuals who are eager to help; qualities that often draw them to library work in the first place. However, unlike some other helping professions like social work, library staff rarely receive training on boundaries before entering the field. Without a refined skill set of establishing and enforcing appropriate boundaries with patrons, some staff unknowingly put themselves at risk or inadvertently harm patrons they're trying so hard to help. We've met library staff who have taken patrons with them to a cash machine to withdraw and provide money out of their bank accounts, which places staff at risk of being robbed or assaulted. We've also talked with library staff who have taken a patron home with them when they didn't have a safe place to stay. We've met staff who have given their personal cell phone numbers to patrons and then report frequent middle-of-the-night calls when the patrons are in crisis. Not only do these types of situations blur the line of a staff member's work-life balance, they also place the staff person at risk of physical harm. In addition to these precarious situations, having loose or invisible boundaries with patrons can be harmful to patrons. Frequent "rescuing" of patrons in the midst of a crisis can create an unhealthy dependence on staff versus assisting individuals to access their own innate resources or coping skills.

Enforcing boundaries can feel unnatural to people focused on helping others, and it takes practice to act in a trauma-informed, compassionate way. Staff can benefit from leaders who set an example with boundaries and give explicit permission for staff to do likewise. This form of modeling can be accomplished through training staff on the expectations for handling patron challenges, role-playing how to navigate common patron scenarios, or creating procedural manuals to communicate policies and expectations for how staff handle challenging situations. Staff often worry that setting boundaries can hurt a patron's feelings, make them feel the library isn't a welcome place, or other negative outcomes. Providing examples of how boundaries can be established in a caring, compassionate way can help staff understand how to do this.

Setting boundaries can be fostered in a number of ways. One can include information about boundaries during orientation of new library employees. This information might include what the boundaries are, positive ways to set them with patrons, and examples of common scenarios they can anticipate. Another way is to incorporate content about boundaries in behavioral guides for staff. These guides can remind staff of library behavioral policies, give examples of common ways they are violated by patrons, and provide sample scripts for how staff might respond. All staff should be trained on the policies and given opportunities to role-play with the scripts. This type of guide and training not only helps ensure staff will remember policies when needed, but role-playing the scripts helps them to learn to put boundaries in their own words and consider how they can correct patron behavior in a way that feels authentic to them. Practicing boundary setting through role play can also help staff recall ways to do this when they are in a stressful situation and need to handle it quickly. These strategies communicate that boundary setting is part of a person-centered, trauma-informed library as it helps ensure the physical and psychological safety of both staff and patrons.

## Encourage Self-Care Strategies for Sustainable Practice

A growing body of literature reflects the fact that library staff are seeking ways to attend to their well-being during or outside of work as a means of reducing stress. Librarians are learning not only about trauma-informed approaches to working with patrons but also how this perspective can help them with secondary trauma they may experience as a result of working with the challenging behavior of patrons. Encouraging self-care is an important strategy for supporting staff. Often when self-care is discussed, people think of relaxing experiences that people do on their own time such as taking walks, soaking in a bubble bath, or getting a massage. However, self-care is much more than this, and it involves management strategies from library leaders as well as expectations for practices used by individual staff.

Zettervall and Nienow build on the notion of self-care by calling on library leaders to encourage "sustainable practice."[20] Such a practice goes beyond mere self-care tips—which often puts the responsibility squarely on the individual to adopt additional tasks on top of their existing work expectations—and instead focuses on how the organization as a whole can support the collective self-care of staff to ensure their ability to continue library work. Often self-care measures are out of reach for individuals due to additional time and expenses. Rather, sustainable practice calls for a transformation of the work culture in which library leaders implement measures to ensure staff are able to flourish in their jobs. This can entail establishing paid, mandatory staff training days that allow for greater participation and sends the message that such professional development measures are valuable. It can also include creating a culture in which debriefing and processing work experiences with supervisors and colleagues is normalized. Encouraging staff to take breaks outside the building and time off after particularly challenging incidents are additional measures that can help ensure staff are able to sustainably continue thriving in their work.

Managers can encourage self-care and sustainable practice in a number of ways. One is by incorporating periodic self-care assessments into staff meetings or retreats. These can be partnered with burnout assessments or other methods of helping staff monitor their levels of stress, which reinforces the need for and increases motivation for self-care strategies. Managers can communicate the expectation that staff will take available vacation or sick time and scheduled breaks while at work. Some encourage taking walks during breaks or engaging in other movement-focused strategies that can be done in groups or individually. Discussions of self-care strategies and check-ins about what staff are doing for self-care can also be incorporated into meetings or supervision conversations. Some workplaces have created spaces for staff to play video games over breaks, another way for them to decompress and relax. Others have volunteers regularly lead staff in meditative practices such as yoga, mindfulness-related exercises, or tai chi. No matter what strategy a library uses, they should ensure these activities happen during work hours. If space and time are made available for staff self-care activities, then more staff will engage in them.

It's also important that the directive to transform library culture—such as implementing self-care measures for sustainable practice—comes with full support from the top down and is incorporated into an overall plan for transforming the culture of the library. It is critical that library administrators and board members initiate, communicate, and model the importance of sustainable practice for staff. Charles Sutton argues that while micro measures such as integrating mindfulness and self-care can be useful for library staff, it is fundamentally more important for library leaders to shift library culture. One way such macro transformations can be ushered in is through providing mentoring and coaching to staff, which can *then* inform and meaningfully support tools such as reflective practices[21] (mentioned further here). When leadership takes the reins in fostering a work atmosphere where staff can thrive, necessary shifts in the culture of libraries have a greater chance of succeeding. In order for this to happen, leadership must "walk the walk" rather than just "talking the talk." Radwa Ali, Director of Roxbury Township Public Library (NJ), finds self-care trainings can have limited impact when administrators tell, rather than show, their staff how to avoid burnout. "What I think works best in times of stress is making sure staff understand that their administration views them as human beings and truly cares."[22] Library leadership must show that they value their staff and their well-being, demonstrating both the importance of self-care and caring for others.

## Healthy Work Environments
### Caseyville Public Library (IL)

To illustrate how libraries create and sustain a culture of care that supports library staff, we want to elevate libraries that are already doing this. At Caseyville Public Library (IL), Director Ashley Stewart encourages her staff to take regular breaks during the day by taking lunch or walks outside the building as needed. She seeks to maintain an open dialogue with her library staff and recognize that they operate as a team: "We are a small library so reliance on one another is essential. We can't do this work alone. We are in this work together."[23] In addition to hosting on-site celebrations for recent student worker graduates, Ashley encourages downtime and "de-stress-ing" together. Caseyville also partnered with a larger, neighboring library to purchase a meditation app for all library staff to use as needed.

Each quarter, Ashley closes the library for one day so she and her staff can dedicate time to professional development and team building, which benefits not only the staff but their wider community as well. To stave off burnout, she instituted a policy limiting the amount of time staff spend assisting each patron. She also initiated a pilot program in which her staff received an hourly pay increase while working fewer hours per week. The aim here is to increase focus and productivity during the shorter times of the week her staff are on-site. During their increased time off, "I encourage them to not think about work . . . so when they are here, they're *here*."

Ashley recognizes that she is able to do her job effectively thanks to the tremendous support she receives from her library's board of directors, the town of Caseyville, her community partners, and the wider Illinois Heartland Library System. The latter provides Ashley with a robust network of regional library directors to connect with. Together, they help Ashley to operate as an excellent leader at Caseville and to be a standout example of a director that is creating and maintaining a healthy work environment.

## Acknowledge and Name the Trauma

Providing ample time and space to process crises and work-related stress is another critical step library administrators can take to support their staff. The reality of contemporary public library work is that it is often stressful, in which staff may experience multiple crises, stressors, and strains. Recent research focuses on library staff experiences that have gone beyond "stress and strain" and actually are experienced as trauma. Dr. Williams, alongside social worker and professor Dr. Lydia Ogden, discusses the importance of acknowledging the reality of what public librarianship involves.[24] They find that in order to transform library culture, we must begin by explicitly naming the mental and emotional labor that public library staff engage in on a daily basis. Naming the reality of library work validates these challenging aspects that cannot be overlooked. Acknowledging what it means to be public library staff today not only elevates the labor but helps to intentionally incorporate necessary components, such as regular and accessible professional development training, into staff's work lives. This helps shift the perspective that these aspects are critical to staff's professional lives rather than being viewed as "add ons" requiring extra work. Williams and Ogden find that even the process of staff participating in focus groups is valuable to staff as it offers a dedicated space to talk through the reality of their work experiences.

We note that some library administrators try to minimize these experiences either out of fear that acknowledging them will somehow make things worse or not knowing how to address them. Denying the reality of the work does not make the challenges disappear. Minimizing the effects of library work or not giving adequate space to name and acknowledge the stressors can generate negativity among staff, which compounds the risk of burnout. In fact, when managers fail to acknowledge the realities of the job or minimize the emotional impact of workplace occurrences, they generate a sense of institutional betrayal among staff, which worsens the impact of the traumatic incident(s) that occurred. In other words, a sense of institutional betrayal can actually magnify or worsen the trauma experienced by an individual from the traumatic incident itself. In Freyd's work on institutional betrayal, she notably includes talk about *institutional courage*.[25] As the opposite of institutional betrayal, institutional courage means that institutions choose to be accountable to employees, assess the prevalence of workplace trauma (such as through employee surveys), reward truth-telling, apologize to staff when necessary, develop strategies for reporting trauma and responding quickly to critical incident reports, educate managers on how to adequately respond, and ultimately take steps to repair harm and protect employees from future harm. Although library-related trauma is a relatively new field of research and we are all still learning what strategies effectively prevent and respond to this trauma, libraries have an obligation to acknowledge the impact of the work on staff and to develop and implement strategies to reduce harm. This is where the design thinking approach that we discussed earlier for addressing patron needs can also be useful for developing staff-supporting strategies.

## Expect, Model, and Create Space for Reflective Practice Techniques

Reflective practice techniques are an integral part of a trauma-informed organization. However, reflective practice is not typically expected or used in most library settings. Library staff will not automatically know how to use reflective practice to process and learn from their work and will need modeling of these skills or someone to initially facilitate these skills. Administrators should set the expectation that staff engage in reflective practice techniques, but they also need to ensure that staff have adequate time and structures placed around this to reinforce the importance of these practices and to set expectations about how and when reflective practice should occur. Similar to other self-care and sustainable practice strategies, it is not reasonable to expect staff to use their own time outside of work for reflective practice. Instead, there should be regular peer supervision or peer support meetings scheduled for library teams during their work hours. Reflective practice can occur during individual supervision, when a single employee meets with their direct supervisor, in planned pairs of mentor/mentee relationships among library staff, or in small groups of staff who are in similar roles and positions.

Reflective practice[26] is a process that allows staff space for processing difficult situations, analyzing these situations, evaluating their own skills, engaging in a process of continuous self-improvement, learning to recognize biases or assumptions that impact their work with the public, generating new ideas, gaining self-awareness, and learning new skills and strategies for handling work-related scenarios. In her book *The Reflective Practice Guide: An Interdisciplinary Approach to Critical Reflection*, Barbara Bassot illustrates reflective practice as a variety of mirrors that help reflects different aspects of ourselves and our work:

- The bathroom mirror: Just as we look at ourselves in our bathroom mirrors and decide whether we're going to style our hair, apply makeup, shave, or otherwise take action to make ourselves presentable, the bathroom mirror analogy in relation to reflective practice means we take a deep look at ourselves and determine if we are going to continue as we are or choose to improve and develop ourselves.

- The full-length mirror: Since we use a full-length mirror to see all of ourselves all at once, in reflective practice we examine our entire self and apply a holistic approach to workplace situations while examining the parts that make up the whole.

- The driver's mirror: When driving a car, we use the mirror to look back and determine if it's safe to move forward. In reflective practice, we review our history or actions we have taken in the past to learn how to proceed in the future.

- The magnifying mirror: When we need to see something closely, we use a magnifying mirror. The same is true in reflective practice. Although sometimes we want a holistic view of ourselves and what happens in our work, other times we are more interested in closely examining a small part of a situation. Attentively examining a situation can help us determine where mistakes were made, and it allows us to learn from mistakes and avoid similar challenges in the future.

- Funhouse mirrors: These mirrors are intentionally distorted and provide an inaccurate reflection of ourselves. Similarly, sometimes when we look at our own practice and skills, our perception is false. We may be too confident about our skills, and our egos prevent us from accurately seeing our mistakes. On the contrary, some of us are too hard on ourselves and may not recognize our existing strengths or the times we appropriately handle difficult situations. In these scenarios, it is essential to have the perspective from someone else who may offer a more accurate reflection of our strengths and weaknesses. This is why reflective practice often takes place in group settings, to allow people to benefit from seeing a truer reflection of themselves from someone else.

---

## Sample Reflective Practice Activities

### For Group Activity or as Individual Reflection

Reflective activities may include having staff respond to prompts such as the following:[27]

1. Describe a recent work-related incident that elicited an emotional response for you. What happened, how did you feel, and did your emotions surprise you?

2. Describe your account of a recent stressful incident at work. Analyze what happened and your initial responses and the responses of people around you. Does this incident highlight any challenges in our library or situations we need to address through policies or standards of practice? What did you learn from this incident? What do you need to be able to improve how you respond to similar incidents in the future?

3. Processing our feelings about work is important to do on a regular basis. This can be done through various approaches such as journaling/writing, recording our thoughts verbally on our phone or other recording device, sharing our feelings with others, or consulting with our supervisor. Which of these strategies for processing feelings will work best for you, and how can the library support you with this strategy? What commitment can you make to sharing your feelings about work consistently and intentionally?

---

## A Note about Reflective Practice Groups

Although many of these types of reflective activities can be done independently, they can be very effective and beneficial to do in groups. Library administrators can create these groups to facilitate staff learning reflective skills, naming difficult situations, gaining peer support, and engaging in continuous improvement. If funds are available, administrators can also hire a trained social worker, social work consultant, or group facilitator to help teach staff reflective practice skills. After a while, staff can self-facilitate the group and will know some useful strategies for leading themselves in a reflective practice process.

Notably, many of the strategies mentioned earlier such as naming/acknowledging the work-related stress and trauma, engaging in critical self-reflection, learning how to better set boundaries, ensuring staff know and consistently apply behavioral policies, and empowering staff to act can all be taught and reinforced through the reflective group process. In these groups, staff not only reflect on incidents that have occurred and process their feelings about these incidents, but they also analyze the event through their own and others' lenses, identify skills and knowledge gaps, and develop plans to address and close those skill and knowledge gaps. If administrators make room and add support for staff reflective practice groups, they will get a lot of "bang for the buck" since multiple strategies for supporting staff can be incorporated into a single group.

## Advocate for Staff Needs

In conjunction with support from library administrators, a shift in library culture can emerge when advocacy is highly valued and demonstrated by leadership. Zettervall and Nienow note a difference between social work and librarianship in this regard: Advocacy is built into the fabric of social work, whereas libraries have a long history of attempting to remain neutral or focusing on very specific types of advocacy such as upholding intellectual freedom. With some libraries losing tax dollars due to recent swells in book banning attempts, Zettervall asserts that advocacy is more urgent than ever for public libraries. Wary staff need to be reminded that they are not being asked to become social workers. In reality, libraries are not neutral spaces. Librarianship has a history of advocating for what they value, such as upholding equal access to library materials and intellectual freedom.

Library administration should actively advocate for staff needs at both the micro/library level and the macro/community or professional level. At the micro level, that means administrators advocate with their boards and city officials for supportive policies, generous leave time, mental health supports, or other strategies to benefit staff well-being. At the macro level, it means that administrators advocate with their state libraries for training, or advocate for other state-level supports for staff mental health. There are currently multiple state library initiatives across the United States aimed at addressing library staff and/or patron well-being and support that all initially began with a single library director or group of directors advocating for their local needs at the statewide level. See the Afterword of this book for some of them. In addition, the current bill before Congress for funding for library social workers and social work interns is an excellent example of the result of macro-level advocacy for more supportive services in America's public libraries.[28] Advocacy takes persistence and dedication but can often end in large-scale initiatives to bring about change that ultimately benefit libraries, their staff, and patrons.

## Build and Maintain Collaborations

Collaborations are essential to supporting the well-being of staff. As we discussed in Chapter 5, collaborations are useful for designing and implementing programming and services for high-needs patrons, which can reduce the demand on staff to "be all things to all people" in the library. Here we want to highlight that collaborations are not only helpful for serving patrons, but some collaborations also directly support staff. For example, organizations facilitating mindfulness-focused services or yoga might be willing to facilitate a group specifically for interested staff. Organizations that focus on mental health or substance abuse treatment might train staff how to de-escalate patrons or how to recognize and interact with patrons using substances. Organizations focused on assisting with accessibility needs can be asked to conduct an assessment of the library to ensure accessibility for staff as well as patrons. Diversity and equity-focused organizations can be asked to do equity assessments to ensure your library demonstrates cultural humility and is a welcoming environment for all staff. Ultimately, collaborations can be developed to help carry out many of the other strategies for supporting staff mentioned in this chapter.

# Summary and Key Takeaway Points

- Public library work can be very difficult, and staff are often not prepared for the challenges of the work.
- There are helpful organizational strategies for creating a positive workplace culture and supporting and fostering the overall health, well-being, and resilience of staff despite the stressors of working with the public.

- Strategies that supervisors or administrators can use include investing in staff training and professional development, clearly defining roles, advocating for library needs, setting clear expectations for staff and patron behavior, creating crisis response plans for both physical and emotional workplace emergencies, empowering staff to take action when needed, and encouraging reflective practice, self-monitoring, and self-care.

- Administrators should foster workplace cultures that develop and demonstrate cultural humility of staff, ensure the library is welcoming and accessible for all employees, acknowledge and identify the emotional stress of the job, and inculcate reflection and a culture of care.

## Notes

1. K. Hagelin, personal communication, August 15, 2022.

2. *Library Staff with Disabilities: What You Need to Know*, American Library Association, 2015, https://www.ala.org/asgcla/resources/tipsheets/staff.

3. C. Getgen, "Cultural Humility in the LIS Profession," *The Journal of Academic Librarianship* 48, no. 4 (2022): 1–4, https://doi.org/10.1016/j.acalib.2022.102538.

4. C. Sharkey, personal communication, February 16, 2022.

5. Zettervall and Nienow, *Whole Person Librarianship*, 121.

6. S. Hassan, "The Importance of Role Clarification in Workgroups: Effects on Perceived Role Clarity, Work Satisfaction, and Turnover Rates," *Public Administration Review* 73, no. 5 (2013): 716–25, https://doi.org/10.1111/puar.12100.

7. *Strategic Plan 2021–2023*, Evansville Vanderburgh Public Library, n.d., https://www.evpl.org/wp-content/uploads/2022/01/2021-2023-strategic-plan-2.pdf.

8. L. P. Ogden and R. D. Williams, "Supporting Patrons in Crisis through a Social Work-Public Library Collaboration," *Journal of Library Administration* 62, no. 5 (2022): 656–72, https://doi.org/10.1080/01930826.2022.2083442.

9. L. T. Dudak, L. Comito, and C. Zabriskie, "You Can't Self-Care Your Way Out of a Broken System," The 2022 Urban Libraries Trauma Forum, *Public Library Quarterly*, 2022, 1–15, https://doi.org/10.1080/01616846.2022.2148826.

10. D. Brawley Sussman, personal communication, August 17, 2022.

11. *Strategic Framework*, Cincinnati & Hamilton County Public Library, December 5, 2022, https://chpl.org/about/strategic-framework/.

**12** Sara Zettervall also discussed the trend she is witnessing of libraries hiring more workers without LIS degrees. Part of this shift stems from an aim to hire workers who are reflective of libraries' immediate communities and generate a workforce of more diverse backgrounds. S. Zettervall, personal communication, September 26, 2022.

**13** A. M. Pfabe, personal communication, November 1, 2022.

**14** *Urban Library Trauma Study,* Urban Librarians Unite, 2022, https://urbanlibrar iansunite.org/ults/.

**15** R. Williams, personal communication, August 3, 2022.

**16** C. Sutton, personal communication, August 23, 2022.

**17** *Emergency Preparedness & Disaster Plan*, Hamburg Library, 2019, https://www .buffalolib.org/sites/default/files/users/ham/files/HPL%20Emergency%20 Preparedness.Disaster%20Plan.B%26G%20Copy.pdf.

**18** *Policies & Procedures*, Charleston County Public Library, April 28, 2022, https:// www.ccpl.org/policies-procedures.

**19** *Library Policies*, Johnston Public Library, March 2011, https://www .johnstonlibrary.com/about-us/library-policies/.

**20** Zettervall and Nienow, *Whole Person Librarianship*.

**21** C. Sutton, personal communication, August 23, 2022.

**22** B. Bonfield, "Supporting Staff Mental Health: Ideas from the Field," *Public Libraries* 59, no. 6 (2020): 8–10.

**23** A. Stewart, personal communication, August 24, 2022.

**24** R. Williams and L. Ogden, personal communication, August 3, 2022.

**25** https://www.jjfreyd.com/project-on-institutional-courage.

**26** B. Bassot, *The Reflective Practice Guide: An Interdisciplinary Approach to Critical Reflection* (New York, NY: Routledge, 2016).

**27** Adapted from reflective activities 5.1, 6.1, 6.6 in Bassot, *The Reflective Practice Guide.*

**28** Congresswoman Garcia Reintroduces Bill to Increase Number of Social Workers in Libraries. (2023, May 1). Representative Sylvia Garcia. https://sylviagarcia. house.gov/media/press-releases/congresswoman-garcia-reintroduces-bill- increase-number-social-workers-libraries.

# 7 Anticipating Challenges to Change

As the common saying goes, "the only constant in life is change" (attributed to Greek philosopher Heraclitus). Yet, as frequently as we encounter change in our day-to-day lives, we nonetheless tend to struggle with it. Organizational change seems to be particularly difficult because, as much difficulty as individuals have with personal change, challenges are multiplied with an entire organization. As leaders in public libraries, it's essential to anticipate difficulty by planning for and managing challenges with change to facilitate the cultural shift required to create and sustain a person-centered library. In this chapter, we set forth realistic expectations about some of the common challenges to change faced by library leaders with the initiatives we've discussed thus far. We also provide helpful strategies to manage and overcome these challenges. For each type of challenge, we include a scenario to illustrate how it can derail the library's efforts to change.

## Challenges from Staff

### Scenario

Maria is the director of a large, urban library. Noticing an increase in patrons who appear to be experiencing homelessness and mental health challenges, she reaches out to a local community mental health provider to explain the library's needs and to see if someone can come to the library on a regular basis to staff an information table, meet with patrons, and conduct staff training. The mental health provider agrees to come to the library twice a week and is happy to be asked, since their agency recently got a grant to do community outreach in that particular city, and a partnership with the library would help them with that outreach. Maria and her assistant director have multiple meetings with the agency to plan what days and times they will come. Both administrators are thrilled to announce this new collaboration at a library staff meeting. Although many staff are happy to have someone come to the library to help with patron mental health and housing-related needs, Maria is surprised when a group of staff sitting in the back of a room appear unhappy with this arrangement and talk among themselves during the meeting. Since these particular staff members seem to be unhappy with many new initiatives, Maria decides to ignore them and move on with her agenda in the meeting.

The first day the mental health provider, David, comes to the library to meet with patrons, a staff member, Dorinda, tells him there is no table or meeting room for him to use and sends him away. After hearing of this, Maria talks to Dorinda and informs her that she is to give the agency a table in the lobby the next time David shows up. Dorinda is also told that a private meeting room should be reserved so David will have space to discuss sensitive matters with patrons if needed. David returns, and this time he is able to set up a table in the lobby to advertise his services. However, when a patron requests to talk to David and he asks for a private meeting space, Dorinda tells him all the meeting spaces are currently occupied. Frustrated, David contacts Maria and says this wastes his valuable time. Since he isn't able to meet with people during both of these visits to the library, he is unable to meet his productivity requirements, which could get him written up at his job. Despite Maria's apologies, David says this collaboration isn't working out and he can't return to the library.

---

As demonstrated in the preceding scenario, one of the most common challenges for library-based change comes directly from the staff. Even when staff do not openly sabotage an initiative (as Dorinda did in the example earlier), they can indirectly prevent its success if they have not accepted its purpose, understand the need it fills, and appreciate how it aligns with the library's mission or strategic plan. Negative attitudes among staff can be contagious if left unaddressed and can sometimes "infect" other staff, particularly newer or more junior staff members. It is essential for library administrators to uncover dissent among staff and directly address it.

There is often disagreement among staff about the role of the library with patrons' psychosocial needs. In Beth's needs assessments with various libraries and library systems, she asks staff about their perceptions of the library's role with patrons who have psychosocial needs. She finds the majority of staff are in favor of libraries providing information, services, programs, or building collaborations to support high-needs patrons. However, there is nearly always a small group of staff who feel this falls outside the library's role. In the branches and library systems she's studied, between 0-10 percent of staff do not agree the library should address mental health, substance use, housing, food insecurity, or other psychosocial needs. Her research finds higher percentages of rural library staff think these services and collaborations are not part of the library's role and responsibilities, compared to urban library staff. Library administrators should encourage open lines of communication with their staff to understand their perspectives and address their concerns before moving forward with new initiatives on behalf of patrons' psychosocial needs.

Even in libraries where there may be broad staff agreement that their library *should* address patrons' psychosocial needs, disagreements are common about the best ways to go about it or exactly *how* that should happen. For example, some staff think the library should collaborate with community partners that can facilitate programming for patrons, come into the library to do outreach with patrons, set up resource tables in the library, or help patrons fill out applications for employment, public benefits, or educational programs. Other staff believe library staff should be trained to provide assistance with applications, referrals, or the like. Others think the library should hire their own social service professionals to work on-site with patrons to address these needs. Such variations among staff beliefs about the role of the library—if the library should address psychosocial needs of patrons and whose responsibility it should be to address these needs—can derail efforts to add new programs, services, or collaborations if not uncovered and handled appropriately.

# Strategies for Preventing and Overcoming Staff-Related Challenges

To address these challenges, there are several strategies library leaders can use. The first strategy to prevent the library's transformation from derailment must occur long before any change is planned and relates back to our earlier discussion on trauma-informed library environments. *Library administrators must work to create an atmosphere of psychological safety.* This entails an atmosphere in which staff feel that their opinions are valued, where they feel comfortable speaking their mind and expressing disagreement without fear of retribution, and a space in which all staff are respected and heard. If a library does not generate this kind of environment, it will be difficult for staff to express disagreement. In the absence of free and safe expression of varying ideas and opinions, library administrators will move forward without knowing the positions and attitudes of their staff. Creating psychological safety isn't something that happens overnight; administrators must earn their employees' trust over time. Administrators must demonstrate concern for their employees' well-being through their actions and soliciting opinions from everyone when new ideas are introduced. For example, ignoring staff in the preceding scenario who seemed unhappy with a pending mental health collaboration was a poor choice for Maria to make. If she had listened to her staff's concerns, she might have had an opportunity to increase their cooperation prior to David visiting the library. Even if the decision remained the same, listening to their concerns would have helped staff feel heard and valued. This discussion could have also uncovered valid concerns that needed to be addressed before the collaboration with David could begin. Administrators must also positively reinforce staff when they take risks by disagreeing or expressing alternative ideas. Yes, this may go too far, so we must also pay attention to *how* staff disagree and express opinions so that there are clear expectations about how discussions and disagreements are to be expressed. Creating psychological safety means that disrespect between staff is immediately addressed and not tolerated. Safe environments create opportunities for all staff to express their true thoughts and feelings, which is necessary for leadership to know before proceeding with new initiatives.

Another important strategy for moving change forward is to *be sure library administration is in agreement about changes that need to be made*. Any new collaboration, program, or service needs to have widespread support from the top down if it is to be successful. If there are significant differences of opinion between administrators, factions of staff can develop who can then interfere with or sabotage the entire initiative. Although staff feedback will be essential for planning the details of the initiative, the administrative team should take the time necessary to reach consensus about the goal prior to moving forward.

After the leadership team is in agreement that they would like to move forward with a new initiative, *library leadership should discuss their ideas and seek feedback from the whole staff*, expecting and even welcoming conflict, disagreement, and challenges. Open communication is key to understanding concerns, having an opportunity to address these concerns, and ultimately being able to reduce barriers to change coming from staff. Leadership should send a clear message about the intent of the discussion, for example saying, "We are seeking your feedback to help us plan the details of a collaboration that will best help our library" rather than, "We are seeking your feedback to help us decide *if* we are going to develop a collaboration." The latter indicates hesitation about whether or not the library wants to move in a particular direction, which sends a message that leadership is not committed to the change being discussed. On the contrary, the former sends a clear message that change is going to happen, and it lets staff know that their feedback will be used to shape the outcome. We make this statement with a caveat: if staff are largely opposed to the change, then library administration should perhaps reconsider their initial plans in response to staff concerns and scale back as needed. It would be foolish to move an initiative forward in the face of significant opposition from staff. In fact, staff may have more knowledge than administration about challenges that occur on the frontlines that may interfere with the initiative in question. At the very least, considerable opposition from staff indicates that more internal work must be done with staff prior to considering any new outward-facing initiatives. It is better to delay the initiative, or to alter the original plans, than to launch something that has to immediately be retracted or cannot be sustained.

## Challenges from Patrons

### Scenario

Stephan is the director of a library and is excited that staff and board members all support the new planned initiatives the library will undertake, including a number of initiatives aimed at increasing equity and sense of belonging for diverse and sometimes underrepresented groups in the community. The library has planned a number of celebrations about diverse religious and cultural groups, is completing a diversity audit to ensure they have diverse collections, has begun offering peer support services for LGBTQ+ teens, and has added support groups for people in recovery and people experiencing mental health concerns. They created a resource table, started a food bank, and connected with a low-income housing provider, including a homelessness-serving organization that comes to the library once a week to help with housing applications. In response to a press release about these new services and events, multiple patrons have come to the library daily and demanded to talk to the director. They express concern about the library's activities attracting more "bums" to the library and that they don't feel safe coming there with people who are "drug dealers," "crazy," and "stink." Other patrons have complained about the LGBTQIA+ peer support groups for teens and have threatened to advocate that the city council pull financial support for the library unless they "stop promoting sin."

---

Another significant source of challenge to the library's transformational change comes directly from the patrons. Although libraries serve the whole public, patrons can often be divided into two groups: (1) individuals who have their basic needs met and are using the library for entertainment, research, or enrichment and (2) individuals who do not have their basic needs met and are using the library for shelter or to access information about social services or health resources (in addition to accessing information for entertainment, research, or enrichment). There can often be animosity among patrons in group 1 about patrons in group 2 based on stereotypes, prejudice, lack of knowledge, and fear.

Beth's research on library patron needs has consistently uncovered the divide between these two groups of patrons across libraries of all sizes and in all types of communities. Following are some direct quotes from library patrons who participated in a survey asking about patrons' unmet psychosocial needs. Note that these comments were entered by patrons in response to a prompt that merely said, "Please make any suggestions for ideas you have about how the library can better meet your needs or the needs of other people visiting this library."

> "The library shouldn't be a halfway house for addicts and homeless."
> "Stick with books—stay in your lane"
> "I don't want it to become another shelter. If those needs have to be addressed they should not be through the library."
> "It should not be a place for help with mental illness or homelessness. . . .I do not want to be surrounded by people who have no other place to hang out."
> "I go to the library just to get books. Is it appropriate for a library to be hosting events better offered by a social worker or someone trained in those issues?"
> "It's not a social club or community or welfare center."
> "I am uncomfortable with the library as a hub for social services."
> "The world has plenty of social service agencies already."
> "Afraid to come because of homeless people there and drug use by them."
> "Drive the bums out of the building."

Notably, in response to the same question on that survey, there are also comments from patrons who support the library attempting to address the needs of all patrons, even those needing social services or access to resources for basic needs. For example, other patrons requested that the library offer some sort of psychosocial support services:

> "I have seen public libraries have community resource offices located in them (i.e. a city liaison, a VA [Veterans Affairs] liaison, social worker) or partner with other social service nonprofits to host services there."
> "Help the homeless people."
> "Employ a social worker."
> "Maybe open far larger . . . so people under less fortunate circumstances can have a place where they feel safe."
> "Support groups for mental health and individuals who can't afford their own programs."

As can be seen in these comments, there are patrons who will support changes you're trying to make and patrons who will actively be against them. The patrons who are against such initiatives might complain, stop coming to the library altogether, or perhaps start arguments with patrons they perceive as "other" who are different from them. We are living in an increasingly divided society, and these factions certainly contribute to struggles experienced by library staff and administrators. Frequently we hear about "first amendment audits" and similar patron challenges from people who believe it's their responsibility to prevent communities from heading in a direction that's viewed as too liberal, "communist," or "sinful." It's important to listen to and understand patron concerns but as library leaders it is also important to help bring people along and not allow some concerns to derail the entire effort.

In this section, please note that we've been primarily talking about verbal or written challenges by patrons. However, in recent years, threats of violence and harm have become more common by patron groups who disagree with the library's offerings or collections. Numerous cases have recently made news of US library directors being harassed to the point they saw no other choice but to quit their jobs. Other libraries have experienced cuts to their budget; some defunding has been severe enough that they can no longer operate. Although we offer some suggestions for managing patron challenges here, we do not minimize challenges serious enough to bring harm to library staff or to cause a library to permanently shut its doors.

## Strategies for Preventing and Overcoming Patron-Related Challenges

Libraries can try several strategies for overcoming patron challenges:

*State your position and calmly stand your ground.* Library staff are trained to be neutral, so sometimes it can feel unnatural to take a stance. However, librarianship is not neutral when it comes to issues of censorship or ensuring the library meets the needs of the whole public.[1] Public libraries have an obligation to allow free access to information of all kinds and cannot censor information. When faced with patron challenges to core values of librarianship, the library should state its official position and publicly stand their ground. Of course this is easier said than done when funding is being pulled from libraries who refuse to remove books from their shelves and lives are threatened for standing up for diversity! We do not minimize that reality in any way. However, the famous quote by Desmond Tutu rings true as efforts are made to silence certain voices: "if you are neutral in situations of injustice, then you have chosen the side of the oppressor." Stating the library's position should be done calmly and assertively. If patrons want to argue or challenge the library's stance, a good strategy can include asking them to write their concerns and let them know you'll present their words to the board or to administration. Schedule a "hearing" or a time for them to express their views. This allows people to feel heard and also diminishes the potential for an unplanned verbal confrontation. For situations in which a library staff or administrator's job is threatened due to taking a stance in this way, there are resources available such as the LeRoy C. Merritt Humanitarian Fund,[2] which can be accessed through the ALA website. The ALA website also maintains a list of additional resources for assisting library staff with navigating patrons' attempts at censorship.[3]

*Ensure services and programs are available for all patrons.* Although services or programs may have been created with the needs of a specific patron subgroup in mind, it is important that all patrons are equally able to access anything the library offers. This is one of the unique attributes of a public library that is different from many nonprofit organizations. Nonprofits are often forced to limit their services to a specific population due to requirements by their funding source or must prioritize people with the most pressing needs. However, libraries do not need to limit their services in this way. Making programs or services accessible to *all* patrons that are typically viewed as only available for *some* helps reinforce the philosophy that all of us need help at times. We want to avoid singling out specific groups. For example, libraries that offer food should ensure it is accessible and available for all patrons no matter their need. Patrons offering job assistance, such as resume writing or help with applications, can make this available to patrons from all socioeconomic statuses. Libraries providing mental health-focused programming or health screenings can ensure that these services are not limited to patrons from vulnerable or oppressed groups. Ensuring access for everyone helps normalize needs while also raising awareness that everyone at some point has needs. It reduces the "us versus them" approach that can emerge when some patrons have more resources than others. Broad accessibility also prohibits the library from being charged with discrimination or limiting access to services which are expected to be fully available to the public.

*Hold community-wide events aimed at educating the public* about populations served by the library to increase acceptance of diverse groups and foster a sense of belonging by all. *Intergroup contact theory* is one of the most consistently researched and supported theories on reducing bias. In short, it states that the more people see, hear, and interact with people different from themselves, the more that prejudice and bias decreases.[4] These effects apply not only to a specific group with which someone interacts but are often generalized by an individual to other groups of people different from them. Thus, the more we interact with people from different cultural groups, not only are we less likely to have prejudice and bias against that particular group, we are also more likely to accept people from cultural groups which we haven't yet interacted with. This effect has even been found for people who consume media that portrays people different from themselves in a positive light.[5] By putting this theory in action, the library can play a key role in community-wide efforts to increase acceptance and belonging for traditionally marginalized or oppressed groups. For example, hosting events that celebrate different communities and cultural groups can be a way to educate the public about one another and can also be a way the library demonstrates its respect and appreciation for everyone. Libraries can enhance interest in cultural events by offering door prizes, entertainment, games, or food to increase attendance by those who may otherwise not be interested. In advance of those events, providing information about a particular cultural group at the library through book displays, social media, or listservs can increase positive exposure to each cultural group by patrons from diverse backgrounds and cultural affiliations.

In addition to the cultural events mentioned earlier, *libraries can also intentionally design programming aimed at facilitating interactions between diverse patrons.*

Libraries often host events or programs which bring people together who have *similar* interests, but an important goal is also to host events which bring people together who come from *different* backgrounds. One factor that contributes to our current social divide is that most people primarily interact with others who are similar in many ways: we are naturally drawn to people who look like us, think like us, talk like us, and act like us. This is called *homophily*, the phenomenon that we tend to surround ourselves with others who share our own views of the world. Social media exacerbates this natural inclination by allowing us to easily block or unfollow people different from ourselves, thus creating a virtual echo chamber. Without intentionally seeking people who are different from us, we limit ourselves to seeing and hearing people who are so similar to ourselves that it's easy to assume people who think or act differently than us must be wrong. As mentioned earlier, intergroup contact theory and the supporting research shows the more we interact with people and groups different from ourselves, the more we learn about, gain respect for, and accept them. Libraries play a key role in creating spaces for us to interact with people and groups different from ourselves. Although the aforementioned strategies were focused on large, community-wide events, public libraries can also offer opportunities for small groups of people to interact with one another in ways they might not be able to do outside of the library. One example is hosting an event similar to the Human Library®[6] in which patrons "check out" human "books" to learn about individuals' diverse backgrounds and lived experiences. Human Library® events facilitate dialogue and encourage people to gain a better understanding of others, thereby aiming to reduce discrimination, bias, and prejudice, and increase cohesion and acceptance.

*Add inclusive signage.* The more your library can help patrons understand the diversity and complexity of *all* populations served, the more patrons will be able to realize their needs do not matter more than others' needs and that they are but one part of a broader community. Libraries can add signage in their spaces about specific groups in their community with posters that may ask, "Did you know that [fill in the blank with examples of a variety of different demographics] live in [fill in blank with community name]? All are welcome at XX Public Library!" Ensuring signage about community events or library programming depicts the diversity of the local community can also help patrons conceive of the broad and varied groups served by the library and the library's obligation to include them all.

# Challenges from Other Library Decision-Makers

## Scenario

The entire staff at a small, rural library decides to offer new services in their library due to growing mental health concerns with patrons. They notice that patrons frequently ask for help accessing mental health services, but the closest mental health provider is about a thirty-minute drive from the library. The staff collaborate to write a grant proposal which, if funded, will allow them to create a telehealth arrangement with a mental health provider and pay for an enclosed "pod" so patrons can meet privately with the provider using the library space. Kris, the library director, excitedly shares their plans with their board of directors. However, the board votes unanimously to not support this grant proposal. The board contends that libraries are not mental healthcare organizations, and they should focus instead on books and literacy programs. Kris dejectedly returns to the library to share the disappointing news with staff. All are devastated that they cannot move forward with their idea for helping to meet the needs of patrons in their community.

---

Library administrators encounter challenges to change based on their library's structure and the fact that many have governing boards as well as city or county administrators that have to endorse changes being made. Operations run smoothly when synchronicity exists among library administrators, the library board, and city/county officials, but that is not always the case. In fact, a degree of disagreements or differences is common between these decision-makers.

Evidence of such friction emerged in data from a statewide needs assessment that Beth completed in a midwestern US state in which library directors frequently described the challenges to change stemming from other library decision-makers. In most cases, these challenges came from city administrators or boards who either (1) lacked accurate knowledge of the library's struggles or the difficulties experienced by front-line staff or (2) had strong opinions of the library's scope and did not think activities aimed at assisting patrons with psychosocial needs were appropriate for a public library.

## Strategies to Prevent and Overcome Challenges from Other Library Decision-Makers

Depending on the nature of the challenges, there are two primary strategies libraries can use to prevent and overcome challenges from other library decision-makers. If the challenge is arising due to lack of knowledge about the reality of work in a public library and an accurate understanding of patron needs, then the best strategy is *to gather and present data* to those decision-makers. Unless they are regular users of the library, often people have little idea what issues public library staff face and the types of resources requested by patrons. Collecting information and presenting it to decision-makers in black and white can open their eyes to patron needs and what the library needs to do in response. This information can be collected through the needs assessment process mentioned earlier in this book. It can also be helpful to prevent data from incident reports, especially if the library is using a comprehensive incident reporting process we mentioned in Chapter 6. In some cases, libraries also request social work practicum students or other types of student internships so the student can focus on collecting data that can be used by the library to understand patron needs, justify planned services, or help determine what services to offer.

However, if lack of data is not the problem and the decision-maker accurately understands the reality of library work and patron needs yet believes addressing patrons' psychosocial needs is outside of the scope of the library, a different strategy is required. In these cases, it can be helpful for library administrators to *present information about the types of programs and services offered in other public libraries and how those activities can fit in the mission and scope of the library*. For example, libraries that request to host a social work student or hire a social worker often face challenges from board members or city officials who think such roles are not part of the library's mission. It can be helpful to inform these board members or city officials about the growing number of public libraries around the United States, Canada, New Zealand, and Australia offering social work services through hosting student interns, contracting with local providers to use library space to meet with patrons, or hiring their own on-staff social workers. Many examples of or descriptions about what these partnerships look like can be found online[7] and shared with these key decision-makers. Although these partnerships began in large, urban libraries, they are growing in libraries of all sizes and community contexts. Awareness of this growth or speaking with folks from these libraries can reduce concerns. According to a survey of 773 public libraries in the United States, 8 percent of surveyed libraries work or employ a social worker in some capacity.[8] Additionally, a map depicting well over 250 social work/library collaborations can be found on the Whole Person Librarianship website.[9] Most libraries highlighted on this website welcome questions from other libraries who are considering the development of their own partnerships. Scheduling a conversation with a similarly sized or situated library with an existing partnership can help answer questions or address concerns about the logistics of partnerships in your local community.

Some library boards or city officials are concerned that "if you build it, they will come" in that by offering library services or programs that might appeal to people who have mental health challenges or are currently unhoused will inadvertently increase the foot traffic of such patrons in libraries. In our experience, this is not the case; rather the libraries are addressing the needs of the high-needs patrons who are *already* visiting their library. Yet even if the number of high-needs patrons grows, they are members of the local community, and the library exists to serve them just as much as higher-resourced library patrons. Public libraries are not designed to appeal only to select demographic groups. Instead, one of the core values of the American Library Association is to "provide the highest level of service to all library users."[10]

## Challenges with Security

### Scenario

A main branch of an urban library began contracting with a security service two years ago due to rising behavioral concerns with patrons and a few incidents in which patrons threatened the safety of staff or destroyed library property. Now there are uniformed, armed security officers at the entrance to the library during open hours and staff have call buttons to alert security of safety concerns. On Tuesday afternoon, a patron enters the library and uses the public computers for a while. She appears to become agitated as she uses the computer and gets up abruptly, slamming the chair back against the desk when she stands up. She rushes to the circulation desk. Looking like she's on the verge of tears, she tells staff that she needs housing immediately because she's about to be evicted and couldn't find any resources online. She seems desperate as she asks the staff for help. Library staff hand her a resource card but she immediately throws it on the floor and tells them she needs more help than that. As staff respond that the library is unable to provide assistance beyond the resource card, she raises her voice and starts screaming that nobody is helping her. Security officers are alerted and one approaches her and says firmly, "Ma'am, you need to calm down. Nobody is allowed to yell in the library, and you can't throw things on the floor." She then grabs items from the circulation desk and starts throwing them, cursing and screaming. Security staff yell for her to stop and tell her to calm down, loudly proclaiming they are going to call the police. Her behavior escalates, so the security officer calls the police, and she is forcibly removed from the property. She is told she can't return to the library due to aggression, throwing things, and being aggressive with staff.

---

Many libraries are struggling with security-related concerns, some of them due to patron needs discussed throughout this book, and other reasons unrelated to mental health problems, poverty-related needs, and the like. Although patrons in heightened states of psychological distress occasionally pose safety concerns, the risk is often overestimated by the public, partially due to media reports which frequently associate acts of violence with mental illness. There is much research to support the opposite notion that patrons with mental illness are more likely to be victims of crime than perpetrators of crime.[11] They are sometimes more of a risk to themselves than to others, which corresponds to recent suicides or suicide attempts occurring in public libraries. Although we are not saying library staff should be unnecessarily fearful of patrons with psychosocial needs, we do not minimize the real risks and concerns associated with serving the public. We acknowledge the multiple, recent cases of violence occurring in public libraries and the increase in general behavioral problems which sometimes escalate to violence. In addition to experiencing threats or violence from patrons—due to the current volatile nature of American society, heightened divisions between political parties, and growth of extremism—some libraries have also received external threats related to their collection materials. There is an increase in people storming libraries to do "first amendment audits" or demand that books on LGBTQ+ topics or systemic racism be removed from the collection. Some of the people making these demands actually threaten harm to library directors or staff. In some communities, it can be a disconcerting and scary time to work in a public library.

One strategy that many libraries have used to address safety concerns and threats is by hiring or contracting with on-site security officers. Although a full examination of the pros and cons of in-library security is beyond the scope of this book, we want to note some aspects of security that library administrators and staff need to consider. The presence of security in libraries is understandably controversial. Libraries aim to create welcoming, inviting spaces for all members of the public, and some hope that having security officers will help to maintain a safe atmosphere. However, due to the history of policing with Black and Latinx communities, including negative interactions with police that patrons experiencing homelessness may have had, guards may actually *increase* fear and anxiety for some patrons. Even for patrons who do not come from groups that have negative associations with police, the presence of uniformed security in a library can send the message that there are potential dangers which need to be controlled. Security may make staff feel safer, but their presence can also transmit a message to others that the library is unsafe.

In addition to fears that can be triggered by seeing uniformed guards, there are realities about on-site security that library staff should be aware of. Many libraries contract with security companies to host on-site guards and expect they are trained to address and de-escalate crises that occur in the library. However, while a few "high-end" security companies hire highly experienced officers who are trained to read body language, identify predictors of violence, and respond swiftly, most security companies that align with limited budgets of public libraries offer the illusion of safety rather than provide actual security. These companies pay little more than minimum wage to their employees, and most require only a high school diploma and a background check to hire for the position. Even with the "high end" security companies mentioned earlier, officers may be retired police or secret service officers who are versed in general security from a law enforcement perspective rather than a harm reduction or trauma-informed approach. Officers rarely undergo training about trauma, de-escalation, crisis intervention, working with people experiencing mental illness; most are no better prepared to act in a crisis than a library worker. In some cases, security personnel may be *less* trained to respond compared to library staff due to sheer inexperience with the populations served at many libraries. Hiring a uniformed security guard from such companies may provide a visual deterrent due to the presence of a guard in uniform and minimal risk protection. Security guards are required to contact police in the case of a true emergency, just like any other library staff member would need to do, yet many can inadvertently escalate a situation by responding in an aggressive or condescending manner toward a patron in crisis. As the preceding scenario illustrates, responding with a forceful tone or failing to validate a patrons' concerns may rapidly escalate a situation rather than reducing it.

## Strategies to Prevent and Overcome Security-Related Challenges

If a public library determines they need to hire on-site security, it is ideal that *security staff be employed by the library, rather than contracted from a security company*. This allows the library to have control over the training and preparation of officers and to fully integrate them into the library and the library staff team. It is essential that security staff utilize the same relationship-focused approach we've emphasized throughout this book, conversing with and getting to know patrons and being present and visible during programming and activities. If possible, have security staff wear casual clothing (although name badges may be necessary to distinguish them as security personnel), since uniforms can escalate people who are triggered by previous negative interactions with security personnel or police officers.

Libraries should also *develop clear behavioral policies and ensure all staff are trained to apply them consistently*. Rather than relying on security alone to handle difficult patron situations, all library staff should be trained to consistently apply policies and to assertively address patron behavioral expectations as needed. Behavioral policies should be worded using a strengths-based, trauma-informed approach in which language is not overly punitive. When patrons violate a behavioral policy, the consequences should be clear and unsurprising due to clear policies and expectations. Patrons should be informed of their rights throughout the process and avenues for appealing consequences and decisions should exist. There should also be consistent timelines for suspensions of library privileges and a process for patrons to access library privileges after their suspension period expires.

If your library has security officers, *ensure they are trained in trauma-informed approaches, behavior management techniques, and the library's philosophy and beliefs*. This is not always the case in libraries! For example, one library Beth is familiar with believes in using a trauma-informed approach yet contracts with security officers who maintain a visible "Wall of Shame" in the main branch of the library. This wall displays pictures and names of people who violate library policy. The pictures primarily include African American men, many who experience homelessness and severe mental illnesses. The security officers find the wall funny and view this form of public humiliation as a deterrent to "bad behavior." This example reflects not only a blatant disregard for patrons depicted on the wall but also a lack of knowledge about effective behavior management techniques. If a library decides to hire security, there are several strategies for ensuring they are prepared and trained to maintain an inclusive, trauma-informed library as mentioned here. Library-based security staff should receive extensive training in effective de-escalation techniques, harm reduction, and trauma-informed approaches.

## Restructuring and Working with Security

### Kalamazoo Public Library

One of Kevin King's roles as head of community engagement is overseeing the security team at KPL. Kevin worked with security to redesign the library's incident reporting system by rating incidents based on severity. He also ensures immediate follow-up with library staff after an incident occurs that involves security (i.e., verbally threatening behavior, physical altercations, drug use) or is potentially traumatizing those involved. Kevin makes a point to cultivate good working relationships between peers, librarians, and security; including the security team's off-site supervisor. One way Kevin aims for this is "treating our security team as part of our library family." This inclusive approach is working to foster and maintain good relationships among all parties at the library. Considering Peer Navigators, Kevin finds that having peers at KPL "boosts everyone's morale, particularly security."[12]

### Cincinnati & Hamilton County Public Library (CHPL)

Beginning in 2020, CHPL took steps to rebrand its security team. In fact, it altered the language of the team in that they are referred to as "public safety specialists"[13] who now wear khaki pants and polo shirts instead of traditional security uniforms. Members of the public safety team do not wear badges or carry weapons though their clothing is distinguishable enough so that patrons can identify who they are. Public safety managers report to the library's chief operating officer, as they are employed, rather than contracted, by the library. Brett says the choices to restructure security and do away with contract security at CHPL are unique when compared to other major metropolitan libraries in Ohio. Additionally, the library has minimized the presence of police officers in that there are now only five officers in all of CHPL's forty-one branches.

### Millennium (Manitoba, Canada) Library

After struggling with incidents of violence and crime, Millenium Library and the City of Winnipeg explored various approaches to safety and security while maintaining a welcoming library environment. In response to a fatal stabbing that occurred in late 2022, the Library now uses an approach combining traditional physical security measures such as metal detectors and bag checks at its entrance with a person-centered strategy of employing warm, helpful "Community Safety Hosts."[14] These Hosts are certified security guards who can handle violent situations if needed, but operate from a trauma-informed, person-centered approach. All Hosts have completed more than 170 hours of training on trauma-informed care, crisis intervention, and harm reduction. Community Safety Hosts patrol the library, not merely to maintain safety and security, but to primarily build relationships with patrons and ensure their needs are met. They do this by offering cups of coffee or snacks, smiling and making conversation, and providing information about community resources. When behavioral policies need to be enforced, they explain to patrons why the policy exists to ensure they understand the rules. A collaboration between the library and community organizations—Fearless R2W and Persons Community Solutions—this program was piloted with three Community Safety Hosts in 2022 and recently expanded to a staff of twenty-one.

### Appleton (WI) Public Library

After experiencing many patron behavioral challenges, including a shooting that happened outside of the library, Appleton Public Library implemented numerous steps to try to increase library safety and security.[15] Committed to using a trauma-informed lens to patron behavior, the library used a multipronged and holistic approach, including strategies for addressing physical security such as:

- Building relationships with local law enforcement to collaboratively problem-solve solutions and ensure timely police response in the case of an emergency

- Installing specialized security equipment such as duress buttons, lock-down buttons, desktop computer alert buttons, and security doors to enable quick facility lock-downs during an emergency incident and immediate notification of law enforcement when needed
- Providing staff with two-way radios to facilitate communication in both emergency situations and day-to-day library services

However, their approach paired trauma-informed strategies with the aforementioned steps to ensure that law enforcement is only called when necessary, including:

- Hiring a consultant for a needs assessment to provide data that would inform the library's decisions about addressing patrons' diverse needs
- Inviting trainers to facilitate workshops with staff on trauma, Whole Person Librarianship,[16] and how to set healthy boundaries with patrons
- Hiring an on-staff security manager (recently promoted to Building Manager) who has a background in case management and social service-related work and focuses primarily on de-escalation approaches with patrons. This security manager supervises contracted security guards to teach them the softer skills needed to work in a person-centered library environment.

Appleton Public Library also was a founding member of the Wisconsin City Library Collective, a collaborative library group that focuses on sharing ideas and resources and collectively seeking solutions for common library challenges. Together, these approaches have helped to improve the sense of safety for library staff, increase staff's efficacy in their ability to address difficult patron situations, and have minimized violent and dangerous interactions with patrons.

## Challenges with Funding

### Scenario

Staff at a midsize suburban library are thrilled to receive an LSTA grant that allows them to hire a social worker for a two-year period. This social worker also supervises four social work interns from a local university, who are paid stipends from the grant. The social work team meets with individual patrons each week to offer support, encouragement, and referrals. The grant also provides bus passes and snacks for patrons. The social work team assists patrons with resume writing, job applications, and applying for public benefits. The team is available during all hours the library is open to ensure they have ample time to meet with patrons. In addition to serving patrons, the team regularly offers support sessions for library staff to process difficult scenarios they face in their work. The team quickly becomes an invaluable asset to the library as both patrons and staff depend on their support. However, at the end of the two-year period, the grant ends and it's determined the library budget cannot support continuation of the program. The social work team departs the library as quickly as they arrive, taking with them their services and support and leaving a noticeable gap for patrons and staff alike.

---

The saying "money comes and money goes" certainly rings true for public libraries, where funding challenges and budget limitations are common and sometimes incessant. Funding is often the main barrier to starting a new program or service. Research shows it is the main concern for public library administrators who consider a social work hire.[17] In fact, most administrators see no drawbacks to employing social workers aside from the capital required to initiate a program.[18] Similarly, based on a study Beth conducted with library administrators across a midwestern US state, the primary concern with starting any type of program or service to address patron psychosocial needs is funding.

Many libraries find alternate funding sources (outside of their normal library budgets) to support initiatives aimed at addressing patrons' psychosocial needs. These include grants from their regional United Way or community mental health organization, statewide funds such as grants from their State Library, or federal funds (often funneled through states) like Library Services and Technology Act (LSTA) grants. Yet most of these funding sources are short-lived and provide support for only one to three years. We know of several libraries that obtained temporary funding, began a fantastic and helpful new initiative, and then terminated the program when the grant ended. Although it can be worthwhile to offer services for a short time, it can also be disruptive and seem almost cruel to begin a program only to have it end; particularly when patrons and staff develop solid working relationships with temporary social workers and or other grant-funded personnel. Of the time-limited collaborations that ceased due to grant expirations, we are aware that patrons lost a much-needed support system and social workers lost their jobs. Both of these losses should be avoided if possible.

## Strategies to Prevent and Overcome Funding-Related Challenges

Because funding is limited, one of the most important things libraries can do is *set priorities to ensure staff are not overextended*. Determine what initiatives are most important for your library: What aligns with your library's mission and vision, what you can include without adding additional burdens on your staff, and use library resources to support those initiatives. It can be overwhelming to remain aware of the varying unmet community needs since library staff often want to address as many factors as possible. Yet it's preferable to select and focus on one need at a time—aiming to do this well rather than trying to address multiple needs simultaneously and risk not assisting anyone effectively.

Similarly, libraries should *start small with new initiatives and scale up when possible*. It is better to make small changes and sustain them versus starting big without being able to continue long term. This strategy addresses funding-related challenges and enables a library to learn lessons from starting with smaller, new initiatives. This allows for adjustments to be made as needed and fosters the program to grow in an intentional way instead of starting with a big "splash" then being forced to backtrack if something fails or is ill-received. An excellent example of partnerships that are successful in part to scaling up after starting small is the New York Public Libraries collaboration with social work students from New York University mentioned in Chapter 5.

*Plan for sustainability before beginning a new program or service.* Although a program may initially be supported through grant funds, a library may acquire additional monies from its city or town council to continue the program. To make the case for the benefits of the program, a library needs to determine what data can help demonstrate the necessity of sustained support. It's important for libraries to consider what data is needed and how to gather it as part of its sustainability plan. Although in-depth evaluations can be complex or require advanced research skills, all libraries are capable of collecting basic data that helps tell a narrative about the initiative and its impact. This "story" may compel the powers-that-be to justify continual funding. Data collected can include anonymous factors such as the number of patrons served during the initiative, the kinds of challenges patrons faced that led them to seek out library services, and the number of referrals to other community partners made. Although quantitative data (numbers, counts, statistics, etc.) demonstrate the number of people assisted by the library's initiative, sometimes it's the *qualitative* data (stories and anecdotes) that is more compelling. It's wise to collect both types of data to appeal to decision-makers about the need for sustained funding of the library's program. Supplementing numerical data alongside the words of patrons who speak to the impact of the library's initiative in their own lives helps make the case for the sustainability of a new library program or service.

*Develop partnerships with other libraries*, to allow the sharing of funding and positions or collaborations. Sometimes groups of libraries are able to compete for larger grants or ongoing funding because of their ability to demonstrate impact on a large geographic region. By sharing the load, library groups may afford the cost of an ongoing initiative without additional grant funds. There are many examples of library consortiums or collaborations that developed to support shared initiatives or to compete for statewide or national funding. The Allegheny County Library Association in Pennsylvania[19] is a system of forty-six independent public libraries, encompassing seventy different locations, that collaborate and share resources to better serve residents of this large county. Together, participating libraries share resources, collaboratively seek funding, and expand what could be offered in any one library.

In contrast to the preceding strategy of partnering with other libraries, *look for opportunities to share funding with other community organizations*. Depending on the most pressing patron needs, libraries can develop partnerships with community organizations whose missions address those specific needs and can contribute to funding a full-time position at the library. For example, libraries with a large number of patrons experiencing homelessness might consider teaming with a local homeless-serving organization to create a shared social work position. Because of similar challenges, some cities have considered sharing positions between the library and the transit center, or between the library and the parks and recreation department. Other libraries are sharing positions with local community mental health organizations. Sometimes these positions work well for many reasons; in addition to sharing the cost of the position, often the individual hired can be employed by the partnering organization, which may already have the necessary liability insurance, record-keeping protocols, and personnel to provide formal supervision for the position.

*Contact relevant departments at your local university to request potential help from student interns or volunteers.* Although less feasible for many rural libraries, urban and suburban libraries often have a university in their vicinity that may be able to provide assistance for free or at a reduced cost. Depending on the initiative your library would like to start, consider contacting your local social work, public health, nursing, community psychology, or human services program to inform them of your needs and inquire about the option of hosting student interns or volunteers. Depending on the research and practice foci of faculty at the institution, you might connect with faculty willing to assist with needs assessments or provide training workshops for library staff. Several library services to address high-needs patrons were initiated or sustained because of university collaborations. In Georgia, social work students from the University of Georgia partnered with the Athens-Clarke County Library to provide training to library staff on trauma-informed approaches. One of the goals of this Trauma-Informed Library Transformation (TILT) program was to further transform libraries into safe and supportive environments for staff and patrons alike.[20] Another university-library partnership is between staff in a Northeastern US library system and social work and library and information science faculty from Simmons University. In this partnership, faculty designed and conducted training for library staff on methods of self-care, boundary setting, and how to respond to patrons experiencing mental health crises.[21] An ongoing, health-focused example of a university-library partnership includes students from multiple disciplines working together to promote healthy living initiatives at various public libraries in Suffolk County, New York.[22] The Stony Brook Medicine Healthy Libraries Program (HeLP) convenes library science, social work, nursing, and public health students from Stony Brook University who address hundreds of patrons' health and social concerns.[23] A final example of a sustained library-based initiative that began through a partnership with a local university is the social work program at the Indianapolis (IN) Public Library. Initially faced with overwhelming patron concerns, library administration reached out to the Indiana University School of Social Work to request a needs assessment and social work practicum students. Through data collected in the needs assessment and by the practicum students, the library was able to justify hiring a full-time, on-staff social work position. They now have a full-time social worker that began in 2021 and supervises a team of social work practicum students. These are all examples of library services or support provided through partnerships with local universities.

## Successful Change Efforts

Although this chapter focuses on challenges to change, we have witnessed libraries overcome these challenges to create sustained long-term improvements in their employees' workplace environments, their available patron-focused programming and services, and the overall well-being of their local communities. Additionally, we have witnessed large community-level changes being made based on the initial efforts of one person or a single library. In the Afterword, we talk about some current large-scale, statewide initiatives aimed at assisting libraries with addressing patron needs and simultaneously supporting their staff. It is worth noting that every one of these examples started with a single person who spoke up about challenges, advocated for resources or help, researched ideas for initiatives to try, and ultimately was willing to never back down. As poet Edward Everett Hale so eloquently stated, "I am only one, but I am one. I cannot do everything, but I can do something. And because I cannot do everything, I will not refuse to do the something that I can do." We want to end this book on a high note and empower all of you to be that person. You can make a difference, whether it is to your patrons, your staff, your coworkers, or your community, if you are willing to take risks, try new initiatives, and speak up and advocate for the needs of yourself, your library, and the patrons you serve.

## Summary and Key Takeaway Points

- Library staff and administrators should expect many challenges to change.

- These challenges can derail change initiatives if not fully anticipated.

- Challenges to change can come from staff, patrons, or other library decision-makers such as board members or city/county administrators.

- Funding and security-related challenges also often derail change attempts.

- With strategies such as intentional planning, collection of data, and efforts to start small and scale up, library staff and administrators can prevent their initiatives from falling flat and maintain and sustain long-term change.

## Notes

1   *ALA Statement on Book Censorship*, American Library Association, November 29, 2021, https://www.ala.org/advocacy/statement-regarding-censorship.

2   *LeRoy C. Merritt Humanitarian Fund*, American Library Association, May 2021, https://www.ala.org/aboutala/affiliates/relatedgroups/merrittfund/merritthumanitarian.

3   *Fight Censorship,* American Library Association, 2022, https://www.ala.org/advocacy/fight-censorship#supporting-library-workers.

4   T. F. Pettigrew, "Advancing Intergroup Contact Theory: Comments on the Issue's Articles," *Journal of Social Issues* 77, no. 1 (2021): 258–73.

5   A. W. O'Donnell, M. T. Friehs, C. Bracegirdle, C. Zuniga, S. E. Watt, and F. K. Barlow, "Technological and Analytical Advancements in Intergroup Contact Research," *Journal of Social Issues* 77, no. 1 (2021): 171–96.

6   *Human Library,* Human Library Organization, 2022, www.humanlibrary.org.

7   Whole Person Librarianship, https://wholepersonlibrarianship.com/.

8   *Public Library Association Public Library Staff and Diversity Report Results from the 2021 PLA Annual Survey*, Public Library Association, 2022, https://www.ala.org/pla/sites/ala.org.pla/files/content/data/PLA_Staff_Survey_Report_2022.pdf.

9   S. Zettervall, *Whole Person Librarianship: Map,* retrieved December 9, 2022, https://wholepersonlibrarianship.com/map/.

10  *Core Values of Librarianship,* American Library Association, 2006, http://www.ala.org/advocacy/intfreedom/corevalues.

11  L. Eisenberg, "Violence and the Mentally Ill: Victims, Not Perpetrators," *Archives of General Psychiatry* 62, no. 8 (2005): 825–6.

12  K. King, personal communication, August 16, 2022.

13  Example of a job posting for a Public Safety Specialist, CHPL (2022, November 2), *Working at the Library* (n.d.), Cincinnati & Hamilton County Public Library (CHPL), https://recruitingbypaycor.com/career/JobIntroduction.action?clientId=8a78826755712ad4015573d869f00055&id=8a7883a8838c33a30183aebfb2992586&specialization=8a7883a86fb6ede6016fe7f3ef7450e1&lang=en.

14  S. Samson, "'Everyone is Equal': Winnipeg Library Security Guards Offer Community-First Approach," *CBC News*, December 8, 2021, https://www.cbc.ca/news/canada/manitoba/winnipeg-community-safety-hosts-program-1.6750010.

15  T. Saecker, personal communication, November 22, 2022.

16  Zettervall and Nienow, *Whole Person Librarianship.*

17  M. Gross and D. Latham, "Social Work in Public Libraries: A Survey of Heads of Public Library Administrative Units," *Journal of Library Administration* 61, no. 7 (2021): 758–75, https://doi.org/10.1080/01930826.2021.1972727.

18  Baum et al., "Bridging the Service Gap."

19  About ACLA, Allegheny County Library Association, https://aclalibraries.org/new/about-acla/.

**20**  A. Shimalla, "ACC Library Staff Trained to Identify Trauma and Offer Help," *Flagpole*, March 6, 2019, https://flagpole.com/news/news-features/2019/03/06/acc-library-staff-trained-to-identify-trauma-and-offer-help/.

**21**  Ogden and Williams, "Supporting Patrons in Crisis through a Social Work-Public Library Collaboration."

**22**  *Healthy Libraries Program (HeLP): About the Program*, Stony Brook Medicine, 2019, https://publichealth.stonybrookmedicine.edu/healthy_libraries_program/about.

**23**  G. Pandolfelli, A. Hammock, L. Topek-Walker, M. D'Ambrosio, T. Tejada, C. Della Ratta, M. E. LaSala, J. A. Koos, V. Lewis, and L. Benz Scott, "An Interprofessional Team-Based Experiential Learning Experience in Public Libraries," *Pedagogy in Health Promotion* 9, no. 1 (2021): 1–10, https://doi.org/10.1177/23733799211048517.

# Afterword

We hope by this point in the book you've come to appreciate how essential your libraries and their staff are. Because of the critical roles you play in our communities, we need to care for and advocate for all staff by preparing them to work in as safe a way as possible, much as we would for other essential service providers. Any steps taken on behalf of librarianship should also consider how to foster staff resilience and protect the library workforce. Would we expect a firefighter to run into a burning building with no preparation for the field, no protective gear, and without ever being in close contact with a fire? Of course not. Nor should we have such equivalent expectations of library workers.

This book was borne from our work with numerous public libraries across the United States and abroad: libraries seeking answers for the situations in which they find themselves. Over the course of our work with libraries and during the interviews we conducted while writing this book, we heard repeated phrases such as, "I wasn't prepared for this," "Nobody told me public library work was going to be like this," and "I've had to figure out how to do this on my own." Although this book is our attempt to provide some guidance and support to library staff seeking solutions and assistance, this is only the beginning. This book focuses on what can be done by individual libraries, yet we would be remiss not to highlight broader strategies libraries can consider to support administrators and front-line library staff with the daily realities of the work. The complex challenges facing libraries today justify the following profession-wide changes.

## Supporting Library Workers Is a Global Priority

Building library capacity and protecting its workforce should be a global priority. At the time we wrote this Afterword, we were contacted by libraries in Australia, Germany, New Zealand, the UK, and multiple regions of the United States looking for solutions. Our websites on the topic of social work and libraries draw frequent visitors from around the world, including Canada, China, France, India,

Iran, Japan, Lithuania, and Switzerland. These factors signify broad international interest in the topic of patrons' psychosocial needs, how libraries can successfully address these needs, how libraries can support their staff, and social work/library collaborations as one solution to these challenges. Because of this global interest, we believe building library capacity for meeting the needs of high-needs patrons and equipping the library workforce to navigate the stressors of this work should be strategic priorities of the International Federation of Library Associations and Institutions. This group is a key voice of libraries across the world by advocating for library support and resources with decision-makers.

## Necessary Leadership from National-Level Professional Associations

In the United States, we call for a number of specific steps to help improve library capacity and support for staff. First, national groups such as the American Library Association and the Public Library Association (PLA) have the power to greatly influence the perception of the public about libraries, the preparedness of librarians entering the field, available resources for libraries and library staff, and available support for front-line library staff. One suggestion emerging from multiple interviews with leaders in the library science (LIS) field and public librarianship is that library associations need to clearly define expectations of how librarianship can address patrons' psychosocial needs, revise the core competencies of the profession,[1] and offer resources and continuing education for individual libraries. Redefining public librarianship to better reflect its present reality can help ensure recruits to the LIS field have a clearer idea of what the work entails. It's promising to see that national groups, such as the PLA, continue to modify their strategic vision for the profession as a whole.[2] They can also support research about effective interventions for staff, effective training needs for staff, and the efficacy of library-based interventions for high-needs patrons. All of the strategies we suggested in this book for organizational change at the level of individual libraries can apply to change at the larger, professional association level as well. Clear communication from the top-down and establishing a shared vision for the profession are essential. National associations also have the ability to advocate for and support library workers across the country, including developing and offering mental health support for staff such as a crisis line.

# Changing LIS Education

A key way to ensure public librarians are adequately prepared for the realities of daily work is to consider LIS curricula. It's not uncommon to hear overwhelmed librarians lament they were not prepared for the realities of the work during their graduate studies. We heard from many librarians in our interviews that they had no idea how stressful public librarianship was going to be. Few LIS programs address the realities of public librarianship or prepare graduates to work with high-needs patrons. Most do not include information about developing collaborations or other strategies to meet patron needs, and none that we are aware of that teach de-escalation or other skills needed for working with the public. Only a few library programs in the United States offer dual degree programs[3] or specific courses[4] on the intersection of social work and librarianship. While more electives are offered in health-related classes, none are required by library programs.[5]

Dr. Rachel D. Williams, a library sciences professor at Simmons College, encourages fellow LIS instructors to consider and incorporate the LIS work experiences of students, as many of them are already employed in libraries.[6] Students' work experiences from their respective libraries can greatly enrich the learning experience of their peers. This is especially important for the LIS professors who are not currently working in the field themselves. Since not all LIS students work in libraries, it also behooves LIS programs to require that students complete an internship as part of their graduate studies. At the very least, opportunities to shadow public librarians can be arranged to offer a sense of what the realities of this work are. On a larger scale, altering accreditation standards for LIS programs should be considered to standardize field placement requirements throughout the United States.

Students should also be taught to begin developing or enhancing tools and practices that can help them navigate the stressors that may accompany working in the field of public librarianship. Smith et al. observe "when librarians are in school they aren't told they will be placed in environments where they may feel they lack control over their well-being or workload. Perhaps library programs do their students a disservice by not emphasizing that public librarianship is a service occupation and may be overwhelming for those without innate coping mechanisms . . . the training of new public librarians should include a grounding in healthy coping mechanisms . . . it is time for library educators to seriously consider how to incorporate self-care into the curriculum."[7] This is essential to support long-term sustainable practice for people working in the LIS field.

# Macro-Level State Library Initiatives

At the time of writing this book, we have seen a recent, significant increase in state library initiatives aimed at supporting both public library staff addressing patrons' psychosocial needs and the staff themselves. State libraries can implement broad initiatives while having a significant influence on the work of libraries in that particular state. They can offer continuing education to staff across the state on patron psychosocial needs, how to develop successful collaborations, or how to de-escalate patron crises. Sometimes there is funding to support statewide needs assessments or a consultant for serving high-needs patrons, a help hotline for library staff, or resource guides. Some laudable state library initiatives include:

*California State Library and California Libraries Learn*. The State of California has made a concerted effort to seek trainers and provide statewide training to library staff and administrators on the effects of trauma and the necessary skills for working with patrons in a trauma-informed manner. They offer regular training for library staff on de-escalation tactics, creating community partnerships with social service providers, becoming trauma-informed, developing a strengths-based perspective to library services, and approaching patrons who have experienced trauma.

*Delaware Division of Libraries*. The Delaware Division of Libraries has developed the first statewide, library-led telehealth program in the world. Initially piloted in three rural library locations, the program recently expanded to include nine additional libraries. Aimed at addressing statewide challenges to accessing healthcare, this program provides access to telehealth technology in private, soundproof booths so community members can access medical and social service providers. This benefits patrons who do not have transportation to travel to a doctor or reliable wi-fi to connect virtually from home. Healthcare "navigators" are located in participating libraries to assist patrons with using the technology, scheduling appointments, or answering questions. Nurses from the program's healthcare partner periodically visit the library to provide health screenings or health information. Telehealth technology was provided for the participating libraries through partnerships with a local healthcare organization, and both local and national funding sources were secured to support the program.

*State Library of Iowa*. To understand concerns from library staff across the state and plan data-informed initiatives, the State Library of Iowa conducted a statewide needs assessment of staff on their perspectives of patrons' unmet psychosocial needs. This included assessing their ideas of the role and responsibility of libraries with types of patron needs, experiences of violence in their libraries, and training needs. This needs assessment also included focus groups of library directors to explore their willingness to pursue collaborations with local social service providers, barriers to such collaborations, and recommendations for how the state library could help. Based on the data obtained from this needs assessment, the State Library is currently planning new initiatives and training for staff.

*Kentucky Department of Libraries and Archives.* The Kentucky Department of Libraries and Archives (KDLA) began a coordinated statewide initiative to plan and pilot social work practicum students in public libraries across the state. Staff from KDLA initiated planning sessions with multiple schools of social work and interested public library administrators. During these sessions, the planning group met with consultants, trainers, and staff from libraries and schools of social work who had previously piloted social work students in their branches to understand and anticipate the challenges and benefits of hosting students. The planning group is conducting workshops for libraries across the state to recruit additional sites and share their lessons learned from piloting social work students in their own libraries.

*New Jersey State Library.* The New Jersey State Library has a multi-year digital equity initiative that aims to provide digital literacy and digital skills education to people from historically underserved communities. It also seeks to improve accessibility to social services at local public libraries and build capacity within the library workforce to provide equitable access and services to New Jersey's communities. As part of this initiative, the State Library has partnered with Rutgers University to position social work students in local libraries who can connect patrons with community resources and offer support as needed. This program will develop a written curriculum, provide training, and create a community of practice for both library supervisors of social work students and the students themselves to help improve their ability to provide services to vulnerable communities and patrons.

Although varying in focus, these statewide initiatives reflect the timeliness and relevance of topics discussed in this book and a positive step toward creating supportive networks to establish and define the roles of public libraries with high-needs patrons. Public libraries in states that do not have initiatives in this arena should consider contacting their state library and advocating for resources and services to help meet their needs. State libraries are often able to support public libraries by offering training and consultation, locating funding sources or providing small grants for programs through Library Services and Technology Act (LSTA) or other national funding sources, or by pulling together groups of libraries to create regional consortiums or collaborative groups.

## Conclusion

Since their inception, public libraries have been constantly adapting to the changing needs of their communities. This resiliency will help sustain the field well into the future. However, now is the time to develop local, statewide, national, and global initiatives to intentionally support the staff who will carry these institutions forward toward future generations.

## Notes

**1**  *Core Competences*, American Library Association, June 10, 2008, https://www.ala .org/educationcareers/careers/corecomp/corecompetences.

**2**  *PLA Strategic Plan 2022–2026*, Public Library Association, June 2022, https://www .ala.org/pla/about/mission/strategicplan.

**3**  Dominican University. (2023). Master of Library and Information Science and Master of Social Work Dual Degree. https://www.dom.edu/academics/majors-programs/mlis-and-master-social-work-dual-degree. University of Michigan. (2023). Master of Science in Information and Master of Social Work. https://www.si.umich.edu/programs/master-science-information/dual-degree-programs/master-science-information-and-master.

**4**  *LIS 582 Library Social Work,* University of Champaign-Urbana, 2022, https://ischool .illinois.edu/degrees-programs/courses/is582.

**5**  G. Pandolfelli, J. A. Koos, and L. Benz Scott, "An Analysis of ALA-Accredited MLS Curricula Indicates Deficiencies in the Initial Training Provided for Public Librarians," *Health Information and Libraries Journal* 39, no. 3 (2022), https://doi.org /10.1111/hir.12443.

**6**  R. Williams, personal communication, August 3, 2022.

**7**  Smith et al., "Public Librarian Job Stressors and Burnout Predictors."

# Appendix A
## Sample Needs Assessment: Patrons

This needs assessment survey was created by Beth and used for a number of patron needs assessments. It is intentionally designed to be brief, and to obtain information about broad areas of patron unmet needs. When she has used it with libraries, the survey is available online, both emailed to library email lists and programmed to pop up on public computers in the library, and is available on paper for patrons who do not use the computer or have access to email. If available on paper, there should be a box placed in a public area that allows patrons to turn in their responses anonymously rather than needing to hand their completed questionnaires directly to a staff person.

*Instructions: The library wants to know what you need and how they can help! Please complete this quick, anonymous survey to let your voice be heard.*

*The survey is voluntary and your answers cannot be linked to you. You may skip any questions which make you uncomfortable. It takes less than five minutes. The survey will be available between (insert dates). You may be asked to participate more than once since this survey is available on paper and electronically. If you have already completed this survey once, please do not answer the questions again.*

*First, we will start by asking you some basic information about yourself. You may skip to the next question at any time.*

**1.** How old are you? _____

**2.** What is your gender?
- **a.** Male
- **b.** Female
- **c.** Other
- **d.** Prefer not to answer

**3.** What is your primary language?

   **a.** English

   **b.** Spanish

   **c.** Other_____

**4.** What is your race (check all that apply)?

   **a.** American Indian or Alaska Native

   **b.** Asian

   **c.** Black/African American

   **d.** Native Hawaiian/Pacific Islander

   **e.** White/Caucasian

   **f.** Other_____

**5.** What is your ethnicity?

   **a.** Hispanic or Latino/a/x

   **b.** Not Hispanic or Latino/a/x

**6.** What best describes your housing situation?

   **a.** Own a home/condo

   **b.** Rent an apartment/house/condo

   **c.** Stay with family/friends (in their home)

   **d.** No permanent address

**7.** On average, how often do you visit the _____ Public Library in person?

   **a.** Weekly or more

   **b.** Monthly

   **c.** Once every 3 months

   **d.** Once every 6 months

   **e.** Once per year or less

   **f.** I do not visit the library in person

**8.** If you answered "I do not visit the library in person" for question 7, please explain your reasons why you do not visit in person. _____

*Next, we will ask you some questions about your needs.*

**9.** Do you have any unmet needs or need assistance in the following areas? Think only about areas in which you are not currently receiving *any* help or in which you are not receiving *enough* help. Check as many as apply.

**a.** Computer and/or internet access

**b.** Help using a computer

**c.** Social connections (to help with loneliness or making friends)

**d.** Fun and safe activities

**e.** Reading/literacy

**f.** Immigration-related needs

**g.** English as a second language

**h.** Education

**i.** Job-related training

**j.** Employment

**k.** Financial needs

**l.** Help applying for food stamps, social security, or other public benefits

**m.** Utilities (help paying for utility bills)

**n.** Housing (help finding safe or permanent housing)

**o.** Clothing

**p.** Not enough food

**q.** Transportation

**r.** Health insurance

**s.** Help with a disability

**t.** Dental problems

**u.** Mental health problems

**v.** Substance use

**w.** Legal needs

**x.** Childcare

**y.** Parenting skills

**z.** Personal hygiene (a place to shower, soap/shampoo, etc.)

**aa.** A place to keep warm or cool

**bb.** A place to store items while I'm at the library

**10.** If the library were to host free workshops or programs on the following topics, how interested would you be?

| Topic | Interest Level | | | | |
|---|---|---|---|---|---|
| | No interest at all | A little interest | A moderate amount of interest | A lot of interest | A great deal of interest |
| Common medical problems | | | | | |
| Mental health problems | | | | | |
| Substance abuse problems | | | | | |
| How to access public benefits | | | | | |
| Community resources | | | | | |
| Budgeting/finances | | | | | |
| Diversity (such as culture, race, religion, or gender-related events) | | | | | |
| Social justice (related to social, economic, or environmental concerns) | | | | | |
| Support groups | | | | | |
| Opportunities for social connection | | | | | |

**11.** How well is _____ Public Library meeting your expectations and needs?

    **a.** Not well at all

    **b.** Slightly well

    **c.** Moderately well

    **d.** Very well

    **e.** Extremely well

**12.** Please make any suggestions for ideas you have about how _____ Public Library can better meet your needs or the needs of other people visiting this library. _____

# Appendix B
## Sample Needs Assessment: Staff

This needs assessment survey was created by Beth and used for a number of staff needs assessments. It is designed to be an electronic survey, emailed to library staff, and using survey software that allows anonymous entries. To obtain the most accurate information from staff, they should be able to submit their responses without administrators being able to identify who gave each response. In most needs assessments, responses have been submitted electronically to Beth or a social work student so individual responses cannot be seen by library administrators. Rather, Beth or the social work student compiles the aggregate responses into a report and submits the final report to library administrators, taking care not to include quotes or responses that could inadvertently identify a staff member. This adds an extra layer of privacy that helps staff feel comfortable providing their honest opinions.

*Instructions: _____ Public Library is interested in obtaining more information about patron needs and the library's ability to meet those needs. We are specifically focusing on "psychosocial needs," which include patron needs related to things such as poverty, mental health problems, substance abuse, or health problems.*

*The first step of the needs assessment is a survey of staff, which will help us understand your perceptions of patron needs and ideas about the library's role in addressing these needs.*

*We are asking you to complete this brief survey and to please be open and honest in your responses. This survey is voluntary and you may skip any questions you prefer not to answer. Your information will remain anonymous, and your name will not be recorded or linked to your responses. The library will receive a report of the overall findings from this survey, but care will be taken so no identifying information or individual responses will be released.*

*The survey will take approximately fifteen to twenty minutes. If you have questions about the needs assessment or this survey, please contact (insert name and contact info).*

1. Is your position public-facing?
   a. Yes
   b. No

2. What do you think is/are the largest unmet need(s) of customers at the library (check all that apply)?
   a. Financial
   b. Housing
   c. Transportation
   d. Food/nutrition
   e. Clothing
   f. Hygiene (supplies, having a place to clean up, etc.)
   g. Employment
   h. Education or literacy-related
   i. Technology (access to or education about technology)
   j. Mental health
   k. Substance abuse
   l. Intimate partner violence (victimization)
   m. Medical or health-related
   n. Disability-related needs
   o. Parenting assistance
   p. Childcare
   q. Safe activities for children
   r. Immigration-related needs
   s. English as a second language
   t. Behavior problems
   u. Anger management/conflict resolution
   v. Relationship problems or interpersonal issues
   w. Social connection/isolation
   x. Entertainment/fun and safe activities
   y. Other_____

3. Some patron needs can cause a great deal of stress to staff, even if they occur infrequently. Which of these patron needs cause stress to you in your library position?
   a. Financial
   b. Housing
   c. Transportation
   d. Food/nutrition
   e. Clothing
   f. Hygiene (supplies, having a place to clean up, etc.)
   g. Employment
   h. Education or literacy-related
   i. Technology (access to or education about technology)
   j. Mental health
   k. Substance abuse
   l. Intimate partner violence (victimization)
   m. Medical or health-related
   n. Disability-related needs
   o. Parenting assistance
   p. Childcare
   q. Safe activities for children
   r. Immigration-related needs
   s. English as a second language
   t. Behavior problems
   u. Anger management/conflict resolution

**v.** Relationship problems or interpersonal issues

**w.** Social connection/isolation

**x.** Entertainment/fun and safe activities

**y.** Other_____

4. What additional services could be offered by or at the library to be helpful to people experiencing poverty and/or homelessness?

   **a.** Hygiene items

   **b.** Snacks/food

   **c.** Warm items such as blankets, hats, coats, or scarves

   **d.** Walk-throughs by various service providers to check on patrons experiencing homelessness

   **e.** Designated days and times for homeless service providers to meet with customers experiencing homelessness

   **f.** Assistance signing up for public benefits like TANF (Temporary Assistance for Needy Families, often referred to as "welfare") or food stamps

   **g.** Assistance signing up for housing programs

   **h.** List of community agencies and their contact information

   **i.** Children and family meal programs

   **j.** Other_____

5. How well do you think the library is doing to meet the needs of patrons experiencing poverty and/or homelessness?

   **a.** Not well at all

   **b.** Slightly well

   **c.** Moderately well

   **d.** Very well

   **e.** Extremely well

   **f.** I don't know

6. In your opinion, what additional services could be offered by the library to be helpful for people experiencing mental health, substance abuse, or medical problems/needs?

   **a.** Assistance signing up for health insurance

   **b.** Workshops by service providers

   **c.** Designated days and times for select service providers to meet with customers experiencing these issues

   **d.** Private room or "pod" for customers to discuss personal issues

   **e.** Assistance signing up for SSI/SSDI ("disability") benefits

   **f.** List of community agencies and their contact information

   **g.** Other_____

**7.** How well do you think the library is doing to meet the needs of patrons experiencing mental health, substance abuse, or medical problems/needs?

    **a.** Not well at all

    **b.** Slightly well

    **c.** Moderately well

    **d.** Very well

    **e.** Extremely well

    **f.** I don't know

**8.** When thinking about services beyond traditional information needs, such as those for patrons' financial, mental health, or physical health needs, do you think these services or programs should be provided by (check all that apply):

    **a.** Trained librarians or other library staff

    **b.** Social services professional(s) hired by the library

    **c.** Partnerships with external community agencies

    **d.** None of the above- These services or programs should not be provided in or by a public library

**9.** In your opinion, are there library policies that create barriers to providing customer service or cause conflict with customers trying to use the library space?

    **a.** Yes

    **b.** No

**10.** If you answered yes to #9, please explain what policies create barriers or cause conflict with customers and any ideas you have for modifying those policies.

_____

_____

_____

**11.** How fearful are you of violence occurring in the library?

    **a.** Not fearful at all

    **b.** Somewhat fearful

    **c.** Very fearful

**12.** Have you ever experienced violence or abuse in your job at the library?

    **a.** Yes

    **b.** No

**13.** Please describe what violence or abuse you have experienced in your job. _____

_____

_____

**14.** Burnout can occur when someone experiences chronic workplace stress, and consists of 1) feelings of exhaustion, 2) increased feelings of negativity or cynicism about one's job, and 3) reduced efficacy at work.[1] Overall, how would you rate your level of burnout?[2]

a. I enjoy my work. I have no symptoms of burnout.

b. Occasionally I am under stress and I don't always have as much energy as I once did, but I don't feel burned out.

c. I am definitely burning out and have one or more symptoms of burnout, such as physical and emotional exhaustion.

d. The symptoms of burnout I am experiencing won't go away. I think about frustration at work a lot.

e. I feel completely burned out and wonder if I can go on. I am at a point where I may need some changes or may need to seek some sort of help.

15. What specific training topics would be helpful to you? You may check as many as apply:

a. Poverty

b. Homelessness

c. Mental health issues

d. Substance abuse

e. Health problems

f. Community resources

g. De-escalation

h. Stress management/self-care

i. How to set boundaries with patrons or others

j. Other _____

16. Please make any additional comments you would like the library to know about how we can better meet the broad and varied needs of our customers and/or better support our staff.

_____
_____
_____

## Notes

1   World Health Organization, accessed November 19, 2022, *Health Workforce*, https://www.who.int/health-topics/health-workforce#tab=tab_1.

2   https://www.ncbi.nlm.nih.gov/pmc/articles/PMC4395610/

# Appendix C
## Sample Needs Assessment: Community

## Direct Methods

This community needs assessment is designed to uncover homelessness-related needs recognized by key community partners that could be addressed by adding programming or services at the public library or by the library doing outreach in the community. In this direct form of a community needs assessment, a representative from the library would contact all homelessness-serving organizations in the local community and ask their administrators to participate in the following survey.

*Instructions: The _____ Public Library is interested in identifying unmet or undermet needs in our local community pertaining to individuals experiencing homelessness. A large number of unhoused individuals use our library on a daily basis and we want to help them feel as welcome as possible while also ensuring we share useful resources with them, offer needed services or programming for them, and fill gaps in services in the local community. Your opinions are needed due to your experience with homelessness in our community and your knowledge of existing services and resources.*

1. At what organization do you work?

2. What is the main purpose of your organization?

3. What services do you offer to people experiencing homelessness?

4. When you consider services offered to people experiencing homelessness in our community, what gaps can you identify?

5. The library's role is to provide resources and information, provide fun and safe activities, create opportunities for diverse groups to interact and socialize, and address literacy-related challenges for our local community. When you consider our role, is there something we could do to improve the experience of people experiencing homelessness in our local community?

6. We often collaborate with other organizations to carry out informational sessions, workshops, or groups in the library that positively impact our local community. We also often collaborate with other organizations for our library staff to take resources into the community to do outreach with vulnerable populations. Is your organization interested in partnering with us? If so, do you have any ideas about how our organizations might work together to better meet the needs of people experiencing homelessness?

# Indirect Methods

This community needs assessment is designed to use indirect methods to assess gaps in services for patrons experiencing homelessness that could be addressed by adding programming or services at the public library or by the library doing outreach in the community. A library representative would search available data sources to look for the following information:

1. What homelessness-serving organizations are in the Library's local community?

2. Who do these organizations serve and what are the criteria for receiving services there? Are there populations (i.e. women, parents of young children, single men, non-veterans, etc.) that have no access to services?

3. What are the hours each organization is open? Do the organizations' clients have to leave the facility for designated hours each day, and if so, what hours will their clients be out in the community?

4. What services are provided by each organization?

5. What other needs often exist for individuals experiencing homelessness (i.e. substance abuse, mental health problems, access to healthcare, education limits/deficits, literacy problems, etc.)?

6. Of the needs identified in question 5, which do not currently appear to be addressed by the existing organizations in the local community?

# Appendix D
## Referral Sheet Template[1]

This referral sheet can be handed to patrons when they are being connected to a community resource. It helps them track needed information and contains helpful hints to increase the success of their contacts.

(Front of Worksheet)

Organization/Agency Name:

Service/Program:

Address:

Phone Number:

Contact person (if known):

Agency Hours/Contact Times:

Date of Call:

Who Did You Speak To:

Name:

Position:

Direct Line/Extension:

What Did They Say:

What Are the Next Steps:

Response Timeframe (When Will You Get a Response):

## Tips for Successful Calls

- Always ask for names.
- Take notes during the call.

- If you try the office in the morning and cannot get through, try in the afternoon.
- Certain times of the day or the month can be busier than others for agencies.
- Many agencies close for lunch between 12 and 1 pm.
- Always leave a detailed voicemail with callback number if you get a voicemail box.
- Ask for direct lines/extension numbers wherever possible.
- If you need to submit documentation, make sure you get a receipt when turning in documents.
- If the person on the phone is not able to help you, ask for a referral or information on who offers similar assistance.
- Be as thorough as possible when giving information, and make sure you advise if you are estimating.
- If the information you get seems inaccurate or does not make sense, seek clarification or a second opinion.
- If you do not hear back in the stated amount of time, follow up.
- If you have been denied, find out the reason and ask whether you can appeal or reapply.

## Note

1   This template was created by Bethany Czernicki, Tajera Morgan, and Shirley Ross, social work students from The College of Saint Rose, in collaboration with the Cobleskill Community Library and the Waterford Library (NY) during their library-based practicum placements.

# Appendix E
## Sample Responses to Patron Behavioral Challenges

## Behavioral Response Guides

A behavioral response guide can be useful to helping staff remember to use a trauma-informed lens, while also ensuring they remember applicable policies and feel empowered to act and set boundaries when needed. Organized by common patron behavioral violations, it's helpful for the guide to include a reminder of why someone might behave in a specific way, relevant policies that apply to the situation, a scenario to demonstrate the violation in action, and sample scripts for how to respond.

Below is an example of a patron behavior violation that could be included in a behavioral response guide. Use your own library policies and common scenarios to build upon this for your library. Once your guide has been created, be sure and train all staff on it and create opportunities to practice the scenarios. The more staff are able to practice, the more they can respond in a way that is genuine to them and feels natural and unforced.

## Patron Behavioral Violation: Aggression

What the behavior looks like: A patron may become escalated and raise their voice, yell at staff or another patron, throw things, get close to someone or "in their face," or threaten to harm them.

Relevant policy/ies: The (insert name) Public Library has a policy prohibiting disruptive or threatening behavior. The conduct policy says patrons can lose library privileges for one week to a year (length of time depends on the severity of the incident) for shouting, swearing, making threats against patrons or employees, destroying property, or aggressive behaviors, and can permanently lose access to the library for committing assault.

Reminder about trauma-informed lens: People who have experienced trauma may have difficulty regulating their emotions and may become easily escalated when things don't go as planned. They may be easily irritable or moody, and become angry by seemingly small minor things that happen around them. They may have difficulty when they are not in control of a situation, such as with other people's behavior. They also may have difficulty reading social cues, which can cause them to interpret someone else's behavior as threatening when it may not be.

## Scenario

You are working the circulation desk when you hear a loud voice. A man is walking up to the desk and yelling at you about how he was using the computer but the person next to him sat down next to him and was talking to himself nonstop, disturbing his concentration. The man seems to be irate, yelling that someone needs to make the other man "shut up" or he's going to "shut him up." He is pacing back and forth by your desk, clenching his fists. You are afraid that he is going to hurt the other man if you do not quickly do something. You are also fearful that this man is going to aim his aggression at you if you don't respond in a way that satisfies him.

---

### Sample Response

1. Show this man that you hear him and care about his experience in the library. For example, say, "I appreciate you coming to get me to help. My name is (insert name) and I am a (insert position) here. We want everyone's experience at our library to be a positive one."

2. Be mindful of your own tone of voice and body language and take deep breaths to try to keep yourself calm. People can become further escalated if they think you're being aggressive with them. Try to stand at a slight angle, with your hands folded together in front of you, in your pockets, or at your side. Keep your voice calm and soft. Often when we speak quieter, the other person will quiet their voice, too.

3. Attempt to get him to move to a different location, separated from the other man, if possible and if you can keep yourself safe. For example, "Can you come to the office with me so we can talk about what happened and come up with a solution?" Once in the other location, give him a chance to voice his concern and talk about what upset him. People want to be heard and understood.

4. Try to relate to him and show him you understand. You can say "I get it! It always bothers me when I'm trying to work on something and people are being loud around me, too." However, only say something like that if you can say it genuinely. Another option is to reflect back what he says to show that you heard him. For example, "I want to be sure I'm getting what you're saying. You were trying to concentrate on filling out a job application, and the man next to you was talking so much that it made it hard to focus. Is that correct?"

5. See if there's an accommodation that can be made to help him calm down while respecting the other person's right to use a computer, too. For example, is there another bank of computers that one of them can be moved to? Is there a designated quiet area that the man can be moved to where people around him won't be talking? Are there earplugs or noise-canceling headphones your library can loan him to shut out the noise around him?

6. If he does not calm down, set a boundary with him about his behavior. Let him know clearly that the library does not allow threatening words or behaviors or yelling. Say, "I really want you to be able to use the library today, but our library has clear policies about yelling or threatening behaviors. If you continue to yell like this, I'm going to have to ask you to leave and I don't want to have to do that. Let's work together here. What can we do to help so you can keep using the computers today?"

7. You may have to remind him that the other person was not violating any library policy (if that's the case), but there are opportunities for him to give feedback to administration if he would like someone to consider a policy change. Often giving someone a voice or an outlet for their frustration can calm them down.

8. If he doesn't calm down, call for the supervisor or person-in-charge to help.

9. If he escalates and attempts to hit you or another patron, yell for help. You are empowered to call 911 if needed.

# Notices of Library Suspension

## Sample Form from Johnston (IA) Public Library

To: _____

Date & Time: _____

At that time, you were engaging in the following conduct which violates the Conduct in the Library Policy:

☐ Disruptive behavior: noise, running, rushing, etc.

☐ No shirt, no shoes, etc.

☐ Non-service animals

☐ Refusing staff direction

☐ Selling, soliciting, proselytizing

☐ Entering non-public areas

☐ Returning while suspended

☐ Alcohol/drugs

☐ Fighting, play-fighting, rough-housing

☐ Vandalism

☐ Other violation of the Conduct in the Library Policy: _____
_____

Because of the conduct noted above, your library privileges have been suspended until the date shown below. If you enter library property before then, police may be called.

Date of suspension: _____

Date library access will be restored: _____

Staff member name and title: _____

Suspension length:

1. Remainder of the day with optional +1 day:
   a. Ignoring repeated warnings about disruptive behavior
   b. Refusing to follow the directions of library staff
   c. Swearing or using foul language
   d. Pushing, hitting, or play fighting

2. One week:

   **a.** Entering or remaining on library property after being asked to leave

   **b.** Being disrespectful to library staff or patrons

   **c.** Repeating or escalating any of the above

3. One month:

   **a.** Damaging library property

   **b.** Threatening or harassing staff or patrons

   **c.** Repeating or escalating any of the above

4. Six months or more:

   **a.** Theft

   **b.** Fighting

   **c.** Assault

   **d.** Sexual harassment

   **e.** Severe damage to library property

   **f.** Stealing

   **g.** Possession or use of illegal drugs and/or alcohol

Re-entry meeting:

Upon restoration of library access, the library director or a department head will meet with you to:

- Review the reason(s) for your suspension
- Review the Conduct in the Library Policy

Appeal procedure:

Any patron suspended for more than one day can appeal the suspension by:

- Contacting library administration, in writing, within five working days of the suspension. The library director or designee will consult with staff, review the incident report and relation documentation, and any written information provided to the patron. The patron may also schedule an appointment with the library director or designee to discuss the decision to suspend library privileges. After reviewing information and/or meeting with the patron, the suspension period may be terminated or shortened, or the suspension may remain in place. The patron will be informed of the library administration decision in the most expedient fashion—via telephone call, email, or mailed letter.

- The patron may appeal the determination of library administration to the Library Board of Trustees via a written notice of appeal within 10 days after receipt of the Library Administration determination. The notice of appeal shall be filed with both the Library Director and the Library Board President, care of (insert library name and address). The Library Board will hold a hearing to discuss the suspension at their next regularly scheduled meeting. The patron will be provided at least ten days' notice of the hearing date. A parent or guardian must accompany a minor (under the age of eighteen) to the hearing.

- The Library Board of Trustees will hear the appeal and will vote to uphold or dismiss the suspension. Library administration will notify the patron by letter of the decision of the Library Board of Trustees. The suspension will remain in effect until the Board's decision.

# Suggested Reading

Association of Rural and Small Libraries. www.arsl.org

Beth Wahler Consulting. https://www.swinthelibrary.com/

Lenstra, Noah. *Healthy Living at the Library: Programs for All Ages* (Santa Barbara, CA: Libraries Unlimited, 2020).

Public Library Association Social Worker Task Force. *A Trauma-Informed Framework for Supporting Patrons: The PLA Workbook of Best Practices* (Public Library Association, 2022). https://www.alastore.ala.org/PLAtiframework

Social Work Students & Public Libraries. https://swlibraryinterns.com/

Whole Person Librarianship. https://wholepersonlibrarianship.com/

Winkelstein, Julie Ann. *Libraries and Homelessness: An Action Guide* (Santa Barbara, CA: Libraries Unlimited, 2021).

Zettervall, S. K., & Nienow, M. C. *Whole Person Librarianship: A Social Work Approach to Patron Services* (Santa Barbara, CA: Libraries Unlimited, 2019).

# Index

# About the Authors

**Elizabeth (Beth) A. Wahler**, PhD, MSW, is the founder/owner of Beth Wahler Consulting and faculty at the UNC Charlotte School of Social Work. She has collaborated with libraries and library systems across the United States to conduct needs assessments of their patrons' psychosocial needs and staff challenges with these types of patron needs and provide training to library staff about trauma-informed librarianship and other approaches to addressing their patron and staff needs. She has created and piloted various interventions to address these patron needs including library/social work collaborations. She has presented internationally on these topics and has published numerous articles on library patron and staff needs in peer-reviewed journals.

**Sarah C. Johnson**, MLIS, LMSW, is Adjunct Lecturer at the School of Information Sciences at the University of Illinois where she teaches a course on Library Social Work. She is a licensed social worker and her research focuses on the impact of social work students conducting their field placements at public libraries. Her aim is to foster quality internships by building alliances among students, public librarians, and social work educators, with the goal of enhancing services to library patrons and their wider community.

Printed in the USA
CPSIA information can be obtained
at www.ICGtesting.com
LVHW010852120224
771452LV00038B/660